Wiley Study Guide for 2017 Level II CFA Exam

Volume 2: Economics & Financial Reporting

Thousands of candidates from more than 100 countries have relied on these Study Guides to pass the CFA® Exam. Covering every Learning Outcome Statement (LOS) on the exam, these review materials are an invaluable tool for anyone who wants a deep-dive review of all the concepts, formulas, and topics required to pass.

Wiley study materials are produced by expert CFA charterholders, CFA Institute members, and investment professionals from around the globe. For more information, contact us at info@efficientlearning.com.

Wiley Study Guide for 2017 Level II CFA Exam

Volume 2: Economics & Financial Reporting

WILEY

Contents

ABOUT THE AUTHORS

Wiley's Study Guides are written by a team of highly qualified CFA charterholders and leading CFA instructors from around the globe. Our team of CFA experts work collaboratively to produce the best study materials for CFA candidates available today.

Wiley's expert team of contributing authors and instructors is led by Content Director Basit Shajani, CFA. Basit founded online education start-up Élan Guides in 2009 to help address CFA candidates' need for better study materials. As lead writer, lecturer, and curriculum developer, Basit's unique ability to break down complex topics helped the company grow organically to be a leading global provider of CFA Exam prep materials. In January 2014, Élan Guides was acquired by John Wiley & Sons, Inc., where Basit continues his work as Director of CFA Content. Basit graduated magna cum laude from the Wharton School of Business at the University of Pennsylvania with majors in finance and legal studies. He went on to obtain his CFA charter in 2006, passing all three levels on the first attempt. Prior to Élan Guides, Basit ran his own private wealth management business. He is a past president of the Pakistani CFA Society.

There are many more expert CFA charterholders who contribute to the creation of Wiley materials. We are thankful for their invaluable expertise and diligent work. To learn more about Wiley's team of subject matter experts, please visit: www.efficientlearning.com/cfa/why-wiley/.

STUDY SESSION 4: ECONOMICS FOR VALUATION

READING 13: CURRENCY EXCHANGE RATES: DETERMINATION AND FORECASTING

LESSON 1: FOREIGN EXCHANGE MARKET CONCEPTS

Level I Recap

An **exchange rate** represents the price of one currency in terms of another currency. It is stated in terms of the number of units of a particular currency (price currency) required to purchase a unit of another currency (base currency).

In this reading, we will refer to exchange rates using the convention "A/B" (or PC/BC), that is, number of units of Currency A (price currency) required to purchase one unit of Currency B (base currency). For example, suppose that the USD/GBP exchange rate is currently 1.5125. From this exchange rate quote we can infer that:

- The GBP is the base currency and USD is the price currency.
- 1 GBP will buy 1.5125 USD or 1 GBP costs 1.5125 USD.
- It will take 1.5125 USD to purchase 1 GBP.
- A decrease in the exchange rate (e.g., to 1.5120) means that 1 GBP will be able to purchase fewer USD.
- Alternatively, fewer USD will now be required to purchase 1 GBP (i.e., the cost of a GBP has fallen).
- This decrease in the exchange rate means that the GBP has depreciated (lost value) against the USD, or equivalently the USD has appreciated (gained value) against the GBP.

It would help you to think of exchange rates in the following manner: An increase in the quoted exchange rate (PC/BC) means an *increase* (appreciation) in the value of the currency in the denominator (base currency) and a *decrease* (depreciation) in the value of the currency in the numerator (price currency).

- The numerical value of the exchange rate and the value of the base currency are *positively* related.
- The numerical value of the exchange rate and the value of the price currency are *negatively* related.

> Just like the price of any product, an exchange rate reflects the price of the currency in the denominator. For example, a price of $5/bag of chips reflects the price of a bag of chips (base or denominator) in terms of the price currency (USD). Similarly, a price (exchange rate) of $2/GBP is the price of GBP (base currency) in terms of USD (price currency). An increase in the price of chips (e.g., to $6/bag) means that the value of a bag of chips (the denominator) in terms of USD has risen. Similarly, an increase in the exchange rate to $3/GBP implies an increase in the value of GBP (the base currency or currency in the denominator).

LOS 13a: Calculate and interpret the bid–ask spread on a spot or forward foreign currency quotation and describe the factors that affect the bid–offer spread. Vol 1, pp 500–505

LOS 13b: Identify a triangular arbitrage opportunity and calculate its profit, given the bid–offer quotations for three currencies. Vol 1, pp 500–505

Spot exchange rates (S) are quotes for transactions that call for **immediate delivery**. For most currencies, immediate delivery means "T + 2" delivery (i.e., the transaction is actually settled 2 days after the trade is agreed upon by the parties).

In professional FX markets, an exchange rate is usually quoted as a two-sided price. Dealers usually quote a bid price (the price at which **they** are willing to **buy**), and an ask price or offer price (the price at which **they** are willing to **sell**). Bid-ask prices are always quoted in terms of buying and selling the **base** currency.

> Remember that the spread results in a profit for the dealer and a loss for the client. The dealer buys the base currency low (at the bid) and sells high (at the ask), while the client buys high (at the ask) and sells low (at the bid).

- For example, a USD/EUR quote of 1.3802–1.3806 means that the **dealer** is willing to buy EUR for 1.3802 USD and is willing to sell EUR for 1.3806 USD. The quote represents the price of the **base currency**, EUR.
- From the **client's perspective**, she will receive 1.3802 USD for selling 1 EUR, but will have to pay 1.3806 USD to purchase 1 EUR.

When working with bid-ask quotes, to determine whether the bid or the offer rate in the exchange rate quote should be used in a particular transaction:

- First identify the base currency of the exchange rate quote; and then
- Determine whether the client is buying or selling the base currency.

Given bid and ask prices for a particular currency, the bid and ask prices for the other currency in the exchange rate quote can be determined as follows:

- The *b/a* ask price is the reciprocal of the *a/b* bid price.
- The *b/a* bid price is the reciprocal of the *a/b* ask price.

In the example that we have been working with, the bid and ask quotes for EUR/USD (with the **USD** as the **base** currency) are calculated as:

$$\text{EUR/USD}_{bid} = 1 / (\text{USD/EUR}_{ask}) = 1 / 1.3806 = 0.7243$$
$$\text{EUR/USD}_{ask} = 1 / (\text{USD/EUR}_{bid}) = 1 / 1.3802 = 0.7245$$

Therefore, EUR/USD = 0.7243–0.7245

> When working with two exchange rate quotes or a currency amount and an exchange rate quote all you really need to do is to express the exchange rate(s) in terms of A/B and determine whether placing a "×" or "÷" sign in between them will result in one currency cancelling out.

Now let's illustrate how these quotes can be used to covert EUR to USD. There are two ways that a person can convert €50,000 into USD:

1. Selling **EUR** at the USD/EUR_**bid** of 1.3802 for $69,010.

- $€50,000 \times \dfrac{\$1.3802}{€} = \$69,010$

- The USD/**EUR** represents the price of the **EUR**.
- The **bid** price is the price at which the **client** can **sell EUR** to the dealer.

2. Purchasing **USD** at the EUR/USD$_{ask}$ of 0.7245 and obtaining $69,010.

- $€50,000 \div \dfrac{€0.7245}{\$} = €50,000 \times \dfrac{\$}{€0.7245} = \$69,010$

- The EUR**/USD** represents the price of the **USD**.
- The **ask** price is the price at which the **client** can **purchase** USD from the dealer.

Currency Cross Rates

A cross rate is an exchange rate between two currencies that is derived from each currency's relationship with a third currency. For example, given the USD/EUR and JPY/USD exchange rates, we can calculate the cross rate between the JPY and the EUR, JPY/EUR as follows:

$$\frac{JPY}{EUR} = \frac{JPY}{USD} \times \frac{USD}{EUR}$$

The given exchange rates should be multiplied such that the USD, the third currency (or common currency) disappears (or mathematically cancels out as it forms the numerator of one quote and the denominator of the other). In determining the cross rate above, the USD cancels out leaving us with the JPY/EUR cross rate.

In order to cancel out the third currency (to compute a cross rate), you might sometimes need to divide one of the exchange rate quotes by the other. For example, if we were given the USD/EUR and USD/GBP exchange rates, we would not be able to calculate the GBP/EUR cross rate by simply multiplying these two exchange rates in their presented forms (because the common currency, the USD, will not cancel out). The GBP/EUR cross rate can be calculated by dividing the USD/EUR exchange rate by the USD/GBP exchange rate:

$$\frac{GBP}{EUR} = \frac{USD}{EUR} \div \frac{USD}{GBP} = \frac{USD}{EUR} \times \left(\frac{USD}{GBP}\right)^{-1} = \frac{USD}{EUR} \times \frac{GBP}{USD}$$

LESSON 2: CROSS RATE CALCULATIONS WITH BID-ASK SPREADS

LOS 13a: Calculate and interpret the bid-ask spread on a spot or forward foreign currency quotation and describe the factors that affect the bid-offer spreads. Vol 1, pp 500–505

LOS 13b: Identify a triangular arbitrage opportunity and calculate its profit, given the bid-offer quotations for three currencies. Vol 1, pp 500–505

Cross Rate Calculations with Bid-Ask Spreads

Calculating bid-ask cross rates (given bid-ask quotes for exchange rates) can be quite complicated unless you understand the underlying procedure very well. Let's work with the following currency quotes to illustrate the process.

$$USD/EUR = 1.3802 - 1.3806$$
$$GBP/EUR = 0.8593 - 0.8599$$

Our aim here is to determine the GBP/USD bid-ask cross rates.

First, we will reiterate some of the things that we have already described in the reading because they serve as the building blocks for our task.

USD/EUR$_{bid}$ = 1.3802	**USD/EUR$_{ask}$ = 1.3806**
• Represents the price of **EUR** (base currency). • An investor can **sell** EUR for USD at this price (as it is the **bid** price quoted by the dealer).	• Represents the price of **EUR**. • An investor can **buy** EUR with USD at this price.
GBP/EUR$_{bid}$ = 0.8593	**GBP/EUR$_{ask}$ = 0.8599**
• Represents the price of **EUR**. • An investor can **sell** EUR for GBP at this price.	• Represents the price of **EUR**. • An investor can **buy** EUR with GBP at this price.

Determining the GBP/USD$_{bid}$ cross rate

> The EUR provides the common link between the exchange rates that we are given.

This rate represents the price at which the **USD** (base currency) can be **sold** by an investor for **GBP**. In order to sell USD in return for GBP given the quotes provided to us (USD/EUR and GBP/EUR), the investor would have to (1) sell her USD for EUR, and then (2) sell those EUR for GBP.

1. In order to sell USD for EUR, the investor needs an exchange rate quote with the **USD** as the base currency. Further, since she is **selling** USD, she needs the **bid** price for the USD in terms of EUR. The exchange rate quote that is provided to us (USD/EUR = 1.3802 – 1.3806) has **EUR** as the base currency, but we can determine the **EUR/USD$_{bid}$** as follows:

$$EUR/USD_{bid} = 1/(USD/EUR_{ask}) = 1/1.3806 = \textbf{0.7243 EUR/USD}$$

2. Once the investor has converted her USD to EUR, she needs to **sell** those EUR for GBP. In order to sell **EUR** for GBP, she needs an exchange rate quote for the EUR. Further, since she is **selling** EUR, she needs the **bid** for the EUR in terms of GBP.

$$GBP/EUR_{bid} = \textbf{0.8593 GBP/EUR} \text{ (provided)}$$

3. Therefore, the bid for the GBP/USD exchange rate can be calculated as:

$$GBP/USD_{bid} = EUR/USD_{bid} \times GBP/EUR_{bid}$$
$$= \frac{0.7243 \; \cancel{EUR}}{USD} \times \frac{0.8593 \; GBP}{\cancel{EUR}}$$
$$= \textbf{0.6224 GBP/USD}$$

Determining the GBP/USD$_{ask}$ cross rate

This exchange rate represents the price at which an investor can **purchase USD** (base currency) with **GBP**. In order to purchase USD with GBP given the quotes provided (USD/EUR and GBP/EUR), the investor would have to (1) purchase EUR with her GBP, and then (2) purchase USD with those EUR.

1. In order to purchase **EUR** using GBP, the investor needs an exchange rate quote with **EUR** as the base currency. Further, since she is **purchasing** EUR, she needs the **ask** price for the EUR in terms of GBP.

$$\text{GBP/EUR}_{ask} = 0.8599 \text{ GBP / EUR (provided)}$$

2. Once the investor has converted her GBP to EUR, she needs to purchase USD with those EUR. In order to purchase **USD**, she needs a quote with the **USD** as the base currency. Further, since she is **purchasing** USD, she needs the **ask** price for the USD in terms of EUR. The exchange rate that is provided (USD/EUR = 1.3802 − 1.3806) has EUR as the base currency, but we can determine the **EUR/USD$_{ask}$** as follows:

$$\text{EUR/USD}_{ask} = 1 / (\text{USD/EUR}_{bid}) = 1 / 1.3802 = 0.7245 \text{ EUR / USD}$$

3. Therefore, the ask for the GBP/USD exchange rate can be calculated as:

$$\text{GBP/USD}_{ask} = \text{GBP/EUR}_{ask} \times \text{EUR/USD}_{ask}$$
$$= \frac{0.8599 \text{ GBP}}{\text{EUR}} \times \frac{0.7245 \text{ EUR}}{\text{USD}}$$
$$= 0.6230 \text{ GBP/USD}$$

We have gone to great lengths to illustrate cross currency calculations with bid-ask quotes step by step in the example above to make sure that you understand the process. Fortunately, there is a quicker way to do this. To illustrate this method, we reproduce the quoted exchange rates below:

$$\text{USD/EUR} = 1.3802 - 1.3806$$
$$\text{GBP/EUR} = 0.8593 - 0.8599$$
$$\text{GBP/USD} = ?$$

Step 1: Bring the bid-ask quotes for the exchange rates into a format such that the common (or third) currency cancels out if we multiply the exchange rates.

We chose to convert the USD/EUR into the EUR/USD exchange rate (and not the GBP/EUR into the EUR/GBP exchange rate) because the exchange rate that we are trying to determine (GBP/USD) has the USD as the base currency and GBP as the price currency. If we were to convert the GBP/EUR exchange rate we would obtain a quote for USD/GBP (not for GBP/USD) by multiplying USD/EUR by EUR/GBP.

In this case, we are provided with USD/EUR and GBP/EUR exchange rates. The common currency is the EUR, but since it represents the base currency (denominator) in both the quotes, the EUR will not cancel out if we multiply them. We need to convert one of the quotes (USD/EUR or GBP/EUR) into a form where EUR is not the base currency. Let's convert the USD/EUR exchange rate into EUR/USD.

$$USD/EUR = 1.3802 - 1.3806$$

$$EUR/USD_{bid} = 1/(USD/EUR_{ask}) = 1/1.3806 = 0.7243 \text{ EUR/USD}$$

$$EUR/USD_{ask} = 1/(USD/EUR_{bid}) = 1/1.3802 = 0.7245 \text{ EUR/USD}$$

Now that we have the EUR/USD exchange rate and the GBP/EUR exchange rate, we know that multiplying the two would cancel out the EUR and leave us with a GBP/USD exchange rate.

Step 2: Multiply the exchange rates in a manner that maximizes the resulting bid-ask spread. The bid-ask spread is maximized when the bid is minimized and ask is maximized.

- The lowest possible exchange rate for GBP/USD would result if we multiply EUR/USD$_{bid}$ by GBP/EUR$_{bid}$. This rate would represent GBP/USD$_{bid}$.

$$GBP/USD_{bid} = EUR/USD_{bid} \times GBP/EUR_{bid} = 0.7243 \times 0.8593 = \mathbf{0.6224 \text{ GBP/USD}}$$

- The highest possible exchange rate for GBP/USD would result if we multiply EUR/USD$_{ask}$ by GBP/EUR$_{ask}$. This rate would represent GBP/USD$_{ask}$.

$$GBP/USD_{ask} = EUR/USD_{ask} \times GBP/EUR_{ask} = 0.7245 \times 0.8599 = \mathbf{0.6230 \text{ GBP/USD}}$$

LESSON 3: FOREIGN EXCHANGE SPREADS AND ARIBTRAGE CONSTRAINTS ON SPOT EXCHANGE RATE QUOTES

LOS 13a: Calculate and interpret the bid-ask spread on a spot or forward foreign currency quotation and describe the factors that affect the bid-offer spreads. Vol 1, pp 500–505

LOS 13b: Identify a triangular arbitrage opportunity and calculate its profit, given the bid-offer quotations for three currencies. Vol 1, pp 500–505

Foreign Exchange Spreads

It is important to distinguish between (1) the bid-ask prices that a **dealer** obtains from the **interbank market** and (2) the bid-ask prices that a **client** receives from a **dealer**.

Dealers buy and sell currencies among themselves in the interbank market to (1) adjust their inventories and risk positions, (2) distribute foreign currencies to clients, and (3) transfer foreign exchange rate risk to market participants who are willing to bear it.

The bid-ask spread that a dealer provides to clients is typically wider than the bid-ask spread observed in the interbank market. For example, if the USD/EUR quote in the interbank market is 1.3802–1.3806, a dealer may provide a client with a quote of 1.3801–1.3807. With the wider bid-ask spread in the quote provided to the client:

- If the dealer purchases the base currency (EUR) from the client (at 1.3801 USD/EUR) she is able to sell the base currency (EUR) in the interbank market (at 1.3802 USD/EUR) and (1) eliminate her risk exposure and (2) make a profit of 1 pip.
- If the dealer sells the base currency (EUR) to the client (at 1.3807 USD/EUR) she is able to purchase the base currency (EUR) from the interbank market (at 1.3806 USD/EUR) and (1) eliminate her risk exposure and (2) make a profit of 1 pip.

Factors Affecting the Size of the Bid-Ask Spread

The size of the bid-ask spread quoted to dealers' clients varies over time and across exchange rates. It is influenced by the factors described below:

The size of the bid-ask spread in the interbank market: The more liquid the interbank market, the narrower the bid-ask spread. Liquidity depends on:

- *The currency pair involved:* Some currency pairs (e.g., USD/EUR, JPY/USD and USD/GBP) see greater market participation (and are therefore more liquid) than others (e.g., MXN/CHF).
- *The time of day:* Interbank FX markets are most liquid when business hours in the two largest FX trading centers (New York and London) overlap (8am-11am EST). Spreads tend to be narrower during this window relative to other times of the day.
- *Market volatility:* The greater the uncertainty in the market, the wider the spread. Uncertainty in the market (e.g., due to geopolitical events or market crashes) leads dealers to charge a higher price to compensate them for the risk of holding those currencies.

The size of the transaction: Generally speaking, the larger the transaction, the wider the spread that a dealer will quote to the client. This is because the dealer would require a higher compensation for taking on the risk associated with having to "lay off" a relatively large quantity of one currency in the interbank market. However, note that the spread in small retail transactions (e.g., individuals converting foreign currency at a local bank, or foreign currency-denominated credit card purchases) can be much higher than the spread in the interbank market.

The relationship between the dealer and the client: Dealers may quote narrower bid-ask spreads to preferred clients based on prospective or ongoing business relationships. Since the settlement cycle for spot FX transactions is relatively short (2 days), credit risk does not play an important role in determining the spread quoted to clients.

Arbitrage Constraints on Spot Exchange Rate Quotes

The bid-ask quotes provided by a dealer in the interbank market must adhere to two arbitrage constraints:

1. The bid quoted by a dealer in the interbank market cannot be higher than the current interbank offer, and the ask offered by a dealer cannot be lower than the current interbank bid; otherwise other dealers in the market would be able to earn riskless arbitrage profits by purchasing low and selling high. To illustrate, assume that the current USD/EUR exchange rate in the interbank market is 1.3802–1.3806.

> The bid-ask spread is sometimes measured in terms of pips. Pips are scaled so that they can be related to the last digit in the spot exchange rate quote. Most exchange rates are quoted to four decimal places. In this case, the bid-ask spread in the interbank market equals 0.0004 or 4 pips, while the bid-ask spread in the quote offered by the dealer equals 0.0006 or 6 pips.

- If a dealer quotes a (misaligned) exchange rate of 1.3807–1.3811, other market participants would buy the EUR in the interbank market (at 1.3806 USD/EUR) and sell EUR to the dealer (at 1.3807 USD/EUR) to make a profit of 1 pip.
- If a dealer quotes a (misaligned) exchange rate of 1.3797–1.3801, other market participants would buy the EUR from the dealer (at 1.3801 USD/EUR) and sell EUR in the interbank market (at 1.3802 USD/EUR) to make a profit of 1 pip.

2. The cross rate bid quoted by a dealer cannot be higher than the implied cross rate ask available in the interbank market, and the cross rate ask quoted by a dealer cannot be lower than the implied cross rate bid available in the interbank market. These constraints are illustrated in detail in the following section.

Triangular Arbitrage

Assume that we are provided with the following exchange rate quotes by a European bank:

$$USD/EUR = 1.3802 - 1.3806$$
$$GBP/EUR = 0.8593 - 0.8599$$

Further, a U.S. bank offers us the following quote:

$$GBP/USD = 0.6216 - 0.6222$$

Calculating the arbitrage profit per USD invested is relatively straightforward given these rates. We would purchase USD from the U.S. bank at 0.6222 GBP/USD and sell USD to the European bank at the implied cross rate of 0.6224 GBP/USD. We would end up with a profit of 0.0002 GBP/USD.

Let's determine if there is an arbitrage opportunity here. An arbitrage opportunity exists when it is profitable for an investor to purchase a currency from one bank and sell it to another. This occurs when the ask price quoted by one bank is *lower* than the bid price provided by another.

- From the cross-currency bid-ask quotes that we calculated in the previous section, we know that the USD/EUR and GBP/EUR quotes provided by the European bank imply a cross exchange rate of GBP/USD = 0.6224–0.6230.
- The **ask** price quoted by the U.S bank for the USD (0.6222 GBP/USD) is *lower* than the implied cross rate **bid** (0.6224 GBP/USD) computed from the European bank's quotes.
- Therefore, we can make an arbitrage profit by purchasing USD (low) from the U.S bank and selling USD (high) to the European bank.

The trades required to make arbitrage profits given that we hold 1,000 GBP are described below:

- Purchase USD (low) from the U.S. bank at the ask price of 0.6222 GBP/USD.
  - We obtain $GBP\ 1,000 \div \dfrac{0.6222\ GBP}{USD} = USD\ 1,607.20$
  - Note: We use the "÷" sign here because we have GBP and the given exchange rate quote has GBP in the numerator.
- Sell the USD (in return for EUR) to the European bank at the EUR/USD bid rate ($EUR/USD_{bid} = 1/1.3806 = 0.7243$)
  - We obtain $USD\ 1,607.20 \times \dfrac{0.7243\ EUR}{USD} = EUR\ 1,164.13$
  - Note: We use the "×" sign here because we have USD and the exchange rate has USD in the denominator.

- Sell the EUR (in return for GBP) to the European bank at the GBP/EUR bid rate (GBP/EUR$_{bid}$ = 0.8593)

  - We obtain EUR 1,164.13 $\times \dfrac{0.8593 \text{ GBP}}{\text{EUR}}$ = GBP 1,000.34

  - Note: We use the "×" sign here because we have EUR and the exchange rate quote has EUR in the denominator.
- We make an arbitrage profit of GBP 0.34 per GBP 1,000 used in the arbitrage. This is a riskless profit and requires no initial investment. See Example 3-1.

The type of arbitrage transaction that we have just illustrated is known as triangular arbitrage. Triangular arbitrage ensures consistency between exchange rates and cross rates and is precluded when:

- The cross rate bid quoted by a dealer is lower than the implied cross rate ask available in the interbank market.
- The cross rate ask quoted by a dealer is higher than the implied cross rate bid available in the interbank market.

Practically speaking, traders and automatic trading algorithms ensure that such price discrepancies almost never occur.

Example 3-1: Calculating Bid-Offer Rates

An analyst gathered the following spot rate quotes from the interbank market:

USD/GBP: 1.5286–1.5289
USD/EUR: 1.4251–1.4254
JPY/USD: 81.79–81.82
CAD/USD: 0.9563–0.9566

Based on these quotes:

1. Calculate the bid-offer on the JPY/GBP cross rate.
2. Calculate the bid-offer on the JPY/CAD cross rate.
3. Is there a possibility of a triangular arbitrage if a dealer quoted a bid-offer rate of 125.0125–125.0239 in JPY/GBP?
4. Is there a possibility of a triangular arbitrage if a dealer quoted a bid-offer rate of 85.5290–85.5688 in JPY/CAD?

Solution:

As mentioned earlier, calculating cross rates with bid-ask quotes is a two-step process:

Step 1: Bring the bid-ask quotes for the exchange rates into a format such that the common (or third) currency cancels out if we multiply the exchange rates.
Step 2: Multiply the exchange rates in a manner that maximizes the resulting bid-ask spread. We multiply the bid by the bid, and the ask by the ask.

---

1. The given exchange rates, JPY/USD and USD/GBP, can be multiplied to cancel out USD (the common currency). Therefore, we compute the implied cross rates by simply multiplying the bid by the bid, and the ask by the ask (to maximize the resulting bid-ask spread).

$$JPY/GBP_{bid} = JPY/USD_{bid} \times USD/GBP_{bid} = 81.79 \times 1.5286 = 125.0242$$
$$JPY/GBP_{ask} = JPY/USD_{ask} \times USD/GBP_{ask} = 81.82 \times 1.5289 = 125.0946$$

2. The given exchange rates, JPY/USD and CAD/USD, cannot be multiplied to cancel out the USD (common currency). Therefore, we must first invert the CAD/USD quotes.

$$USD/CAD_{bid} = 1/(CAD/USD_{ask}) = 1/0.9566 = 1.0454 \, USD/CAD$$
$$USD/CAD_{ask} = 1/(CAD/USD_{bid}) = 1/0.9563 = 1.0457 \, USD/CAD$$

Now that the JPY/USD and USD/CAD exchange rates can be multiplied to cancel out the USD, we multiply the bid by the bid, and the ask by the ask to compute the JPY/CAD cross rates.

$$JPY/CAD_{bid} = JPY/USD_{bid} \times USD/CAD_{bid} = 81.79 \times 1.0454 = 85.5007$$
$$JPY/CAD_{ask} = JPY/USD_{ask} \times USD/CAD_{ask} = 81.82 \times 1.0457 = 85.5589$$

3. Triangular arbitrage is possible if the dealer's bid (offer) is above (below) the interbank market's offer (bid).

The dealer's offer for JPY/GBP (125.0239) is actually below the interbank market's implied cross rate bid (125.0242). This implies that the dealer is selling GBP too cheap. Therefore, triangular arbitrage would involve buying GBP from the dealer for JPY 125.0239 and selling GBP in the interbank market at the implied cross rate bid of JPY 125.0242, making a profit of JPY 0.0003 (= 125.0242 − 125.0239) per GBP transacted. Note that selling the GBP for JPY in the interbank market would entail first selling the GBP for USD and then converting those USD into JPY.

4. Triangular arbitrage is not possible in this case.
   - The dealer's JPY/CAD bid (85.5290) is less than the interbank market's implied cross rate offer (85.5589),
   - The dealer's offer (85.5688) is greater than the interbank market's implied cross rate bid (85.5007).

LESSON 4: FORWARD MARKETS

LOS 13c: Distinguish between spot and forward rates and calculate the forward premium/discount for a given currency. Vol 1, pp 507–513

Going forward, in order to focus on the intuition behind the computation of forward rates, we will ignore the bid-ask spread on exchange rate quotes and money market interest rates. Further, we will work with exchange rates quoted as indirect exchange rates (FC/DC) as is the case in the CFA Program curriculum. Wherever possible, we will also try to express our conclusions, equations, and expressions in terms of price and base currencies so that you can apply them when questions do not explicitly direct you to treat a particular currency as the domestic currency.

Forward exchange rates (F) are quotes for transactions that are contracted (agreed upon) today, but settled at a pre-specified date in the **future** (settlement occurs after a period longer than the two days for spot transactions). Forward exchange rates (just like spot exchange rates) are also quoted in terms of bid and ask prices.

> Covered interest rate parity is also discussed later in the reading.

Forward exchange rates are calculated in a manner that ensures that traders are not able to earn arbitrage profits (a condition known as covered interest rate parity). This means that a trader with a specific amount of domestic currency should be able to earn the exact same amount from both the following investment options:

Option 1: She invests the funds at the domestic nominal risk-free rate (i_{DC}) for a particular period of time.

- If she invests 1 unit of DC at i_{DC} for 1 year, the value of her investment after 1 year would equal $(1 + i_{DC})$.

Option 2: She converts the funds into a foreign currency (at the current spot rate, $S_{FC/DC}$), invests them at the foreign nominal risk-free rate, i_{FC} (for the same period of time as in Option 1) and then converts them back to the domestic currency at the forward exchange rate ($F_{FC/DC}$) which she locks in today.

- When she converts her 1 unit of DC into FC today, she receives $1DC \times S_{FC/DC} = S_{FC}$ units of FC.
- She invests S_{FC} units of FC at the foreign risk-free rate (i_{FC}).
  - After one year, she receives $S_{FC} \times (1 + i_{FC})$.
- This amount is converted back into DC at the 1 year forward rate (which was determined at the time of initial investment) given by $F_{FC/DC}$
  - After 1 year, the value of her investment (in DC terms) equals $[S_{FC} \times (1 + i_{FC})] \div F_{FC/DC}$.

Both these investment options are **risk-free** because they require the money to be invested at risk-free interest rates. Further, the exchange rate risk in the second option is eliminated (hedged) by locking in the forward rate at the time of investment. Since these two investments have identical risk characteristics, it follows that they must have the same return (to preclude arbitrage profits), leading to the following equality:

$$(1 + i_{DC}) = \frac{(1 + i_{FC}) \times S_{FC/DC}}{F_{FC/DC}}$$

The above equality can be used to derive the formula for the forward rate:

$$F_{FC/DC} = S_{FC/DC} \times \frac{(1 + i_{FC})}{(1 + i_{DC})}$$

We can also express this equation in terms of the standard exchange rate quoting convention (price currency/base currency) as follows:

$$F_{PC/BC} = S_{PC/BC} \times \frac{(1 + i_{PC})}{(1 + i_{BC})}$$

> This version of the formula is perhaps easiest to retain as it contains the FC term in the numerator for all three components: $F_{FC/DC}$, $S_{FC/DC}$, and i_{FC}. You may also find it useful to remember that the numerator-denominator rule applies for all parity relations. If you are given an A/B exchange rate quote, the Country A interest rate will be in the numerator and the Country B interest rate will be in the denominator.

For simplicity, we worked with a 1-year investment horizon in the illustration above. However, the no-arbitrage argument holds for any investment horizon. Since the risk-free rates typically used in this arbitrage relationship are LIBOR rates for the currencies involved, the formulas above can be expressed as:

$$F_{FC/DC} = S_{FC/DC} \times \frac{1 + (i_{FC} \times {Actual}/{360})}{1 + (i_{DC} \times {Actual}/{360})}$$

$$F_{PC/BC} = S_{PC/BC} \times \frac{1 + (i_{PC} \times {Actual}/{360})}{1 + (i_{BC} \times {Actual}/{360})}$$

Currencies Trading at Forward Premium/Discount

- If the forward exchange rate is *higher* than the spot exchange rate, the **base currency** is said to be trading at a forward premium because it is expected to **appreciate** in the future (the price of the base currency is expected to be higher going forward).
    - At the same time, the price currency would be trading at a forward discount, which means that it is expected to depreciate.
- If the forward rate is *lower* than the spot rate, the **base currency** is trading at a forward discount as it is expected to **depreciate** in the future (the price of the base currency is expected to be lower going forward).
    - At the same time, the price currency would be trading at a forward premium and is expected to appreciate.
- The forward discount/premium equals the difference between the forward exchange rate and the spot exchange rate. See Example 4-1.

$$F_{FC/DC} - S_{FC/DC} = S_{FC/DC} \left(\frac{(i_{FC} - i_{DC}) \times {Actual}/{360}}{1 + (i_{DC} \times {Actual}/{360})} \right)$$

$$F_{PC/BC} - S_{PC/BC} = S_{PC/BC} \left(\frac{(i_{PC} - i_{BC}) \times {Actual}/{360}}{1 + (i_{BC} \times {Actual}/{360})} \right)$$

Example 4-1: Calculating the Forward Premium (Discount)

An analyst gathered the following information:

Spot USD/EUR = 1.4562
180-day LIBOR (USD) = 1.05%
180-day LIBOR (EUR) = 2.38%

Calculate the forward premium (discount) for a 180-day forward contract for USD/EUR.

Solution:

$$\text{Forward premium (discount)} = F_{PC/BC} - S_{PC/BC} = S_{PC/BC}\left(\frac{(i_{PC} - i_{BC}) \times \text{Actual}/360}{1 + (i_{BC} \times \text{Actual}/360)}\right)$$

$$= 1.4562\frac{(0.0105 - 0.0238) \times 180/360}{1 + (0.0238 \times 180/360)}$$

$$= -0.00957$$

In professional FX markets, forward exchange rates are quoted in terms of points (pips), which simply represent the difference between the forward rate and the spot rate (forward premium or discount). Note however, that these points (pips) are scaled so that they can be related to the last digit in the spot quote (usually the fourth decimal place). We will use the hypothetical spot exchange rates and forward points in Table 4-1 to illustrate this:

Table 4-1: Sample Spot and Forward Quotes (Bid-Offer)

Maturity	Spot Rate or Forward Points
Spot USD/EUR	1.3802/1.3806
One month	− 5.4/− 4.9
Three months	− 15.8/− 15.2
Six months	− 36.9/− 36.2
Twelve months	− 93.9/− 91.4

Note that:

- The bid rate is always lower than the ask rate.
- In this case, the forward points are negative, which indicates that the EUR (base currency) is trading at a forward discount and that the USD (price currency) is trading at a forward premium.
- The absolute number of forward points increases with time to maturity.
- The quoted forward points are scaled to each maturity (they are not annualized) so they do not need to be adjusted before adding them to the spot rate to compute the forward rate.
- To convert any of these forward point quotes to an actual forward exchange rate, we divide the number of pips by **10,000** (to scale them down to the fourth decimal place) and then add the resulting number to the quoted spot exchange rate.
  - For example, if the client wants to sell EUR 3 months forward, the applicable number of forward points is −15.8.
    - We use the **bid** rate because the **client** is **selling** the **base** currency in the currency quote.
    - We first divide −15.8 by 10,000 to get −0.00158 and then simply add this number to the spot USD/EUR bid rate.
    - 3 month forward USD/EUR$_{bid}$ = 1.3802 + (−0.00158) = 1.37862 USD/EUR

In the swap market, it is standard practice to use the mid-market spot exchange rates for the transaction. However, the forward points will still be based on the bid or offer rate depending on the investor's position. This is because in a swap transaction, there are simultaneous spot and forward transactions in that the base currency is being bought (sold) spot and sold (bought) forward. FX swaps are used for swap financing as well as rolling over (hedging or speculative) positions as the underlying forward contract matures.

Factors Affecting the Bid-Ask Spread in Forward Exchange Rate Quotes

In addition to the factors mentioned earlier in the reading (that affect spreads in the spot market) spreads in the forward market are influenced by the term of maturity of the contract. Generally speaking, spreads tend to widen with longer terms. This is due to:

- Lower liquidity of longer term contracts.
- Greater credit risk in longer term contracts.
- Greater interest rate risk in forward contracts. Forward rates are based on interest rate differentials. Longer maturities result in greater duration or higher sensitivity to changes in interest rates.

LOS 13d: Calculate the mark-to-market value of a forward contract.
Vol 1, pp 517–520

Mark-to-Market of Forward Contracts

Mark-to-market adjustments on various forward contracts (including currency forwards) are described in much more detail in the section on Derivatives.

A forward contract is priced to have zero value to either party at contract initiation. In the case of currency forwards, this no-arbitrage forward price is determined based on **interest rate parity**. However, once the counterparties have entered the contract, changes in the forward price (due to changes in the spot exchange rate or changes in interest rates in either of the two currencies) will result in changes in the mark-to-market value of the contract as the contract holds positive value for one counterparty, and an equivalent negative value for the other. See Example 4-2.

The "all-in" forward rate is simply the sum of the spot rate and the forward points, appropriately scaled to size.

Example 4-2: Valuing a Forward Contract Prior to Expiration

An investor purchased GBP 10 million for delivery against AUD in 6 months (t = 180) at an "all-in" forward rate of 1.5920 AUD/GBP. Four months later (t = 120), the investor wants to close out his position. Given that a dealer quotes him the bid-offer rates for the spot exchange rate and forward points in Table 4-2, answer the questions that follow. Assume that LIBOR-60 at t = 120 is 4.20%.

Table 4-2: Spot Exchange Rate and Forward Points at t = 120

Maturity	Spot Rate or Forward Points
Spot AUD/GBP	1.6110/1.6115
One month	5.1/5.2
Two months	10.3/10.5
Three months	15.9/16.2
Four months	26.4/26.8

1. What position would the investor take, and on which contract, to effectively eliminate (close out) his forward position at t = 120?
2. Calculate the gain or loss that the investor would incur to close out his forward position at t = 120.

Solution:

1. The investor took a **long** position on the GBP in the **initial** contract which had a term of 6 months (t = 180). Four months into this contract (at t = 120), in order to close out his forward position, the investor must take the (opposite) short position on GBP 10 million in an **offsetting** forward contract that expires in another 2 months (at t = 180).

2. To sell GBP (the base currency) forward, the relevant exchange rate would be the all-in AUD/GBP$_{bid}$. The appropriate all-in two-month forward exchange rate is calculated based on the spot rate at t = 120 and the forward points on the two-month forward bid exchange rate:

$$1.6110 + (10.3/10,000) = 1.61203 \text{ AUD/GBP}$$

This means that the investor initially purchased 10 million GBP (for delivery at t = 180) at 1.5920 AUD/GBP and then (at t = 120) sold 10 million GBP (for delivery at t = 180) at 1.61203 AUD/GBP. The GBP amounts will net to zero at settlement, but the AUD amounts will not (because the forward rate has changed over the four months). At contract expiration, the investor stands to make a profit (loss) of:

$$\text{Profit (loss)} = (1.61203 - 1.5920) \text{ AUD/GBP} \times 10,000,000 \text{ GBP} = \text{AUD } 200,300$$

The investor makes a profit because he had a long position on the GBP and the forward rate increased (the base currency, GBP, appreciated) during the four month period (from t = 0 to t = 120). Note that the investor would stand to "pocket" this profit at t = 180 (when both the forward contracts actually settle). In order to compute the mark-to-market value of the investor's position at t = 120 (when the forward position is effectively closed out via the offsetting contract) we must discount the settlement payment for two months (time remaining until contract expiration) at the two-month discount rate. Given that LIBOR-60 at t = 120 equals 4.20%, the mark-to-market value of the original long GBP 10m six-month forward contract two months prior to settlement is calculated as:

$$\frac{\text{AUD } 200,300}{1 + (0.042 \times 60 / 360)} = \text{AUD } 198,907.65$$

Below, we summarize the steps involved in marking-to-market a position on a currency forward:

- Create an equal offsetting forward position to the initial forward position.
  - Make sure that the settlement dates and the notional amounts of both the contracts are the same.
- Determine the all-in forward rate for the offsetting forward contract.
  - If the base currency in the exchange rate quote should be sold (purchased) in the offsetting contract, use the bid (ask) side of the quote.
- Calculate the profit/loss on the net position as of the settlement date.
  - If the currency that the investor was long on in the initial forward contract has appreciated (depreciated), there will be a profit (loss).
  - If the currency that the investor was short on in the initial forward contract has appreciated (depreciated), there will be a loss (profit).
- Calculate the present value (as of the date of initiation of the offsetting contract) of the profit/loss.
  - Remember to use the appropriate LIBOR rate and to unannualize it (if necessary).

LESSON 5: INTERNATIONAL PARITY RELATIONS: PART I: IMPORTANT CONCEPTS, COVERED AND UNCOVERED INTEREST RATE PARITY

LOS 13e: Explain international parity relations (covered and uncovered interest rate parity, purchasing power parity, and the international Fisher effect).
Vol 1, pp 516–537

LOS 13f: Describe relations among the international parity conditions.
Vol 1, pp 516–537

LOS 13g: Evaluate the use of the current spot rate, the forward rate, purchasing power parity, and uncovered interest parity to forecast future spot exchange rates.
Vol 1, pp 516–537

Before moving into international parity relations, we must understand the following concepts:

- **Long run versus short run:** Parity relations offer estimates of exchange rates in the long run, and are typically poor predictors of exchange rates in the short run. Long-term equilibrium values act as an "anchor" for exchange rate movements (short run exchange rates revolve around them).
- **Real versus nominal values:** Most of the discussion that follows in this section focuses on predicting future nominal exchange rates. Real exchange rates (that are adjusted for inflation) will also be discussed, but not as much as nominal exchange rates (which are tradable and are used to determine mark-to-market adjustments).
- **Expected versus unexpected changes:** Expected changes are generally reflected in current prices (and exchange rates). Unexpected changes are sources of risk as they can lead to more significant price movements. As a result, investors demand a premium for bearing the risk associated with unpredictable outcomes.
- **Relative movements:** Relative changes, (not absolute or isolated changes) in economic factors across countries determine exchange rates. Since an exchange rate represents the price of one currency in terms of another, the inflation rate in one country must be evaluated relative to the inflation rate in the other country to determine the impact on the exchange rate between their currencies.

Bear in mind that there is no simple formula, model, or theory that would enable investors to accurately forecast exchange rates. However, the theories that we will now discuss do offer us a framework for developing a view on exchange rates and for thinking through some of the forces that influence them.

Covered Interest Rate Parity

We already described **covered interest rate parity** earlier in this reading when we were illustrating the determination of forward exchange rates (using domestic vs. foreign nominal risk-free rates). Basically, covered interest rate parity describes a no-arbitrage condition where the **covered** or **currency-hedged** interest rate differential between two currencies equals zero. What this means is that there is a no-arbitrage relationship among risk-free interest rates and spot and forward exchange rates.

$$\text{Covered interest rate parity: } F_{PC/BC} = S_{PC/BC} \times \frac{1 + (i_{PC} \times \text{Actual}/360)}{1 + (i_{BC} \times \text{Actual}/360)}$$

The forward premium (discount) on the base currency can be expressed as a percentage as:

$$\text{Forward premium (discount) as a\%} = \frac{F_{PC/BC} - S_{PC/BC}}{S_{PC/BC}}$$

The forward premium (discount) on the base currency can be estimated as:

$$\text{Forward premium (discount) as a \%} \approx F_{PC/BC} - S_{PC/BC} \approx i_{PC} - i_{BC}$$

- If the risk-free rate on one currency is *greater* than the risk-free rate on another currency, the currency with the higher risk-free rate will trade at a forward *discount* relative to the other currency, such that the benefit of the higher interest rate will be offset by a decline in the value of the currency.
    - If the risk-free rate of the price currency is **greater** than that of the base currency, the base currency will trade at a forward premium (as the forward exchange rate will be greater than the spot exchange rate. Since the base currency will trade at a forward premium, it implies that the price currency will trade at a forward discount, and is expected to **depreciate** in the future.
- The currency with the lower risk-free rate will trade at a forward *premium* relative to the other currency, such that the benefit of the expected appreciation of the currency will be offset by the lower interest rate.

For covered interest rate parity to hold, we must assume zero transaction costs, free mobility of capital and that the underlying money market instruments are identical in terms of liquidity, maturity and default risk. Generally speaking, covered interest rate differentials tend to be close to zero under normal market conditions, which indicates that covered interest parity tends to hold.

Uncovered Interest Rate Parity

Uncovered interest rate parity states that the **expected return** on an **uncovered** or **unhedged** foreign currency investment should equal the return on a comparable domestic currency investment. Uncovered interest rate parity states that an investor's expected return from the following investment options should be the same.

Option 1: She invests the funds at the domestic nominal risk-free rate (i_{DC}) for a particular period of time.

- If she invests 1 unit of DC at i_{DC} for 1 year, the value of her investment after 1 year would equal $(1 + i_{DC})$.

Option 2: She converts her funds into a foreign currency (at the current spot rate, $S_{FC/DC}$), invests them at the foreign nominal risk-free rate, i_{FC}, (for the same period of time as in Option 1) and then converts them back into the domestic currency after 1 year at the expected spot exchange rate one year from today ($S^e_{FC/DC}$).

- When she converts her 1 unit of DC into FC today, she receives $1DC \times S_{FC/DC} = S_{FC}$ units of FC.
- She invests S_{FC} units of FC at the foreign risk-free rate (i_{FC}). After one year, she receives $S_{FC} \times (1 + i_{FC})$.
- This amount is converted back into DC at the expected spot exchange rate one year from today given by $S^e_{FC/DC}$.
    - After 1 year, the value of her investment (in DC terms) equals $[S_{FC} \times (1 + i_{FC})] \div S^e_{FC/DC}$.

Therefore, the uncovered interest rate parity equation (assuming a time horizon of 1 year) is given by:

$$(1 + i_{DC}) = \frac{(1 + i_{FC}) \times S_{FC/DC}}{S^e_{FC/DC}}$$

The above equality can be used to derive the formula for the expected future spot exchange rate:

$$S^e_{FC/DC} = S_{FC/DC} \times \frac{(1 + i_{FC})}{(1 + i_{DC})}$$

Notice that the numerator-denominator rule applies here as well. If you are given an A/B exchange rate quote, the Country A interest rate will be in the numerator and the Country B interest rate will be in the denominator for the uncovered interest rate parity equation.

The expected percentage change in the spot exchange rate can be calculated as:

$$\text{Expected \% change in spot exchange rate} = \%\Delta S^e_{PC/BC} = \frac{S^e_{PC/BC} - S_{PC/BC}}{S_{PC/BC}}$$

The expected percentage change in the spot exchange rate can be estimated as:

$$\text{Expected \% change in spot exchange rate} \approx \%\Delta S^e_{PC/BC} \approx i_{PC} - i_{BC}$$

Covered versus Uncovered Interest Rate Parity

- In **covered interest rate parity**, we consider the **hedged** (against all currency risk) return on the foreign risk-free rate.
    - The investor locks in the **forward exchange rate** today so she is not exposed to currency risk.
    - If covered interest rate parity holds, the **forward premium/discount** offsets the yield differential.
- In **uncovered interest rate parity**, we consider the **unhedged** (against currency risk) return on the foreign risk-free rate (see Example 5-1).
    - The investor leaves his foreign exchange position uncovered (unhedged) and expects to convert foreign currency holdings back into her domestic currency at the **expected future spot rate**.
    - If uncovered interest rate parity holds, the **expected appreciation/depreciation** of the currency offsets the yield differential.

Example 5-1: Covered versus Uncovered Interest Rate Parity

Consider the following information:

- Risk-free rate on the USD = i_{USD} = 4%
- Risk-free rate on the GBP = i_{GBP} = 5%
- Current spot USD/GBP exchange rate = $S_{USD/GBP}$ = 1.5025

1. Compute the 1-year USD/GBP forward rate and the forward premium/discount assuming interest rate parity holds.
2. Compute the expected USD/GBP spot rate in 1 year and the expected change in the spot exchange rate over the year assuming that uncovered interest parity is expected to hold.

Solution:

Given how the spot rate is presented (USD/GBP), we will assume that the USD is the foreign currency and the GBP is the domestic currency in the discussion that follows:

1. Covered interest rate parity states that the holding period return on (1) an investment in a domestic money-market instrument and (2) an investment in a fully currency-hedged foreign money-market instrument must be the same.

   If covered interest rate parity holds, we can compute the **forward exchange rate** today as:

$$F_{USD/GBP} = S_{USD/GBP} \times \frac{(1+i_{USD})}{(1+i_{GBP})}$$

$$= 1.5025 \times \frac{1.04}{1.05} = 1.4882 \, USD/GBP$$

The forward premium (discount) on the GBP can be computed as:

$$\frac{F_{USD/GBP} - S_{USD/GBP}}{S_{USD/GBP}} = \frac{1.4882 - 1.5025}{1.5025} = -0.952\%$$

or approximately: $i_{USD} - i_{GBP} = 0.04 - 0.05 = -1\%$

Interpretation: Under covered interest rate parity, the GBP would trade at approximately a 1% forward discount versus the USD. This forward discount on the GBP is explained by its relatively high interest rate versus the USD (5% versus 4%). At the same time, the USD would trade at approximately a 1% forward premium versus the GBP (due to its lower interest rate).

2. Uncovered interest rate parity states that the expected holding period return on (1) an investment in a domestic money-market instrument and (2) an unhedged (against currency risk) investment in a foreign money-market instrument would be exactly the same. If uncovered interest rate parity holds, we can compute the **expected future spot rate** as follows:

$$S^e_{USD/GBP} = S^e_{USD/GBP} \times \frac{(1+i_{USD})}{(1+i_{GBP})}$$

$$1.5025 \times \frac{1.04}{1.05} = 1.4882\, USD/GBP$$

The change in the spot exchange rate for the GBP against the USD over the next year is expected to be:

$$\frac{S^e_{USD/GBP} - S_{USD/GBP}}{S_{USD/GBP}} = \frac{1.4882 - 1.5025}{1.5025} = -0.952\%$$

or approximately: $\%\Delta S^e_{USD/GBP} = i_{USD} - i_{GBP} = 0.04 - 0.05 = -1\%$

Interpretation: Under uncovered interest rate parity, the GBP would be expected to depreciate by approximately 1% over the next year. The spot exchange rate is expected to fall from 1.5025 USD/GBP to 1.4882 USD/GBP. The GBP is expected to depreciate against the USD over the year to offset its higher interest rate relative to the USD (5% versus 4%). At the same time, the USD is expected to appreciate against the GBP by approximately 1% over the year.

Important:

- Note that under uncovered interest rate parity, the direction of the predicted change in spot rates is counterintuitive. All other factors constant, an increase in interest rates would be expected to lead to an appreciation of the currency, but uncovered interest rate parity implies that the opposite would be the case.
    - In our example, the GBP has the **higher** interest rate, but if uncovered interest rate parity holds, the GBP is expected to **depreciate** against the USD.
- Uncovered interest rate parity asserts that the **expected return** on the unhedged foreign investment is the same as the return on the domestic investment. However, the **distribution of possible return outcomes** is different. The domestic currency return is known with certainty, but the unhedged foreign investment return could:
    - *Equal the domestic currency return.* This would be the case if the percentage appreciation of the USD equals the interest rate differential (1%) as is the case in Example 5-1 Part 2.
    - *Be less than the domestic currency return.* This would be the case if the percentage appreciation of the USD is less than the interest rate differential (1%).
    - *Be greater than the domestic currency return.* This would be the case if the percentage appreciation of the USD is more than the interest rate differential (1%).

Due to this uncertainty associated with the future spot exchange rate, uncovered interest rate parity is often violated as investors (who are generally not risk-neutral) demand a risk premium for accepting the exchange rate risk inherent in leaving their positions unhedged (uncovered). As a result, future spot exchange rates typically do not equal the forward exchange rate. Forward rates (that are based purely on interest rate differentials to preclude covered interest arbitrage) are therefore, poor (biased) predictors of future spot exchange rates.

> If uncovered interest rate parity holds, the expected future spot rate would equal the forward rate ($S^e_{FC/DC} = F_{FC/DC}$), in which case the forward rate would be an unbiased predictor of the future spot rate. Covered interest rate parity always holds (as it is a no-arbitrage condition) but only when uncovered interest rate parity also holds would the forward rate be an unbiased forecast of the future spot exchange rate.

- As you may have noticed, the uncovered interest parity equation is quite similar to the covered interest parity equation except that the expected future spot exchange rate replaces the forward rate. To conclude:
    - Covered interest rate parity is a **no arbitrage condition** that uses the forward exchange rate.
    - Uncovered interest rate parity is a **theory** regarding expected future spot rates.

Empirical evidence suggests that:

- Uncovered interest rate parity does not hold over the short and medium terms, but works better over the long term. Over the short and medium terms, interest rate differentials do not explain changes in exchange rates, so forward rates (that are computed based on interest rate differentials) tend to be poor predictors of future exchange rates.
- Current spot exchange rates are also not good predictors of future spot exchange rates because of the high volatility in exchange rate movements. This suggests that exchange rates do not follow a random walk.

So far we have been looking at the relationship between exchange rates and **interest rate differentials**. We shall now be turning our attention towards exchange rates and **inflation differentials**.

LESSON 6: INTERNATIONAL PARITY RELATIONS PART II: PURCHASING POWER PARITY AND THE REAL EXCHANGE RATE

LOS 13e: Explain international parity relations (covered and uncovered interest rate parity, purchasing power parity, and the international Fischer effect).
Vol 1, pp 516–537

LOS 13f: Describe relations among the international parity conditions.
Vol 1, pp 516–537

LOS 13g: Evaluate the use of the current spot rate, the forward rate, purchasing power parity, and uncovered interest parity to forecast future spots exchange rates.
Vol 1, pp 516–537

Purchasing Power Parity (PPP)

Purchasing power parity (PPP) is based on the law of one price, which states that identical goods should trade at exactly the same price across countries when valued in terms of a common currency. For example, suppose the price of a pen in the U.S. is 2 USD, and the price of an identical pen in Europe is 3 EUR. Assuming that there are no transaction costs and no trade restrictions, the USD/EUR exchange rate must be 0.667 (as 3 EUR × 0.667 USD/EUR = 2 USD).

$$\text{Law of one price: } P_{pen}(\text{USD}) = P_{pen}(\text{EUR}) \times S_{\text{USD/EUR}}$$
$$\text{Law of one price: } P_{FC}^{X} = P_{DC}^{X} \times S_{\text{FC/DC}}$$
$$\text{Law of one price: } P_{BC}^{X} = P_{BC}^{X} \times S_{\text{PC/BC}}$$

If the price of these pens rises in Europe, pens would be traded from the U.S. to Europe, leading to an increase in supply of EUR (and demand for USD) to purchase pens. Eventually, the USD/EUR exchange rate would fall until the price differential is eliminated.

To summarize, according to the law of one price, a relative increase (decrease) in prices in one country will result in depreciation (appreciation) of its currency so exchange rate-adjusted prices are constant across countries. There are various versions of PPP.

1. **Absolute Purchasing Power Parity (Absolute PPP)**

Absolute PPP extends the law of one price to a broad range of goods and services consumed in different countries. Instead of focusing on just one individual good (like we focused on pens to illustrate the law of one price), absolute PPP states that the broad or general price level (GPL) in a country should equal the currency-adjusted general price level in the other country:

$$\text{Absolute PPP: } \text{GPL}_{FC} = \text{GPL}_{DC} \times S_{\text{FC/DC}}$$
$$\text{Absolute PPP: } \text{GPL}_{PC} = \text{GPL}_{BC} \times S_{\text{PC/BC}}$$

Note that absolute PPP assumes that all goods are tradable and that prices indices (used to determine the GPL) in both countries include the same goods and services with identical weights. We can rearrange the equations above to make the nominal exchange rate ($S_{\text{FC/DC}}$) the subject:

$$\text{Absolute PPP: } S_{\text{FC/DC}} = \text{GPL}_{FC} / \text{GPL}_{DC}$$
$$\text{Absolute PPP: } S_{\text{PC/BC}} = \text{GPL}_{PC} / \text{GPL}_{BC}$$

Notice once again that the numerator-denominator rule applies here. If you are given an A/B exchange rate quote, the Country A GPL will be in the numerator and the Country B GPL will be in the denominator.

Therefore, absolute PPP asserts that the equilibrium exchange rate between two countries is determined by the ratio of their respective national price levels. However, since (1) product-mixes and consumption baskets differ across countries and (2) there are transaction costs involved in international trade as well as trade restrictions, generally speaking, absolute PPP does not hold.

2. Relative Purchasing Power Parity (Relative PPP)

Instead of assuming that there are no transaction costs and other trade impediments (as is the case with absolute PPP), relative PPP merely assumes that these are constant over time. Relative PPP claims that **changes** in exchange rates are linked to relative **changes** in national price levels, even if the relation between exchange rate *levels* and price *levels* does not hold.

$$\text{Relative PPP: } E\left(S_{FC/DC}^{T}\right) = S_{FC/DC}^{0}\left(\frac{1+\pi_{FC}}{1+\pi_{DC}}\right)^{T}$$

Once again, notice that the numerator-denominator rule applies. If you are given an A/B exchange rate quote, the Country A inflation rate will be in the numerator and the Country B inflation rate will be in the denominator.

According to relative PPP, changes in the spot exchange rate can be approximated as:

$$\text{Relative PPP: } \%\Delta S_{FC/DC} \approx \pi_{FC} - \pi_{DC}$$
$$\text{Relative PPP: } \%\Delta S_{PC/BC} \approx \pi_{PC} - \pi_{BC}$$

Relative PPP suggests that the percentage change in the spot exchange rate ($\%\Delta S_{FC/DC}$) will be entirely determined by the difference between foreign and domestic inflation. For example, if U.S. inflation is 5% and Eurozone inflation is 8%, then the USD/EUR exchange rate should fall by 3%. Note that this means that the USD (low-inflation currency) will **appreciate**, while the EUR (high-inflation currency) will **depreciate**. In order to keep relative purchase power constant across countries, currencies of countries with higher (lower) rates of inflation should see their currencies depreciate (appreciate).

3. Ex Ante Version of PPP

The ex ante version of the PPP is based on relative PPP. While relative PPP asserts that *actual* changes in the exchange rate are driven by *actual* relative changes in inflation, ex ante PPP asserts that *expected* changes in spot exchange rates are entirely driven by *expected* differences in national inflation rates. According to ex ante PPP, countries that are expected to see persistently high (low) inflation rates should expect to see their currencies depreciate (appreciate) over time.

$$\text{Ex ante PPP: } \%\Delta S_{FC/DC}^{e} \approx \pi_{FC}^{e} - \pi_{DC}^{e}$$
$$\text{Ex ante PPP: } \%\Delta S_{PC/BC}^{e} \approx \pi_{PC}^{e} - \pi_{BC}^{e}$$

Real Exchange Rates

The real exchange rate of a currency measures the real purchasing power of a currency in terms of the amount of real goods and services that it can purchase internationally. The real exchange rate ($q_{FC/DC}$) equals the ratio of the domestic price level expressed in the foreign currency to the foreign price level.

- The domestic price level in terms of the foreign currency can be expressed as $P_{DC} \times S_{FC/DC}$.
- The foreign price level is represented by P_{FC}.

Therefore, the real exchange rate, $q_{FC/DC}$, can be expressed as:

$$q_{FC/DC} = \frac{P_{DC} \text{ in terms of FC}}{P_{FC}} = \frac{P_{DC} \times S_{FC/DC}}{P_{FC}} = S_{FC/DC} \left(\frac{P_{DC}}{P_{FC}} \right)$$

The numerator-denominator rule does NOT apply for the real exchange rate. If you are given A/B real or spot exchange rate, the Country A price level will be in the denominator and the Country B price level will be in the numerator.

Note that for a domestic consumer, an increase in the real exchange rate ($q_{FC/DC}$) indicates that the purchasing power or the real value of the domestic currency (base currency) is increasing. Further, the real exchange rate, $q_{FC/DC}$ (purchasing power of domestic citizens) is:

Understanding these three bullets (reproduced from Level I) will help you see why the formula for the real exchange rate is structured the way it is (with the nominal exchange rate and the domestic price level in the numerator and the foreign price level in the denominator).

- An *increasing* function of the nominal exchange rate ($S_{FC/DC}$). An increase in the nominal exchange rate means appreciation of the domestic currency (DC is the base currency), so domestic citizens can purchase more foreign goods.
- An *increasing* function of the domestic price level (P_{DC}). The assumption here is that the domestic price level is directly proportional to domestic income. Therefore, if the domestic price level increases, domestic income will also increase, so domestic citizens will be able to purchase more foreign goods.
- A *decreasing* function of the foreign price level (P_{FC}). An increase in the foreign price level would mean that domestic citizens would be able to purchase fewer foreign goods.

Studies have found that in the long run, real exchange rates tend to stabilize around their mean (mean reversion). Stable or constant real exchange rates in the long run imply that relative PPP holds in the long run. See the math below:

$$q_{FC/DC} = S_{FC/DC} \times \frac{P_{DC}}{P_{FC}}$$

Since the real exchange rate stabilizes in the long run, $\Delta q_{FC/DC} = 0$. We make the nominal exchange rate the subject of the equation for the real exchange rate and express the equation in terms of growth rates:

$$S_{FC/DC} = q_{FC/DC} \times \frac{P_{FC}}{P_{DC}}$$
$$\Delta S_{FC/DC} = \Delta q_{FC/DC} + (\Delta P_{FC} - \Delta P_{DC})$$
$$q_{FC/DC} = 0; \text{ Therefore:}$$
$$\Delta S_{FC/DC} \approx \pi_{FC} - \pi_{DC} \dots \dots (\text{Relative PPP})$$

Historically, it has been observed that:

- Over the short run, nominal exchange rates tend to not follow the path predicted by PPP.
- However, in the long run nominal exchange rates tend to move towards their long-run PPP equilibrium values, so PPP does serve as a valid framework for assessing the long-run fair value of a currency.
- So far we have discussed the relation between (1) exchange rates and interest rate differentials and (2) exchange rates and inflation differentials. In the next section, we examine how exchange rates, interest rates, and inflation rates interact.

LESSON 7: INTERNATIONAL PARITY RELATIONS PART III: THE FISHER EFFECT AND BRINGING ALL PARITY RELATIONS TOGETHER

LOS 13e: Explain international parity relations (covered and uncovered interest rate parity, purchasing power parity, and the international Fischer effect).
Vol 1, pp 516–537

LOS 13f: Describe relations among the international parity conditions.
Vol 1, pp 516–537

LOS 13g: Evaluate the use of the current spot rate, the forward rate, purchasing power parity, and uncovered interest parity to forecast future spots exchange rates.
Vol 1, pp 516–537

The Fisher Effect

The **Fisher effect** asserts that the nominal interest rate (i) in a country equals the sum of the real interest rate in that country (r) and the expected inflation rate (π^e).

> Fisher Effect: $i = r + \pi^e$

Therefore, the expressions for the domestic and foreign nominal interest rates are given as:

$$i_{DC} = r_{DC} + \pi_{DC}^e$$
$$i_{FC} = r_{FC} + \pi_{FC}^e$$

Real Interest Rate Parity and the International Fisher Effect

To illustrate real interest rate parity, we undertake the following steps:

First, we subtract the expression for the domestic nominal interest rate (i_{DC}) from the expression for the foreign nominal interest rate (i_{FC}):

$$(i_{FC} - i_{DC}) = (r_{FC} + \pi_{FC}^e) - (r_{DC} + \pi_{DC}^e)$$
$$(i_{FC} - i_{DC}) = (r_{FC} - r_{DC}) + (\pi_{FC}^e - \pi_{DC}^e)\ldots(\text{Expression 1})$$

Expression 1 tells us that the nominal interest rate spread between the foreign and domestic countries $(i_{FC} - i_{DC})$ equals the sum of:

1. The foreign-domestic real yield spread $(r_{FC} - r_{DC})$; and
2. The foreign-domestic expected inflation differential $(\pi_{FC}^e - \pi_{DC}^e)$

Then, we make the foreign-domestic real yield spread $(r_{FC} - r_{DC})$ the subject of Expression 1:

$$(r_{FC} - r_{DC}) = (i_{FC} - i_{DC}) - (\pi_{FC}^e - \pi_{DC}^e)$$

Now recall that:

- If uncovered interest rate parity holds, the nominal interest rate spread $(i_{FC} - i_{DC})$ approximately equals the expected change in the exchange rate $(\%\Delta S_{FC/DC}^e)$.
- If ex ante PPP holds, the difference in expected inflation rates $(\pi_{FC}^e - \pi_{DC}^e)$ approximately equals the expected change in the spot rate $(\%\Delta S_{FC/DC}^e)$.

> Real interest rate parity may be interpreted as the law of one price holding for securities internationally (real interest rates represent the real prices of securities).

Therefore, assuming that both (1) uncovered interest rate parity and (2) ex ante PPP hold, the real yield spread between the foreign and domestic countries ($r_{FC} - r_{DC}$) will equal 0. This proposition that real interest rates will converge to the same level across different countries (as real yield spreads across countries equal zero) is known as the **real interest rate parity** condition.

$$\text{Real interest rate parity} : (r_{FC} - r_{DC}) = (i_{FC} - i_{DC}) - (\pi^e_{FC} - \pi^e_{DC}) = \%\Delta S^e_{FC/DC} - \%\Delta S^e_{FC/DC} = 0$$

Further, if the real yield spread ($r_{FC} - r_{DC}$) equals zero in all markets, it follows that the foreign-domestic nominal yield spread will be determined by the foreign-domestic expected inflation rate differential. This is known as the **international Fisher effect**:

$$(i_{FC} - i_{DC}) = (r_{FC} - r_{DC}) + (\pi^e_{FC} - \pi^e_{DC})$$

$$\text{If } (r_{FC} - r_{DC}) = 0 \text{ then: } (i_{FC} - i_{DC}) = 0 + (\pi^e_{FC} - \pi^e_{DC})$$

$$\text{International Fisher effect: } (i_{FC} - i_{DC}) = (\pi^e_{FC} - \pi^e_{DC})$$

International Parity Relations: Bringing Everything Together

Covered interest rate parity: Arbitrage ensures that differences in nominal interest rates equal the forward premium/discount.

- Currencies with higher (lower) nominal interest rates will trade at a discount (premium) in the forward market.

Uncovered interest rate parity: The expected change in the spot rate equals the nominal interest rate spread.

- Currencies with higher (lower) nominal interest rates will be expected to depreciate (appreciate) in the future.

If both covered and uncovered interest rate parity hold, the nominal interest rate spread will equal the forward premium (discount) and the expected appreciation (depreciation) in the exchange rate. Therefore, the forward rate will be an unbiased predictor of the future spot exchange rate.

Ex ante PPP: Differences in expected inflation rates lead to changes in spot rates in the future.

- Currencies with higher (lower) expected inflation will be expected to depreciate (appreciate) in the future.

International Fisher effect: Given that (1) the Fisher effect holds in each market (i.e., the nominal interest rate in each country equals the real interest rate plus the expected inflation rate) and (2) real interest rate parity holds (i.e., real interest rates across markets are the same) then the difference between domestic and foreign nominal interest rates will equal the difference between domestic and foreign expected inflation rates.

If ex ante PPP and Fisher effects hold, then the expected inflation differential equals both the (1) expected change in the spot exchange rate and (2) nominal interest rate differential. This implies that uncovered interest rate parity holds (i.e., the expected change in the spot exchange rate equals the nominal interest rate differential): (1) equals (2).

If all the international parity relations hold, the expected percentage change in the spot rate would equal:

- The forward premium or discount (expressed as a percentage).
- The nominal yield spread between countries.
- The difference in expected inflation rates across countries.

If all these parity relations held it would not be possible for global investors to earn consistent profits on currency movements.

- If forward exchange rates accurately predicted the path to be taken by spot exchange rates, there would be no way of making money on future exchange rate speculation.
- If high-yield currencies depreciated in value versus low-yield currencies in line with the path implied by nominal interest rate spreads, currency-adjusted returns would be the same across the globe. In such a scenario, carry trades (discussed later in the reading) would not be profitable.

See Figure 7-1

Figure 7-1: Spot Exchange Rates, Forward Exchange Rates, and Interest Rates[1]

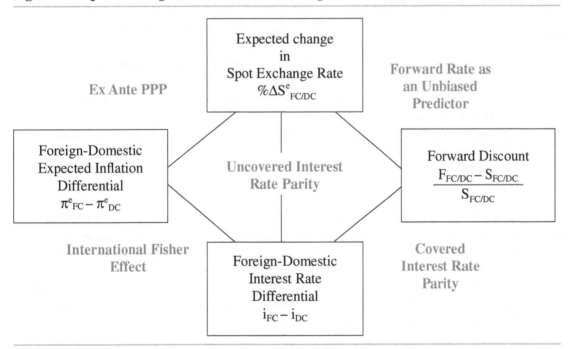

1 - Exhibit 4, Volume 1, CFA Program Curriculum 2017

LESSON 8: ASSESSING AN EXCHANGE RATE'S EQUILIBRIUM LEVEL

LOS 13h: Explain approaches to assessing the long-run fair value of an exchange rate. Vol 1, pp 538–539

Assessing an Exchange Rate's Equilibrium Level

The IMF uses a three-pronged approach to determine long-term equilibrium exchange rates:

1. The macroeconomic balance approach aims to determine how much exchange rates would need to adjust in order to close the gap between a country's current account imbalance over the medium term and its normal or sustainable current account imbalance.
2. The external sustainability approach aims to determine how much exchange rates would need to adjust in order to ensure that a country's net foreign asset (liability)-to-GDP ratio stabilizes at a particular desired level.
3. A reduced-form econometric model aims to determine the equilibrium path that a country's currency should take based on several macroeconomic variables (e.g., net foreign asset position, terms of trade and relative productivity).

A country's balance of payments accounts must always balance. A current account deficit (surplus) must be matched by a surplus (deficit) on the capital account. The IMF's three approaches basically represent different perspectives on this equilibrating mechanism:

- The macroeconomic balance approach focuses on flows required to achieve long term equilibrium on the current account. For example, a country running persistent current account deficits will eventually need its currency to depreciate to become competitive on the international market.
- The external sustainability approach focuses on flows required to achieve long-term equilibrium on the capital account.
- The reduced-form econometric model is a hybrid approach that combines elements of both the current and capital accounts into a statistical equation.

These different approaches to calculate the long-run equilibrium values of exchange rates often do not agree on the exchange rate level that represents long-run equilibrium. For example consider a study that uses both PPP and the macroeconomic balance approach to assess long-run fair value:

- If the currency is overvalued according to PPP and the country has an unsustainably large current account deficit then both approaches suggest that the currency should depreciate.
- If the currency is undervalued according to PPP and the country has an unsustainably large current account surplus then both approaches suggest that the currency should appreciate.
- If (1) the currency is undervalued according to PPP and the country has an unsustainably large current account deficit, or (2) the currency is overvalued according to PPP and the country has an unsustainably large current account surplus, the recommended course of action is unclear.

A Model that Includes Long-Term Equilibrium

Another model that is used to predict exchange rates in the long run is based on the assumptions that (1) uncovered interest rate parity holds in the long run and (2) real exchange rates converge to an equilibrium value ($\overline{q}_{FC/DC}$) in the long run. Further, it incorporates risk premia that reflect the perceived sustainability of the country's external balances.

$$q_{FC/DC} = \overline{q}_{FC/DC} + [(r_{DC} - r_{FC}) - (\Phi_{DC} - \Phi_{FC})]$$

$q_{FC/DC}$ = Real exchange rate
$\overline{q}_{FC/DC}$ = Long-run equilibrium real exchange rate
r_{DC} = Domestic currency real interest rate
Φ_{DC} = Domestic currency risk premium

According to this model, the real exchange rate can be expressed as:

- A *positive* function of the long-run equilibrium real exchange rate, $\overline{q}_{FC/DC}$.
- A *positive* function of the domestic-foreign real interest rate differential ($r_{DC} - r_{FC}$).
- A *negative* function of the difference between the domestic and foreign risk premia ($\Phi_{DC} - \Phi_{FC}$).

This model is used later in the reading to (1) explain the impact of capital flows on the exchange rate and (2) to describe monetary models of exchange rate determination.

LESSON 9: THE CARRY TRADE

LOS 13i: Describe the carry trade and its relation to uncovered interest rate parity and calculate the profit from a carry trade. Vol 1, pp 539–543

The Carry Trade

Uncovered interest rate parity asserts that countries with higher (lower) interest rates should expect their currencies to depreciate (appreciate). If uncovered interest rate parity held at all times, investors would not be able to profit from a strategy that involved taking long positions in high-yield currencies and short positions in low-yield currencies (as the change in the spot rate over the investment horizon would offset the interest rate differential).

Studies however have found that, on average, high-yield currencies do not depreciate to the levels predicted by interest rate differentials; nor do low-yield currencies appreciate to the levels predicted by interest rate differentials. These findings imply that FX carry trades can be potentially profitable. An **FX carry trade** involves taking long positions in high-yield currencies and short positions in low-yield currencies (also known as **funding currencies**). See Example 9-1.

> **IMPORTANT:**
> Note that this equation uses real exchange rates and we know that the formula for the real exchange rate does not follow the numerator-denominator rule. Therefore, in this equation, the interest rate and risk premia differentials do not take the form of FC − DC (as they do with all the parity relations); instead they take the form of DC − FC.

Example 9-1: Carry Trade

Consider the following information:

- $i_{JPY} = 1\%$
- $i_{AUD} = 3\%$
- $S_{JPY/AUD}$ today $= 85$

1. Compute the profit on a carry trade between the JPY and the AUD assuming that $S_{JPY/AUD}$ in one year equals 85.
2. Compute the profit on a carry trade between the JPY and the AUD assuming that $S_{JPY/AUD}$ in one year equals 84.

Solution:

In the given scenario, a carry trade would involve borrowing the low-yield currency (JPY) and investing in the high-yield currency (AUD). The investor would stand to earn a reward equal to the interest rate differential adjusted for the depreciation of the high-yield currency versus the low-yield currency.

1. Given that the JPY/AUD exchange rate stands at the same initial level after 1 year ($S_{JPY/AUD}$ in one year = 85), the investor's profit from the carry trade is calculated as:

   Interest earned on investment
   − Interest paid on funding currency
   −/+ Depreciation (appreciation) of investment currency

   Therefore, the profit on this carry trade equals $3\% - 1\% - 0\% = 2\%$

2. Given that the JPY/AUD exchange rate falls to 84 in one year, the depreciation of the AUD (investment currency) in percentage terms is calculated as:

   $$\%\Delta AUD = (84 - 85)/85 = -1.18\%$$

   If uncovered interest parity held, the AUD would have depreciated by 2% (the interest rate differential) over the course of the year and the investor's total return would have been 1% on either investment (1% nominal interest rate in JPY versus 3% nominal interest rate in AUD offset by 2% depreciation of AUD).

   However, the AUD only depreciated by 1.18%, which means that the investor was able to earn an excess return on the carry trade equal to $3\% - 1\% - 1.18\% = 0.82\%$. The return on the investment in AUD ($3\% - 1.18\% = 1.82\%$) was greater than the return on the JPY (1%).

Studies have shown that carry trades have earned positive excess returns in most (normal) market conditions. During periods of low turbulence, investors do not see much potential for sudden, substantial, adverse exchange rate movements and are relatively confident of earning excess returns through the strategy. However, in relatively turbulent times (during which asset price and/or FX volatility rise significantly) realized returns on long high-yield currency positions have declined dramatically, and funding costs have risen significantly as well.

Going back to our example, in relatively stable conditions, the JPY/AUD exchange rate would not deviate significantly from 85 JPY/AUD over the short term. The investor would earn excess returns around 2% (the interest rate differential) over the course of the year. Even if the JPY/AUD were to gradually move towards a level that is in line with uncovered interest rate parity (depreciate by 2%), the carry trade investor has a cushion of up to 2% (the interest rate differential between the AUD and JPY).

However, in turbulent market conditions, the return on the AUD investment can decline significantly and very quickly as a result of (1) rapid depreciation of the AUD and/or (2) decline in AUD asset prices. At the same time, the investor's funding costs can rise substantially due to appreciation of the JPY.

Returns of carry trades have not followed the normal distribution; instead the returns distribution has been more peaked with fatter tails that are negatively skewed.

- The peaked distribution around the mean indicates that carry trades typically earn small gains (more frequently than would be expected were the returns normally distributed, which is good).
- The negative skew and fat tails indicate that carry trades have resulted in (1) larger losses and (2) more frequent than implied by a normal distribution. This relatively high probability of a large loss is referred to as **crash risk**.

The primary reason for crash risk is that the carry trade is essentially a leveraged trade.

- Investors borrow in one currency and invest the proceeds in another. Like all leveraged trades, investor gains and losses (relative to their equity bases) are magnified in carry trades. As soon as an adverse shock hits the market, investors quickly move to close their positions (to avoid the potentially large losses associated with adverse exchange rate movements). They often leave stop-loss orders with their brokers to mitigate losses from carry trades, and these orders are triggered with the onset of adverse exchange rate movements. Therefore, there is a cascading effect as more and more investors move to close their carry trade positions resulting in extended adverse currency movements.
- Further, in periods of turbulence, there is generally a "flight to safety." Investors lean towards investing in (as opposed to borrowing) low-yield currencies (with their low risk premia) and move away from (as opposed to investing in) high-yield currencies (with their high risk exposures). Therefore, exchange rates tend to move quickly in a direction unfavorable to those with open carry trade positions.

Managing Downside Risks Associated with Carry Trades

Using volatility filters: Under this approach the level of implied volatility (implied in equity and currency options markets) is used to determine whether carry trades should be undertaken. If implied volatility rises above (falls below) a certain level, carry trade positions are closed or reversed (opened or initiated).

Using valuation filters: Under this approach, benchmarks based on purchasing power parity are used to determine whether carry trade positions should be opened or closed.

- If high-yield currencies were to become overvalued (undervalued) relative to their prescribed PPP threshold bands, the risk of a significant adverse exchange rate movement (i.e., depreciation of the investment currency), would increase (decrease) so investors would close or reverse their positions (leave their positions open).
- If low-yield currencies were to become undervalued (overvalued) relative to their prescribed PPP threshold bands, the risk of a significant adverse exchange rate movement (i.e., appreciation of the funding currency), would increase (decrease) so investors would close or reverse their positions (leave their positions open).

From the perspective of policy makers, there is a risk that carry trades could result in exchange rate misalignments. For example, high-yield currencies could become overvalued and monetary authorities in those countries may have to resort to imposing restrictions on the movement of capital (e.g., capital controls) to prevent any undesired appreciation of their currencies. Further, the search for yield encourages carry traders to take heavily leveraged positions, and the cascades of selling that arise when there are adverse shocks to the system can lead to serious currency and financial crisis. For example, in 2008, the unwinding of carry trades and the flight of capital from high-yield countries resulted in significant depreciation of currencies like the AUD and NZD even though neither of these economies was at the heart of the 2007 to 2008 global financial crises.

LESSON 10: THE IMPACT OF BALANCE OF PAYMENTS FLOWS

LOS 13j: Explain how flows in the balance of payment accounts affect currency exchange rates. Vol 1, pp 543–554

The Impact of Balance of Payments Flows

Balance of payments (BOP) accounts are an accounting record of all monetary transactions between a country and the rest of the world. Sources of funds for a nation, such as exports or the receipts of loans and investments, are recorded as positive or surplus items. Uses of funds, such as for imports or to invest in foreign countries, are recorded as negative or deficit items. The BOP equation is given by:

$$\text{Current account} + \text{Capital account} + \text{Financial account} = 0$$

- The current account balance represents the sum of transactions in traded goods and services, income receipts and unilateral transfers.
- The capital account balance represents the sum of capital transfers and transactions in nonproduced, nonfinancial assets.
- The financial account includes official reserve assets and government assets.

For our purposes, we will break the balance of payments into just two components: (1) the current account and (2) the capital account (which will include the impact of financing decisions as well). Since the balance of payments account must always balance, the current account balance must be matched by an equal and opposite balance in the capital account.

Studies that have examined the impact of the nature of a country's current and capital account balances on the exchange rate have found that in the short to medium term, capital account flows (investing and financing decisions) are the dominant factor in determining exchange rates. This is because capital flows are much larger and respond to changing economic conditions more quickly than trade flows. In the sections that follow, we evaluate the impact of current account and capital account balances on the exchange rate.

Current Account Imbalances and the Determination of Exchange Rates

Generally speaking, persistent current account deficits lead to depreciation of the domestic currency. The following mechanisms explain this relationship:

The flow supply/demand channel: If the country sells less (more) goods and services than it purchases, demand for its currency should fall (rise). Therefore, countries with persistent currency account deficits (surpluses) should see their currencies depreciate (appreciate) over time. In the long run, exchange rates movements should help to eliminate the initial imbalances (as long as the Marshall-Lerner condition is satisfied):

> The Marshall-Lerner condition and its implications were discussed at length at Level I.

- For countries running persistent current account deficits, depreciation of the domestic currency should make exports more competitive and imports more expensive over time.
- For countries running persistent current account surpluses, appreciation of the domestic currency should make exports more expensive and imports relatively cheaper over time.

The magnitude of the exchange rate adjustment required to remove the initial current account imbalances depends on the following factors:

- The initial gap between imports and exports. The larger the current account deficit, the more significant the currency depreciation required to bring about a meaningful adjustment in the trade imbalance.
- The response of export and import prices to changes in the exchange rate. For a country with a current account deficit, the greater the pass through of depreciation of the domestic currency to prices of traded goods, the lower the exchange rate adjustment required to eliminate the deficit.
- The response of export and import demand to changes in export and import prices. For a country with a large current account deficit, the greater the price elasticity of demand of exports and imports, the more effective currency depreciation would be in increasing exports and reducing imports. However, note that the actual impact of changes in export and import prices on quantities traded can be quite sluggish.

The portfolio balance channel: If China has a persistent current account surplus versus the United States, the surplus on its current account would be offset by a deficit on its capital account. The deficit on China's capital account arises from capital flows from China to the United States (as China purchases assets denominated in USD). Over time, as the weight of USD-denominated assets in China's overall portfolio increases, China may decide to rebalance its investment portfolio and reduce the weight of USD-denominated assets. The ensuing sell-off of USD-denominated assets would result in USD depreciation.

<table>
<tr><td>Note that the debt sustainability channel is the mechanism that underlies the IMF's external sustainability approach to determining the long-run equilibrium exchange rate.</td></tr>
</table>

The debt sustainability channel: Countries that run large, persistent current account deficits finance these deficits by borrowing from their trade partners (resulting in capital account surpluses). However there will come a point in time when the ratio of national debt to GDP grows to such a high level that investors will begin to reason that a depreciation of the currency would be required to ensure that the current account deficit narrows and that national debt stabilizes at a sustainable level. As a result, over time, the market will make downward revisions to its expectations of the currency's real long term equilibrium value.

Capital Flows and the Determination of Exchange Rates

We mentioned earlier that capital flows (capital account balances) tend to have a more immediate impact on exchange rates than trade flows (current account balances). With greater financial integration of the world's capital markets and increased capital mobility, capital flows are now the dominant force in influencing exchange rates, interest rates, and asset price bubbles.

Recent history provides numerous cases of capital inflows bringing boom-like conditions to some emerging markets. The initial surges in capital inflows to emerging markets have contributed to:

- Unwarranted appreciation of emerging market currencies;
- A significant buildup of external debt by emerging market governments and businesses;
- Financial and property market bubbles;
- A boom in consumption with explosive growth in domestic credit and/or the current account deficit;
- Overinvestment in risky projects and questionable activities.

However, sometimes (in more than one-third of the cases according to an IMF study), these inflows have stopped abruptly and then actually reversed, often resulting in major economic downturns, banking crises, and substantial currency depreciation in those markets. Since these surges of capital flows into emerging markets have often ended badly, emerging market policy makers have recently chosen to intervene in the FX market and/or impose capital controls to prevent their currencies from becoming overvalued. This has been discussed in detail later in the reading.

Real Interest Rate Differentials, Capital Flows, and the Exchange Rate

Earlier, in the section on real interest rates, we introduced a model (Equation 1) which asserted that real exchange rate movements around long-run equilibrium levels $\left(q_{FC/DC} - \overline{q}_{FC/DC}\right)$ are driven by (1) real interest rate differentials and (2) risk premia differentials:

$$q_{FC/DC} - \overline{q}_{FC/DC} = [(r_{DC} - r_{FC}) - (\Phi_{DC} - \Phi_{FC})]\ldots\text{Equation 1 (reconfigured)}$$

This equation can help us understand several economic phenomena including:

Long-run cyclical trends in the value of currencies: The equation above suggests that relative interest rate trends play an important role in exchange rate movements. When we evaluate the performance of the USD in light of interest rate differentials since the late 1970s, a clear pattern emerges:

- The decline of the USD in the late 1970s, its rise in the first half of the 1980s, and its subsequent decline in the late 1980s can be explained in large part by changes in the U.S.-foreign real yield spreads.
- The USD's decline in the 1990s and subsequent rise in the latter half of the 1990s are also correlated with movements in the U.S.-foreign real yield spreads.

The persistence of excess returns on carry trades: The excess returns on carry trades can come from (1) gradual accrual of the interest rate differential and/or (2) favorable movements in spot exchange rates. To understand why a high-yield currency can attract significant inflows of capital such that its value appreciates persistently (as opposed to depreciating in line with the assertions of uncovered interest rate parity), we express Equation 1 in the following form:

> For a carry trade, a favorable movement in the exchange rate would be an appreciation of the high-yield currency (depreciation of the funding currency).

$$q_{L/H} = \bar{q}_{L/H} + [(r_H - r_L) - (\Phi_H - \Phi_L)]$$

r_H = real interest rate in high-yield currency
r_L = real interest rate in low-yield currency

Next, we express the real interest rate differential as the difference between the nominal interest rate differential and the expected inflation differential.

$$q_{L/H} = \bar{q}_{L/H} + (i_H - i_L) - (\pi_H^e - \pi_L^e) - (\Phi_H - \Phi_L)$$

According to this equation, the real value of the high-yield currency, $q_{L/H}$, (the base currency) will tend to rise in the long run when its long-run equilibrium value ($q_{L/H}$) is trending higher.

Finally, we make the difference between the real exchange rate and its long-run equilibrium value the subject.

$$q_{L/H} - \bar{q}_{L/H} = (i_H - i_L) - (\pi_H^e - \pi_L^e) - (\Phi_H - \Phi_L)$$

Based on this equation, we can conclude that relative to its long-run equilibrium value $\left(\bar{q}_{L/H}\right)$, the real exchange rate ($q_{L/H}$) will rise as:

- The nominal yield spread between high- and low-yield markets ($i_H - i_L$) rises.
- The difference in expected inflation rates in the high-yield market and the low-yield market ($\pi_H^e - \pi_L^e$) declines.
- The difference in risk premia associated with the high-yield market and the low-yield market ($\Phi_H - \Phi_L$) declines.

For our purposes, the important takeaway is that the profitability of FX carry trades can come from factors other than just the level and trend of the nominal yield spread ($i_H - i_L$). These other factors include expected inflation differentials and risk premium differentials. Further, movements or changes in all these differentials tend to be gradual but persistent, so movements in exchange rates tend to be gradual and persistent as well. For example:

- Monetary policy makers (in both high- and low-yield countries) tend to adjust official lending rates slowly over time.
- It can take several years to bring inflationary expectations down to reasonably low and stable levels.

Since the fundamental criteria that drive exchange rates over time (the three differentials mentioned above) tend to proceed gradually, we should expect to see observable trends in exchange rate movements and persistence in FX carry trade returns.

Equity Market Trends and the Exchange Rate

Generally speaking, it has been difficult to predict exchange rate movements based on equity market performance.

- The long-run correlation between the value of the USD and U.S. equity returns is close to 0.
- Over the short to medium term, correlations have swung from being highly positive to highly negative.

LESSON 11: MONETARY AND FISCAL POLICIES

LOS 13k: Describe the Mundell–Fleming model, the monetary approach, and the asset market (portfolio balance) approach to exchange rate determination. Vol 1, pp 555–567

LOS 13l: Forecast the direction of the expected change in an exchange rate based on balance of payment, Mundell–Fleming, monetary, and asset market approaches to exchange rate determination. Vol 1, pp 555–567

LOS 13m: Explain the potential effects of monetary and fiscal policy on exchange rates. Vol 1, pp 555–567

Monetary and Fiscal Policies

The Mundell-Fleming Model

The Mundell-Fleming model describes how changes in monetary and fiscal policies affect interest rates and the level of output in a country, which in turn lead to changes in trade and capital flows, and eventually to changes in the exchange rate. Before getting into the model, it is important for you to understand that the model focuses on aggregate demand, so the implicit assumption here is that there is enough of an output gap in the economy to allow changes in output without having a significant impact on price levels and inflation.

Expansionary Monetary Policy

Expansionary monetary policy stimulates growth by lowering interest rates, thereby increasing investment and consumption. Since expansionary monetary policy entails lower interest rates, there are capital outflows which put a downward pressure on the exchange rate.

With flexible exchange rates, expansionary monetary policy will lead to depreciation of the domestic currency as low interest rates cause a flight of capital to higher-yielding markets. The more responsive capital flows are to interest rate differentials, the more significant the depreciation of the domestic currency. Over time, the depreciation of the currency will also increase net exports and reinforce the aggregate demand impact (on investment and consumption spending) of expansionary monetary policy.

With fixed exchange rates, since there will be downward pressure on the currency due to the capital flight triggered by the low interest rates, the monetary authority will have to buy its own currency (using its foreign exchange reserves) in the FX market to keep the exchange rate at the desired (fixed) level. As a result, the monetary base will shrink and domestic credit will dry up, offsetting the desired expansionary effect of the monetary stance. Further, note that the central bank's ability to maintain the fixed exchange rate will be limited by its stock of foreign exchange reserves.

Expansionary Fiscal Policy

Expansionary fiscal policy stimulates growth by increasing government expenditure and/or lowering taxes. Since the resulting budget deficits must be financed with government borrowing, expansionary fiscal policy typically leads to an increase in interest rates, which stimulate capital inflows and exert an upward pressure on the exchange rate.

With flexible exchange rates, expansionary fiscal policy will lead to appreciation of the domestic currency as high interest rates stimulate capital inflows. If capital flows are relatively sensitive to interest rate differentials, the domestic currency should appreciate considerably. However, note that if capital flows are relatively insensitive to interest rate differentials (which is rarely the case), the currency may actually depreciate as the increase in aggregate demand will worsen the trade balance (increase imports with no direct impact on exports).

With fixed exchange rates, since there will be upward pressure on the currency due to the capital inflows triggered by the high interest rates, the monetary authority will have to sell its own currency in the FX market to maintain the exchange rate at the desired (fixed) level. The resulting expansion of domestic money supply will reinforce the aggregate demand impact of expansionary fiscal policy.

The Mundell-Fleming model offers the following insights:

If domestic policy makers try to (1) pursue independent monetary policy, (2) permit capital to flow freely through its borders, and (3) commit to a fixed exchange rate regime, it would not be possible for them to satisfy all three of these objectives.

Also, the degree of capital mobility has a significant influence on the effectiveness of monetary and fiscal policy in an open economy. Capital controls are important for central banks that want to retain monetary policy independence and at the same time manage their exchange rate.

Capital controls are discussed in more detail later in the reading.

With high capital mobility:

- A restrictive (expansionary) monetary policy under floating exchange rates will result in appreciation (depreciation) of the domestic currency. The change in the exchange rate will be more significant if capital mobility is high.
- A restrictive (expansionary) fiscal policy under floating exchange rates will result in depreciation (appreciation) of the domestic currency.
- If monetary and fiscal policies are both restrictive or both expansionary, the overall impact on the exchange rate will be unclear.

Table 11-1 below summarizes the impact of monetary and fiscal stances on the exchange rate under conditions of high capital mobility.

Table 11-1: Monetary-Fiscal Policy Mix and the Determination of Exchange Rates under Conditions of High Capital Mobility

	Expansionary Monetary Policy	Restrictive Monetary Policy
Expansionary Fiscal Policy	Ambiguous	Domestic currency appreciates
Restrictive Fiscal Policy	Domestic currency depreciates	Ambiguous

With low capital mobility, the impact of monetary and fiscal policy changes on domestic interest rates does not result in major changes in capital flows. With limited capital mobility, the impact of monetary and fiscal policy on the exchange rate comes more from trade flows rather than capital flows. Therefore, with low capital mobility:

- A restrictive (expansionary) monetary policy will lower (increase) aggregate demand, resulting in an increase (decrease) in net exports. This will cause the domestic currency to appreciate (depreciate).
- A restrictive (expansionary) fiscal policy will lower (increase) aggregate demand, resulting in an increase (decrease) in net exports. This will cause the domestic currency to appreciate (depreciate).
- If monetary and fiscal stances are not the same (i.e., one is restrictive while the other is expansionary) the overall impact on the exchange rate will be unclear.

Table 11-2 below summarizes the impact of monetary and fiscal stances on the exchange rate under conditions of low capital mobility.

Table 11-2: Monetary-Fiscal Policy Mix and the Determination of Exchange Rates under Conditions of Low Capital Mobility

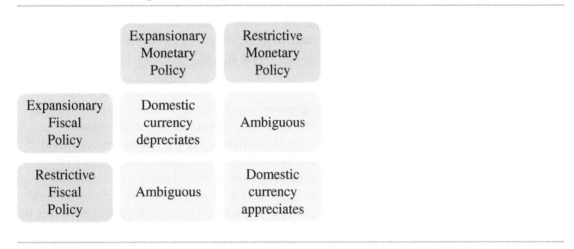

	Expansionary Monetary Policy	Restrictive Monetary Policy
Expansionary Fiscal Policy	Domestic currency depreciates	Ambiguous
Restrictive Fiscal Policy	Ambiguous	Domestic currency appreciates

Monetary Models of Exchange Rate Determination

Recall that under the Mundell-Fleming model, monetary policy has an impact on exchange rates through its impact on interest rates and output; changes in the price level and inflation play no role. Monetary models of exchange rate determination take the opposite perspective—output is fixed and monetary policy's primary impact on exchange rates is through the price level and inflation.

The Monetary Approach with Flexible Prices

This approach is based on the quantity theory of money, which asserts that money supply changes are the primary determinant of price level changes. If purchasing power parity holds, then the increase (decrease) in domestic price levels relative to foreign price levels that results from a relative increase (decrease) in domestic money supply will lead to a proportional decline (increase) in the value of the domestic currency.

The major shortcoming of the monetary approach is that it assumes that PPP always holds. We know (from earlier in the reading) that PPP only tends to hold in the long run. Therefore, the monetary model does not offer an accurate explanation for the impact of monetary policy on the exchange rate in the short and medium terms.

The Dornbusch Overshooting Model

The Dornbusch overshooting model overcomes this weakness of the monetary approach by assuming that prices are relatively inflexible in the short run, but are completely flexible in the long run. As a result the model predicts that:

- In the long run, since prices are completely flexible, an increase in domestic money supply will lead to a proportional increase in domestic prices and result in a depreciation of the domestic currency. Note that this conclusion is consistent with that of the monetary model (and PPP).
- In the short run, since prices are relatively inflexible, an increase in nominal money supply translates into an increase in real money supply. As real money supply increases, real interest rates fall, resulting in capital outflows and a substantial depreciation of the domestic currency in nominal and real terms. In fact, the domestic currency would overshoot its long-run level, and actually fall to a level lower than predicted by PPP. Eventually, over the long run, as domestic prices and domestic interest rates rise, the nominal exchange rate will recover and approach the level predicted by the conventional monetary approach (in line with PPP) and the real exchange rate will converge towards its long-run equilibrium level.

The Taylor Rule and the Determination of Exchange Rates

The Taylor rule is a mathematical rule that can be used to determine the appropriate policy rate for an economy given the its neutral rate, its inflation and output targets, and the economy's current deviation from those targets:

$$i = r_n + \pi + \alpha(\pi - \pi^*) + \beta(y - y^*)$$

where
i = the Taylor rule prescribed central bank policy rate
r_n = the neutral real policy rate
π = the current inflation rate
π^* = the central bank's target inflation rate
y = the log of the current level of output
y^* = the log of the economy's potential/sustainable level of output

The Taylor rule prescribes that the policy rate should rise (fall) in real terms relative to the neutral rate in response to positive (negative) inflation and output gaps. While the rule is used largely for explaining and predicting the path of policy rates, it also offers valuable insights in determining exchange rates.

First we manipulate the Taylor rule equation by deducting the current inflation rate from both sides (so that we come up with an expression for the real interest rate).

$$r = (i - \pi) = r_n + \alpha(\pi - \pi^*) + \beta(y - y^*) \qquad \text{... Equation 2}$$

We then use Equation 2 to substitute for the real interest rate differential in Equation 1 (described earlier).

$$q_{PC/BC} = \bar{q}_{PC/BC} + \left(r_n^{BC} - r_n^{PC}\right) + \alpha\left((\pi_{BC} - \pi^*{}_{BC}) - (\pi_{PC} - \pi^*{}_{PC})\right)$$
$$+ \beta\left((y_{BC} - y^*{}_{BC}) - (y_{PC} - y^*{}_{PC})\right) - (\Phi_{BC} - \Phi_{PC}) \qquad \text{... Equation 3}$$

Equation 3 suggests that the base currency should strengthen versus the price currency in real terms if:

- There is an *increase* in the market's estimate of the base currency's long-run equilibrium value $(\bar{q}_{PC/BC})$.
- There is an *increase* in the policy-neutral interest rate in the base currency relative to the price currency $(r_{BC}^n - r_{PC}^n)$.
- There is an *increase* in the output gap in the base currency relative to the output gap in the price currency $[(y_{BC} - y^*{}_{BC}) - (y_{PC} - y^*{}_{PC})]$.
- There is an *increase* in the inflation gap in the base currency relative to the inflation gap in the price currency $[(p_{BC} - \pi^*{}_{BC}) - (\pi_{PC} - \pi^*{}_{PC})]$.
- There is a *decrease* in the risk premium demanded for holding base currency-denominated assets relative to the risk premium on price currency-denominated assets $(\Phi_{BC} - \Phi_{PC})$.

The important takeaway here is that this framework suggests that an increase in base currency inflation implies *appreciation* of the base currency (as higher inflation would induce the central bank to raise real interest rates). On the other hand, the pure monetary/purchasing power parity model suggests that an increase in base currency inflation would lead to *depreciation* of the base currency.

Fiscal Policy and the Determination of Exchange Rates

Earlier in the reading, we studied the impact of fiscal policy on exchange rates under the Mundell-Fleming model. However, the Mundell-Fleming model is a short-term model that does not consider the long-term effects of budgetary imbalances. On the other hand, the portfolio balance approach focuses on the long-term exchange rate implications of sustained fiscal imbalances. The approach assumes that global investors hold diversified baskets of foreign and domestic assets (including bonds), and their desired allocation across markets is based on return and risk considerations. If a particular economy has persistent budget deficits, its government would need to issue bonds to finance those deficits so there would be a steady rise in the supply of that country's bonds. This persistent demand for financing would eventually lead to (1) investors demanding a higher risk premium to invest in those bonds and (2) currency depreciation.

The Mundell-Fleming and portfolio balance models can also be combined into a single framework. Initially, over the short run, when a government undertakes expansionary fiscal policy, real interest rates rise so the domestic currency appreciates. However, over the long run, sustained fiscal deficits can result in a substantial pile-up of government debt. If the market believes that debt levels are unsustainable, the government may feel pressured into taking one of the following courses of action (see Figure 11-1):

- Monetize the debt: The central bank would increase money supply and buy the government's debt with the newly created money. This would lead to rapid depreciation (or reversal of the initial currency appreciation).
- Reverse the fiscal stance: In order to restore a longer-run sustainable balance on its fiscal position, the government may have to reverse its initial expansionary fiscal stance that drove the currency higher. The new contractionary fiscal stance would lead to depreciation of the domestic currency.

Figure 11-1: The Short- and Long-Run Response of Exchange Rates to Changes in Fiscal Policy[2]

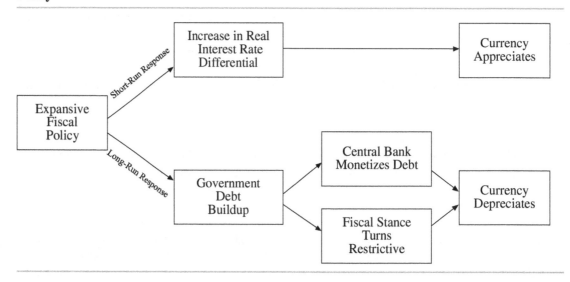

LESSON 12: EXCHANGE RATE MANAGEMENT: INTERVENTION AND CONTROLS, CURRENCY CRISES, AND SHORTER-TERM FORECASTING TOOLS

LOS 13n: Describe the objectives of central bank intervention and capital controls and describe the effectiveness of intervention and capital controls. Vol 1, pp 571–576

Exchange Rate Management: Intervention and Controls

Capital flows can be a double-edged sword for emerging economies. On the one hand, they can help these economies grow by financing the gap between domestic investment needs and domestic savings. On the other hand however, they can create boom-like conditions, fuel asset price bubbles,

---

2 - Exhibit 9, Volume 1, CFA Program Curriculum 2017

and take the domestic currency into overvalued territory. Problems arise when currency inflows abruptly reverse, as they can then trigger a major economic downturn, decline in asset prices, and significant depreciation of the currency (e.g., the Asian financial crisis of 1997 and 1998).

Surges in capital flows can arise due to "pull" and "push" factors.

Pull factors represent a favorable set of developments in the **domestic economy** that attract capital from foreign countries. These factors include:

- Better economic management;
- Expected decline in the inflation rate;
- A more flexible exchange rate regime;
- An improving current account balance;
- A decline in public and private debt burdens;
- A sovereign credit rating upgrade;
- An improving fiscal position; and
- Strong and sustained economic growth.

On the other hand, push factors represent a favorable set of factors in **foreign economies** that drive capital flows abroad. These factors include:

- Low interest rates in developed countries (that tend to be the primary sources of internationally mobile capital);
- Changes in long-run trends in asset allocation such as increasing weights for emerging market assets in global portfolios.

Objectives of Central Bank Intervention and Capital Controls

Given the possible negative consequences that their economies would have to bear if there were an abrupt reversal of capital inflows, emerging market policy makers can resort to intervention in the FX market and/or capital controls to achieve the following objectives:

- Prevent their currencies from appreciating too strongly in the wake of surges in capital inflows;
- Reduce excessive capital inflows; and
- Enable the monetary authority to pursue independent monetary policy without having to worry about the repercussions of changes in policy rates on capital flows (and the exchange rate).
  - For example, an economy with high inflation may want to reduce money supply and increase interest rates to cool down the economy. Restrictions on capital flows may enable the country to pursue contractionary monetary policy without worrying about the possibility of the currency overappreciating.

Emerging Market Responses to Unwanted Surges of Capital Inflows

- If the emerging market (EM) country's currency is **undervalued**, then the appropriate response to a surge in capital inflows would be to let the currency appreciate (as long as it does not overappreciate and compromise the competitiveness of the economy).
- If the EM currency is **fairly valued or overvalued**, the appropriate response would be to intervene in the FX market.
  - If there is **no inflation threat**, then unsterilized intervention is the best option. The central bank would sell the EM currency on the FX market (to offset the upward pressure on the currency coming from capital inflows) and the resulting increase in the monetary base would lower interest rates, which would discourage capital inflows.
  - If **inflation is a threat**, then sterilized intervention would be the way to go. The central bank would sell the EM currency on the FX market (to offset the upward pressure on the currency coming from capital inflows) and at the same time it would sell domestic securities to the private sector to absorb excess liquidity in the market. Money supply and short-term interest rates would then remain unaffected by the intervention.
- If **all of the above fail** to relieve the capital inflow-induced upward pressure on the EM currency, policy makers should consider capital controls.

Evidence on the Effectiveness of Central Bank Intervention

- In the case of **developed countries**, studies have shown that the effect of central bank intervention in the FX market on the level and path of their exchange rates is insignificant. This is because the volume of intervention is dwarfed by the average trading turnover of these currencies on the global FX market.
- In the case of **emerging market currencies**, studies have shown that the effect of central bank intervention in the FX market is relatively more significant but still mixed overall.
  - Intervention has reduced the volatility of EM exchange rates.
  - Intervention has had limited (but more than in the case of developed countries) influence on the level and path taken by exchanges rates. This is because emerging markets' holdings of foreign currency reserves have swelled over the last decade and the ratio of their reserves to global FX market turnover in their currencies is quite sizeable.

Evidence on the Effectiveness of Capital Controls

Studies have suggested that capital controls on inflows:

- Make monetary policy more independent;
- Can alter the composition of capital flows;
- Can lower the pressure on the real exchange rate in certain cases.

However, studies have also concluded that capital controls on inflows do not reduce the volume of **net flows**. Further, the larger the magnitude of capital flows and the greater their persistence, the less effective capital controls will be in relieving the upward pressure on the real exchange rate.

LOS 13o: Describe warning signs of a currency crisis. Vol 1, pp 572–575

If currency crises were expected by most market participants, we would expect to see the following as a crisis drew nearer:

- A widening of the interest rate differential to reflect the chances of substantial currency depreciation in the near term.
- A lower future value of the currency built into consensus forecasts by leading economists.
- Credit rating downgrades to reflect the increased risk of banking and other forms of financial crises.

Unfortunately, none of these signals have been generated in the lead up to currency crises in the past, which indicates that these episodes have not been adequately anticipated by market participants.

There are two primary schools of thought regarding the underlying causes of currency crises. One contends that currency crises tend to be precipitated by deteriorating economic fundamentals. The other contends that even though deterioration of economic fundamentals may explain a relatively large number of crises, there can be instances when economies with relatively sound fundamentals see their currencies come under severe pressure due to (1) an adverse change in market sentiment completely unrelated to economic fundamentals or (2) spillover effects from changes in push factors that discourage investment overseas.

An IMF study on potential early warning signs of a currency crisis found that:

- In the period leading up to the crisis, the real exchange rate is much higher than its mean level during tranquil periods.
- The trade balance displays no significant difference in the pre-crisis period versus relatively tranquil periods.
- Foreign exchange reserves tend to decline drastically in the lead up to a crisis.
- There is some deterioration in the terms of trade in the lead up to a crisis.
- Inflation tends to be relatively high in the pre-crisis period relative to tranquil periods.
- The ratio of M2 (money supply) to bank reserves tends to rise in the 2-year period leading up to a crisis, and then declines sharply following the crisis.
- Broad money growth in nominal and real terms rises sharply in the 2-year period leading up to a crisis.
- Nominal private credit growth also rises sharply in the period leading up to a crisis.
- A boom-bust cycle in equity prices generally comes before a currency crisis.
- Real economic activity shows no real pattern before a crisis, but falls significantly following the crisis.

The IMF and leading investment banks have tried to create composite early warning systems that could alert policy makers and investors to the possibility of a currency crisis. An ideal early warning system would need to:

- Have a strong record in (1) predicting actual crises and (2) avoiding frequent issuances of false signals.
- Be based on macroeconomic indicators that are available on a timely basis and can signal an impending crisis well in advance of its actual onset.
- Be based on a wide range of potential crisis indicators.

LOS 13p: Describe uses of technical analysis in forecasting exchange rates.
Vol 1, pp 576–581

Shorter-Term Forecasting Tools

The fundamentals-based models that we described earlier in the reading are generally useful in explaining longer-term trends in exchange rates. They have not enjoyed much success in explaining trends in exchange rates over the short and medium terms. Portfolio managers have now turned to other types of forecasting tools to help them forecast exchange rates over shorter time horizons. Examples include technical analysis and order flow, sentiment, and positioning indicators.

Technical Analysis

Investors who follow technical analysis believe that past price trends can be used to determine the magnitude and direction of future price movements. Technical trading rules have been used to identify market trends, market reversals, overbought/oversold conditions, relative strength, and support/resistance levels. Studies on the effectiveness of technical analysis have found that:

- Technical trading rules would have generated significant profits if applied to Forex trading from the 1970s to the early 1990s. However, when applied over the period 1995 to 2010, these technical trading rules would not have generated such impressive profits. This is because persistent and pronounced exchange rate swings have become relatively infrequent occurrences over time.
- Technical trading rules could still be applied in the early years of a country's floating exchange rate regime to earn excess returns. This can be explained by the markets in these currencies being relatively less crowded, which allows mispricings to persist as they are not quickly arbitraged away.
- Even though technical trading rules have largely been unsuccessful in enhancing returns, they can play a significant role in controlling risk. The standard deviation of returns on strategies based on technical trading rules tends to be lower than for strategies that ignore technical rules completely. A key takeaway here is that carry trade investors (where returns have significant downside tail risk) could benefit from using technical analysis to identify warning signs of widespread carry trade unwinds.

Order Flow, Sentiment, and Positioning

FX Dealer Order Flow

Unlike the equity market (where there are mandatory disclosure requirements), the FX market is relatively less transparent as volume and price data are not immediately available to all parties. Therefore, the order books of large FX dealers could have predictive value in the short run (as they contain information that is not available to the public). Studies have found that:

- There is a strong, positive, contemporaneous correlation between customer order flow and the current trend in exchange rates over short periods (on an intraday or daily basis).
- There is no conclusive evidence on the relationship between lagged order data and future exchange rates so we cannot draw any clear conclusions regarding the predictive value of order flow data.

Currency Options Market

FX traders often use risk reversals to gauge whether the FX market is attaching a higher probability to a currency appreciation or to a currency depreciation. Without getting into the technicalities, a risk reversal basically represents the implied volatility spread between call and put options on a particular currency, where both the options have the same delta and expiration date.

- A positive risk reversal indicates that the implied volatility built into the call price is greater than the implied volatility built into the put price. This means that the market is attaching a higher probability to a large appreciation of the base currency than to a large depreciation.
- A negative risk reversal indicates that the implied volatility built into the put price is greater than the implied volatility built into the call price. This means that the market is attaching a higher probability to a large depreciation of the base currency than to a large appreciation.

Studies have found that:

- There is a high contemporaneous relationship between the trend in risk reversals and the trend in exchange rates so risk reversals do explain current trends in exchange rates.
- However, there is no statistically significant relationship between lagged risk reversal data and future exchange rate movements so risk reversals cannot be used to predict future exchange rates.

Information on the Size and Trend in Net Speculative Positions

FX market participants closely watch the net positions of speculative accounts in the FX futures market to determine whether speculative flows are moving into/out of particular currencies and whether any positions are overbought/oversold. Studies have found that:

- There is a strong, positive, contemporaneous correlation between changes in net positions of speculative accounts and exchange rate movements so changes in net positions of speculative accounts do explain current trends in exchange rates.
- However, changes in net speculative positions cannot be used to predict changes in exchange rates.

READING 14: ECONOMIC GROWTH AND THE INVESTMENT DECISION

LESSON 1: GROWTH IN THE GLOBAL ECONOMY: DEVELOPED VERSUS DEVELOPING COUNTRIES

A country's standard of living and its level of economic development are usually evaluated based on its **gross domestic product (GDP)** and **per capita GDP**. **Economic growth** is calculated as annual percentage change in *real GDP* or in *real per capita GDP*.

- Growth in *real GDP* measures how rapidly the total economy is expanding.
- Growth in *real per capita GDP* implies that real GDP is growing at a faster rate than the country's population, which means that the average person's standard of living is improving.

One approach for comparing standards of living across countries is to convert domestic-currency denominated numbers into USD at current market exchange rates. This approach entails two problems:

- Market exchange rates are very volatile and can result in significant changes in measured GDP even if there is little or no growth in the country's economy.
- Market exchange rates are determined by financial flows and trade flows, while nontradable goods and services, which actually represent a large portion of global consumption, do not have much of an influence on exchange rates. For example, labor is typically cheaper in developing countries compared to developed countries. Therefore, prices of labor-intensive products (e.g., haircuts) are lower in developing countries. Failing to account for differences in prices of nontraded goods and services across countries has the effect of *understating* the standard of living in developing countries.

The second (preferred) approach for comparing standards of living across countries is to convert domestic-currency denominated numbers based on purchasing power parity.

Countries may be broadly divided into two categories:

- **Developed (or advanced) countries** are those with higher per capita GDP, such as the U.S., Canada, Australia, Japan, and other major economies. Generally speaking, growth in developed countries has slowed over the last few decades.
- **Developing countries** have a per capita GDP that is lower than that of advanced countries. These include countries like China, India, and Brazil. GDP in these countries is growing at a faster rate than in the developed countries.

Reasons for differences in economic growth between developed and developing countries generally focus on the role of capital and labor resources and the use of technology as sources of growth. These aspects are discussed at length later in the reading. For now, we begin by examining some of the key institutions and requirements for growth.

LOS 14a: Compare factors favoring and limiting economic growth in developed and developing economies. Vol 1, pp 598–604

Preconditions from Economic Growth

Savings and investment: Developing countries have low average levels of income, which translates into lower savings and lower investment. Low levels of investment mean lower levels of capital per worker, which in turn lead to slower GDP growth, and persistently low income and savings. However, developing nations can try to get out of this vicious cycle by attracting foreign investment (to plug the gap between domestic savings and investment requirements).

Financial markets and intermediaries: Financial markets and intermediaries, such as banks, can promote growth in the following ways:

- They screen those who seek funding and monitor those who obtain funding to ensure that capital is devoted to projects with the highest risk-adjusted returns.
- They encourage saving and risk-taking among investors by creating attractive investment instruments that are liquid and facilitate diversification and transfer of risk.
- By pooling savings from a number of investors, they are able to finance projects on a larger scale than would otherwise be possible.

However, one should note that financial sector intermediation can sometimes result in declining credit standards and/or higher leverage, which tend to increase risk but not necessarily help economic growth.

Political stability, rule of law, and property rights: Stable and effective governments, well-developed legal and regulatory systems, and respect for property (including intellectual property) rights are all key preconditions for economic growth. Unfortunately for developing countries, their recent history has been tarnished by wars, military coups, corruption, and other sources of political instability that increase economic uncertainty, and in turn increase investment risk, discourage foreign investment, and hinder growth.

Education and health care systems: A major obstacle to growth for many developing countries is inadequate education, as workers do not acquire the skills needed to use and apply new technologies. Another problem in developing countries is "brain drain" where highly educated individuals leave for more developed nations. Developed countries tend to invest more in post-secondary education, which has been shown to foster innovation. On the other hand, developing countries tend to invest primarily in primary and secondary education, which helps them apply existing technologies that have already been developed elsewhere.

Another impediment to growth in developing countries is poor health care, which leads to lower life expectancy.

Tax and regulatory systems: Studies have shown that limited regulations and low administrative start-up costs encourage entrepreneurial activity and the entry of new companies. This in turn leads to competition and improvements in average productivity levels.

Free trade and unrestricted capital flows: Free trade provides domestic residents with goods at lower costs. Further, it offers domestic companies access to larger overseas markets and helps them become more efficient (as they strive to remain competitive in the face of stiffer competition from foreign companies).

Foreign investment helps developing nations meet domestic investment requirements. Foreign investment can increase a developing economy's physical capital stock, resulting in higher productivity, employment, and wages, and can even lead to higher domestic savings. Further, it gives developing countries access to advanced technologies that are developed and used in developed countries. Foreign investment can be classified as:

- Direct investment, which occurs when foreign companies build or buy property, plant and equipment in the domestic country.
- Indirect investment, which occurs when foreign companies and individuals purchase securities issued by domestic companies.

LOS 14b: Describe the relation between the long-run rate of stock market appreciation and the sustainable growth rate of the economy. Vol 1, pp 606–611

LOS 14c: Explain why potential GDP and its growth rate matter for equity and fixed income investors. Vol 1, pp 606–611

Why Potential GDP Matters to Investors

One of the primary factors that influence equity market performance is the anticipated growth in aggregate corporate earnings. Growth in potential GDP matters to investors because it places a limit on how fast the economy (and therefore, aggregate corporate earnings) can grow. An economy's potential GDP is the maximum amount of output it can sustainably produce without resulting in an increase in the inflation rate. Once actual real GDP exceeds potential GDP, the economy suffers from inflationary pressures, which prompts the government to move to cool down economic activity. Therefore, it is very important for investors to evaluate the growth in potential GDP as it can serve as a limiting factor for earnings growth.

The relationship between economic growth and stock prices can be illustrated by expressing the aggregate value of the stock market as the product of (1) GDP, (2) the share of corporate earnings in GDP, and (3) the market P-E ratio:

$$P = GDP\left(\frac{E}{GDP}\right)\left(\frac{P}{E}\right)$$

where:
P = Aggregate price or value of earnings
E = Aggregate earnings

This equation can also be expressed in terms of growth rates:

$$\Delta P = \Delta(GDP) + \Delta(E/GDP) + \Delta(P/E)$$

The above equation implies that growth in stock market prices is a function of (1) the percentage change in GDP, (2) the percentage change in the share of earnings in GDP, and (3) the percentage change in the market price-earnings multiple.

Over the short term, all three factors influence stock market performance. However, over the long term, stock market performance is primarily driven by the growth rate of GDP.

- The ratio of earnings to GDP cannot rise forever, nor can it decline forever.
  - It cannot keep rising because a declining share of the overall economic pie for labor will decrease aggregate demand, jeopardizing future profit growth.
  - It cannot keep declining because unprofitable businesses will eventually disappear.
  - Therefore, over the long term, the second term in the equation above approximately equals zero.
- Similarly, the price-to-earnings ratio cannot grow or contract forever.
  - It cannot rise forever as there will come a point where investors will feel that equity prices are inflated and will not pay an arbitrarily high price for each unit of earnings.
  - It cannot keep declining forever (towards zero) as investors will not give away earnings for nothing.
  - Therefore, the third term in the equation above also approximately equals zero over the long term.

Aside from its impact on equity values, growth in potential GDP is also relevant for fixed-income investors through its influence on nominal and real interest rates.

- Potential GDP is used to measure inflationary pressures in the economy. Actual GDP growth above (below) growth in potential GDP puts an upward (downward) pressure on inflation, which result in an increase (decrease) in nominal interest rates. This is a negative (positive) for bond prices.
- The real interest rate is the return that consumers/savers demand in order to postpone consumption. Higher growth rates of potential GDP translate into higher real interest rates. This is because, faster growth in potential GDP means that consumers expect their incomes to rise substantially in the future, which encourages them to spend in the current period. All else remaining the same, the real interest rate would then have to be higher in order to stimulate the saving required to fund capital accumulation.

Other ways in which potential GDP growth plays a role in fixed-income security analysis are listed below:

- A higher growth rate of potential GDP improves the general credit quality of fixed-income securities. The reduction in risk results in higher values.
- The nature of the output gap (difference between actual real GDP and potential GDP) in the economy has important implications for monetary policy. When actual real GDP exceeds potential GDP, the resulting inflationary pressures in the economy encourage policy makers to increase interest rates to cool down the economy, which is a negative for fixed-income security values.
- Slower estimated growth in potential GDP has negative consequences for credit ratings of sovereign and government-issued debt.

- A government's fiscal stance (whether it is expansionary or contractionary) is evaluated based on the structural or cyclically-adjusted balance (i.e., the budgetary balance that would exist were the economy operating at full employment).

LESSON 2: DETERMINANTS OF ECONOMIC GROWTH

LOS 14d: Distinguish between capital deepening investment and technological progress and explain how each affects economic growth and labor productivity. Vol 1, pp 613–615

Production Function

To examine the impact of capital investment on economic growth and labor productivity, we will work with the Cobb-Douglas production function. To simplify our analysis, we use the following two-factor (labor and capital) production function:

$$Y = AK^{\alpha}L^{1-\alpha}$$

where:
Y = Level of aggregate output in the economy
L = Quantity of labor
K = Quantity of capital
A = Total factor productivity. Total factor productivity (TFP) reflects the general level of productivity or technology in the economy. TFP is a scale factor (i.e., an increase in TFP implies a proportionate increase in output for any combination of inputs).
α = Share of GDP paid out to capital
$1- \alpha$ = Share of GDP paid out to labor

The Cobb-Douglas production function exhibits the following two important properties:

- Constant returns to scale: This means that if quantities of all inputs are increased by the same percentage, then output would also increase by that same percentage. For example, all other things (including the state of technology, A) remaining the same, if the quantities of labor and capital were increased by 10%, total output would also increase by 10%. Based on this assumption, the Cobb-Douglas production function can be modified and expressed in terms of output per worker as follows:

> Note that the lowercase letters denote variables measured on a per capita basis.

$$y = Y/L = A(K/L)^{\alpha}(L/L)^{1-\alpha} = Ak^{\alpha}$$

where:
y = Y/L = Output per worker or labor productivity
k = K/L = Capital per worker or capital-labor ratio

> As mentioned, TFP is a scale factor that multiplies the impact of factor inputs. Changes in TFP are measured using growth accounting, which is discussed in the next section.

This equation tells us that labor productivity (the amount of goods that can be produced by a worker) depends on:
  ○ The capital-labor ratio (K/L or k)
  ○ Total factor productivity (A)
  ○ The share of capital in GDP (α)

- Diminishing marginal productivity of factor inputs: Marginal productivity refers to the additional output produced from a one-unit increase in an input, keeping the quantities of all other inputs unchanged. The Cobb-Douglas production function exhibits diminishing marginal productivity of labor and capital, which implies that if we keep on increasing quantities of one of these inputs while holding quantities of the other input constant, the additional output produced will keep declining. The significance of diminishing marginal returns in the production function depends on the value of α.

  ○ If α is close to zero, diminishing marginal returns to capital are very significant. In other words, the extra output produced by each additional unit of capital declines quickly as more units of capital are employed.

  ○ If α is close to one, diminishing marginal returns to capital are not very significant. The extra output produced by the marginal unit of capital is almost the same as the extra output produced by the previous unit of capital employed.

The terms diminishing marginal productivity and diminishing marginal returns can be used interchangeably.

Note that the sum of the exponents on K and L in the Cobb-Douglas production function equals one, which indicates constant returns to scale. If quantities of both inputs are increased proportionately, there are no diminishing marginal returns.

In the analysis above, we simply stated that α equals the share of capital in GDP. It would facilitate your understanding if you were to learn to derive this outcome (as it will help you understand growth theories later in the reading). We do this below:

In a competitive economy, factors of production are paid their marginal product. Profit maximization occurs at the point where the marginal product of capital equals the rental price of capital and the marginal product of labor equals the real wage rate. Based on the Cobb-Douglas production function, the marginal product of capital, MP_K, is derived as:

Marginal product of capital is determined by differentiating the expression for Y with respect to K.

$$Y = AK^{\alpha}L^{1-\alpha}$$

$$=> MP_K = \alpha AK^{\alpha-1}L^{1-\alpha}$$

$$\text{Since } Y = AK^{\alpha}L^{1-\alpha}; MP_K = \alpha Y/K$$

Setting MP_K equal to the rental price (r) of capital, we get $\alpha Y/K = r$. Then solving for α, we get α equals rK/Y, which represents the share of GDP paid out to suppliers of capital.

The two things that you must take away from this section (in order to understand growth theories) are that:

- In a competitive economy, profit maximization occurs when:
  ○ $MP_K = r$ and MP_L = real wage rate.
- The marginal product of capital can be expressed as $\alpha Y/K$. We will use this expression in neoclassical growth theory.

Capital Deepening versus Technological Progress

Diminishing marginal productivity plays an important role in evaluating the role of capital and technology in economic growth. Figure 2-1 shows the relationship between output per worker (y = Y/L) and the capital-labor ratio (k = K/L).

Figure 2-1: Per Capita Production Function: Capital Deepening versus Technological (TFP) Progress

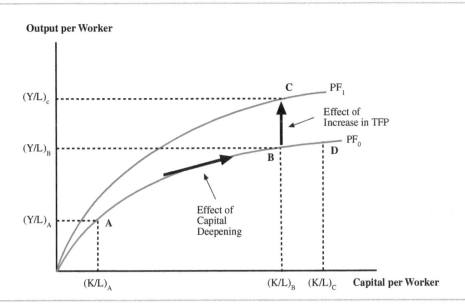

As the figure suggests, growth in output per worker can come from two sources:

- Capital deepening: Capital deepening refers to an increase in the capital-labor ratio and is reflected in a movement along the same per-capita production function (e.g., from Point A to Point B on PF_0). The capital-labor ratio will increase as long as the growth rate of capital exceeds the growth rate of labor. However, the increase in output per worker from increasing the capital-labor ratio becomes relatively insignificant once the capital-labor ratio reaches a relatively high level (e.g., moving from Point B to Point D). This is because the marginal product of capital declines as more capital is added to fixed quantities of labor.

  As long as MP_K is greater than r (the real interest rate), economies will continue to increase investment in capital and capital deepening will raise per capita growth. However, when MP_K equals r, capital deepening will stop. Once the economy reaches this steady state, capital deepening cannot be a source of sustained growth in the economy.
- Technological progress: While capital deepening results in a movement along the same per-capita production function, improvements in TFP cause the entire production function to shift upwards (e.g., from PF_0 to PF_1). Improvements in technology enable the economy to produce a higher output per worker for a given level of capital per worker. Technological progress can therefore result in a permanent increase in output per worker despite the diminishing marginal productivity of capital.

Developed markets typically have high capital-labor ratios, while developing countries typically have low capital-labor ratios. Therefore:

- Developed countries have relatively little to gain from capital deepening and must rely on technological progress for growth in potential GDP. You would expect a developed country to lie somewhere close to Point B on Figure 2-1.
- Developing countries on the other hand, have the potential to grow from both capital deepening and technological progress. You would expect a developing country to plot somewhere close to Point A on Figure 2-1.

LOS 14e: Forecast potential GDP based on growth accounting relations. Vol 1, pp 615–616

Growth Accounting

Solow's growth accounting equation is used to analyze the performance of economies. It is basically the production function written in the form of growth rates:

$$\Delta Y/Y = \Delta A/A + \alpha \Delta K/K + (1-\alpha)\Delta L/L \quad \dots \text{(Equation 1)}$$

According to the growth accounting equation, the growth rate of output ($\Delta Y/Y$) equals the sum of:

- The rate of technological change ($\Delta A/A$)
- α times the growth rate of capital ($\Delta K/K$)
- $(1-\alpha)$ times the growth rate of labor ($\Delta L/L$)

In the previous section, we learned that α and $(1-\alpha)$ refer to the relative shares of capital and labor in GDP. In the context of growth accounting, these exponents can be viewed as the elasticites of output with respect to capital and labor respectively. For example, if the share of capital in a country's GDP is 0.6, it implies that, all other things remaining the same, a 1% increase in the amount of capital increases output by 0.6%.

Uses of the Growth Accounting Equation

- Estimating the contribution of technological progress to economic growth. **Data on output, capital, labor, and the elasticities of capital and labor (shares of capital and labor in national income) are usually available (at least for most developed countries), but the rate of technological change is not directly observable and therefore must be estimated. Given values for the growth in output, capital, labor, and the share of capital and labor in national income, the growth accounting equation can be used to estimate the amount of output that cannot be explained by growth in capital and labor. This residual represents progress in TFP.**
- Empirically measure the sources of growth in an economy. **Studies use the growth accounting equation to quantify the contribution of each factor to long-term economic growth and answer questions such as:**
  - What is the contribution of capital and how important is the contribution of capital deepening to economic growth?
  - What is the impact of improvement in TFP on economic growth?
- Measure potential GDP. **Growth in factor inputs is estimated using trend analysis, α is estimated using GDP data, and growth in TFP is estimated using time-series analysis. These estimates are then applied as inputs in Equation to measure potential output.**

Note that potential GDP may also be measured using the labor productivity growth accounting equation, which models potential GDP as a function of (1) labor input quantities and (2) labor productivity.

$$\text{Growth rate in potential GDP} = \text{Long-term growth rate of labor force} + \text{Long-term growth rate in labor productivity} \quad \dots \text{(Equation)}$$

The advantage of using this equation is that there is no need to estimate the capital input or total factor productivity (TFP). However, one drawback is that it incorporates both capital deepening and TFP progress in the productivity term.

LOS 14f: Explain how natural resources affect economic growth and evaluate the argument that limited availability of natural resources constrains economic growth. Vol 1, pp 617–619

There are two categories of natural resources:

- Renewable resources are those that are replenished, such as forests.
- Nonrenewable resources are those that are limited in supply and are depleted once they are consumed, such as oil and coal.

The relationship between *ownership* of natural resources and economic growth is not straightforward. Some countries (e.g., Brazil) that have an abundance of natural resources (agricultural land) have grown rapidly because of their resource base. Others, however, (e.g., Venezuela) have shown relatively unimpressive growth despite being well-endowed with resources (oil). Further, some countries (e.g., Singapore) have experienced rapid economic growth despite having few natural resources. The conclusion is that *ownership* and *production* of natural resources is not necessary for an economy to grow; it is more important for a country to be able to *access* natural resources (e.g., via trade).

Note that the presence of natural resources may sometimes even restrain economic growth, resulting in a "resource curse." This may happen because of the following reasons:

- Countries with abundant reserves of natural resources may focus too much on recovering those resources, while neglecting the development of economic institutions necessary for growth.
- Appreciation of the domestic currency driven by export demand for natural resources may result in other segments of the economy (e.g., manufacturing) becoming globally uncompetitive. This is referred to as the Dutch disease. If the manufacturing sector contracts, the country would fall behind in terms of technological progress, which would hinder long-term productivity growth.

Another concern is that countries that grow rapidly as a result of their large reserves of nonrenewable natural resources will eventually witness a decline in growth due to resource depletion. However, this concern is overstated as over time, scarcity will inflate prices of such resources and encourage a shift towards substitutes in greater supply.

LOS 14g: Explain how demographics, immigration, and labor force participation affect the rate and sustainability of economic growth. Vol 1, pp 619–624

Labor Supply

The potential quantity of labor input in the economy is measured in terms of the total number of hours available for work, which can be estimated as:

> Total number of hours available for work = Labor force × Average hours worked per worker

The **labor force** is defined as the working age population (16 to 64 years old) that is either (1) employed or (2) available for work, but not working (unemployed).

Factors Affecting Labor Supply

Population growth: Population growth is a function of birth rates and mortality rates. Generally speaking, population growth rates in developing countries are higher than in developed countries. While population growth may increase the growth rate of the GDP, it has no impact on the rate of increase in per capita GDP.

Another important consideration is growth of the working age population. Some economies (e.g., Japan) face a demographic burden as the proportion of nonworking elders in their populations is relatively high. On the other hand, in many developing countries the proportion of the population below the age of 16 is relatively high, which suggests that labor supply will grow in the future in those economies.

Labor force participation: The labor force participation rate equals the percentage of the working age population that is in the labor force. In the short run, changes in labor force participation may lead to differences between the growth rate of the labor force and the population growth rate. Given the population, an increase in labor force participation would lead to an increase in the growth of per capita GDP. Over the last few decades, the increasing number of women in the workforce has led to an increase in the labor force participation rate in most countries.

Net migration: Immigration offers a solution for slowing labor force growth in developed countries where (1) birth rates are relatively low and/or (2) the proportion of nonworking elders is relatively high. In recent years, immigration has led to an increase in the labor force in Ireland and Spain, which has allowed them to experience GDP growth above the European average.

Average hours worked: The average number of hours worked is very sensitive to the business cycle. Generally speaking however, it has declined over the long term in most developed countries as a result of legislation, collective bargaining agreements, growth of part-time and temporary work, and the impact of the "wealth effect" and high tax rates on labor income, which have encouraged individuals to take more leisure time.

LOS 14h: Explain how investment in physical capital, human capital, and technological development affects economic growth. **Vol 1, pp 624–631**

Labor Quality: Human Capital

Human capital refers to the accumulated knowledge and skills that workers acquire from education, training, and life experience. Better-educated and more skilled workers are generally more productive and more adaptable to changes in technology and to other shifts in market demand and supply.

The quality of human capital can be improved through education, on-the-job training, and better health care. Further, education can result in innovation and technological progress, which can lead to a permanent increase in the growth rate of an economy.

Capital: ICT and Non-ICT

Generally speaking, there is a high positive correlation between investment in physical capital and GDP growth. This may seem inconsistent given that we earlier stated that capital deepening cannot result in long-term sustainable growth, but there are several explanations to reconcile this apparent disconnect.

First, although the positive impact of capital deepening on economic growth may be limited by diminishing marginal productivity, investment-driven growth can last for a considerable period of time. This is especially true for countries that start off at relatively low capital-labor ratios.

Second, the composition of investment spending on physical capital stock is also very important. Capital spending can be separated into two categories: (1) ICT investment (i.e., spending on information, computers, and telecommunications equipment) and (2) non-ICT investment, which includes nonresidential construction, transport equipment, and machinery.

- ICT investment is a measure of the impact of the information technology (IT) sector on economic growth. Growth in the IT sector has led to network externalities (i.e., it has enabled people to interconnect and work more productively), which has led to increasing TFP and economic growth.
- Non-ICT investment results in capital deepening, and therefore has more of a temporary impact on economic growth.

A growing share of ICT investment in economies has boosted the growth rate of potential GDP (through network externalities and growth in TFP). Therefore, the positive relation between capital spending and economic growth over the long run can be explained by a relatively higher portion of capital spending being allocated to ICT investment (which results in improving TFP).

Technology

Improvements in technology result in an upward shift in the production function, and allow economies to overcome limits on growth imposed by diminishing marginal returns to capital. Stated differently, they allow economies to produce more goods and services with the same quantity of factor inputs.

Technological change may be brought about through investment in human capital, and/or new machinery, equipment, and software (especially ICT goods).

Expenditures on research and development, R&D, (both public and private) usually encourage innovation. Developed countries tend to spend a higher percentage of GDP on R&D as they primarily rely on innovation and the development of new products and production methods for growth. In contrast, developing countries tend to spend less on R&D as they (1) can acquire new technology through imitation, and (2) can foster economic growth in the short run through capital deepening.

Public Infrastructure

Investment in public infrastructure such as roads, bridges, municipal water, and dams improves the productivity of private investment. Therefore, public infrastructure is an important source of productivity growth (similar to that of R&D) and should be included in the production function.

LESSON 3: CLASSICAL GROWTH THEORY AND NEOCLASSICAL GROWTH THEORY (PART I)

LOS 14i: Compare classical growth theory, neoclassical growth theory, and endogenous growth theory. Vol 1, pp 637–652

LOS 14k: Describe the economic rationale for governments to provide incentives to private investment in technology and knowledge. Vol 1, pg 651

The subsistence real wage rate is the minimum real wage rate required to maintain life. If the real wage rate is lower than the subsistence real wage rate, some people cannot survive and the population decreases. If the real wage rate is greater, there is a population explosion.

Theories of Growth

Classical Model (Malthusian Model)

This model asserts that growth in real GDP per capita is **temporary**. GDP per capita only grows until it rises above the subsistence level. Once it rises above the subsistence level, real GDP per capita falls due to a population explosion. See Figure 3-1.

To understand this theory, assume that technological advancement has led to investment in new capital, which improves labor productivity. Labor demand therefore rises, and real wages increase. At this stage, economic growth has occurred and the standard of living appears to have improved. However, once the real wage rate exceeds the subsistence real wage rate, there is a population explosion, which eventually (due to diminishing marginal returns to labor) reduces marginal product of labor to zero. Labor productivity and per capita income fall back to the subsistence level.

Figure 3-1: Classical Growth Model

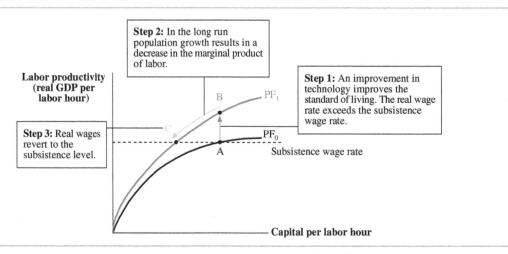

Basically this theory predicts that standards of living remain constant over time even with technological progress as there is no growth in per capita output. In the long run, new technologies result in a larger population, but not a richer population.

Empirically, this theory has not proven to be true because:

- Per capita income growth has not resulted in population growth (as assumed by the theory). In fact, population growth has historically slowed with economic growth.
- The positive impact of technological progress on per capita income has outweighed the negative impact of diminishing marginal returns.

Neoclassical Model (Solow's Model)

This model is based on the Cobb-Douglas production function. Both labor and capital are variable factors of production and both suffer from diminishing marginal productivity.

The neoclassical model seeks to find the economy's equilibrium position, which it asserts occurs when the economy grows at the steady state rate of growth (see Example 3-1). In this state:

- The output-capital (Y/K) ratio is constant. This ratio is denoted by Ψ and calculated as:

$$\frac{Y}{K} = \left(\frac{1}{s}\right)\left[\left(\frac{\theta}{(1-\alpha)}\right) + \delta + n\right] \equiv \Psi \qquad \ldots\text{(Equation 3)}$$

where:
s = Fraction of income that is saved
θ = Growth rate of TFP
α = Elasticity of output with respect to capital
y = Y/L or income per worker
k = K/L or capital-labor ratio
δ = Constant rate of depreciation on physical stock
n = Labor supply growth rate

- Capital per worker (k = K/L) and output per worker (y = Y/L) grow at the same rate, which is given by:
  - Growth rate in k and y: $\theta/(1 - \alpha)$
- Growth in total output (Y) equals the sum of (1) the growth rate in output per worker, $\theta/(1 - \alpha)$, and (2) growth in labor supply, n. Notice that this assertion is in line with the labor productivity growth accounting equation (Equation 2).
  - Growth rate in output (Y) = $\theta/(1 - \alpha) + n$
  - $n = \Delta L/L$ = Growth in labor supply
- The marginal product of capital is also constant, and equals the real interest rate:
  - $MP_K = \alpha Y/K = r$ (derived earlier)

Important takeaways:

- Even though the capital-labor ratio (k = K/L) is increasing [at the rate $\theta/(1 - \alpha)$] in the steady state, which indicates that capital deepening is occurring in the economy, the marginal product of capital remains constant (at $MP_K = \alpha Y/K = r$). This can be explained by growth in TFP offsetting the impact of diminishing marginal returns to capital.
- Further, capital deepening has no effect on the growth rate of the economy in the steady state. The economy continues to grow at a constant rate of $\theta/(1 - \alpha) + n$.

Example 3-1: Steady State Growth Rates

Consider the following information:

Country	Growth Rate of Potential GDP (%)	Labor Cost in Total Factor Cost (%)	Growth Rate of TFP (%)	Growth Rate of Labor Force (%)
A	11.5	45	2.6	1.3
B	0.6	58	0.3	0.0
C	1.7	56	0.9	0.0

1. Calculate the steady state growth rates from the neoclassical model for the three countries.
2. Compare the steady state growth rates to the potential GDP growth rates and explain the results.

Solution:

1. According to the neoclassical model, the steady state growth rate of GDP is calculated as the sum of (1) the growth rate of TFP, θ, scaled by labor factor share, $(1 - \alpha)$ and (2) the labor force growth rate, n.

   Growth rate in output $(Y) = \theta / (1 - \alpha) + n$

   Using this equation, the steady state growth rates for the three countries are estimated as:

   Country A: 2.6%/0.45 + 1.3 = 7.08%
   Country B: 0.3%/0.58 + 0.0 = 0.52%
   Country C: 0.9%/0.56 + 0.0 = 1.61%

2. For Countries B and C, their estimated steady state growth rates are very close to their growth rates in potential GDP (B: 0.52% vs. 0.6%; C: 1.61% vs. 1.7%). Changes in growth rates of TFP (θ) and labor (n), and labor's share in GDP $(1 - \alpha)$, which are the three variables considered in the steady state rate calculation, explain the growth in potential GDP (almost) in its entirety. Therefore, improvements in the capital-labor ratio (capital deepening) will not have a significant impact on the growth rate of potential GDP for these economies, and we can conclude that these economies are in (or very close to) equilibrium according to the neoclassical theory.

   On the other hand, for Country A, the estimated steady state growth rate is significantly lower than the growth rate in potential GDP (7.08% vs. 11.5%). This implies that after accounting for changes in growth rates of TFP and labor, and labor's share in GDP (which are the three variables considered in the steady state rate calculation), there is still some growth in potential GDP that remains unexplained. This growth can be harnessed by increasing the capital-labor ratio in this economy. Therefore, we can conclude that this economy is not in equilibrium as defined by the neoclassical model since capital deepening can play an important role in the growth rate of potential GDP.

We can also analyze steady state equilibrium by applying the following savings/investment equation (which is basically a transformed version of Equation 3):

$$sy = \left[\left(\frac{\theta}{(1-\alpha)}\right) + \delta + n\right]k$$

You will not be required to transform Equation 3 into this form on the exam. However, you are required to understand its implications and the analysis that follows.

According to this equation, steady state equilibrium occurs at the point where savings per worker (and actual gross investment per worker), sy, are sufficient to:

- Provide capital to new workers entering the workforce at the rate, n.
- Replace worn-out plant and machinery that is depreciating at the rate, δ.
- Deepen the capital stock at the rate $\theta/(1-\alpha)$, which is the required growth rate of capital in the steady state. When the capital-labor ratio increases at this rate, the marginal product of capital remains constant.

Think of it this way: We know that in the steady state, capital-labor grows at $\theta/(1-\alpha)$ and the marginal product of capital remains constant (equal to the real interest rate, r). We have now introduced the impact of depreciation and labor growth into the mix. Depreciation and labor growth have a negative impact on the capital-labor ratio. In order to keep the overall or net growth rate of the capital-labor ratio constant at $\theta/(1-\alpha)$, gross investment per worker (sy) must first offset the negative impact of depreciation (δ) and labor growth (n) on the capital-labor ratio and still be sufficient to grow the capital-labor ratio at the rate of $\theta/(1-\alpha)$. Therefore, overall gross investment per worker must equal the sum of $\theta/(1-\alpha)$, δ and n in the steady state.

The steady state is represented graphically in Figure 3-2.

- The curved line (sy_0) represents the amount of actual saving/ gross investment per worker.
- The straight line $[\delta_0 + n_0 + \theta_0/(1-\alpha_0)]k$ indicates the amount of investment per worker required to keep the physical capital stock growing at the required rate of $\theta/(1-\alpha)$. We shall refer to this line as the required investment line.

The point of intersection of the investment per worker curve and the required investment line represents the steady state (Point A) at a particular point in time. Note that at any point in time, the exogenous factors (i.e., labor supply and TFP) are fixed.

Figure 3-2: Steady State in Neoclassical Model at a Point in Time (t=0)

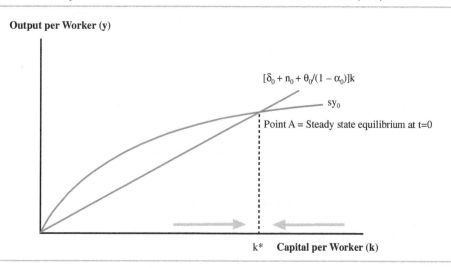

Note that over time, TFP grows at θ, so output per worker, y, grows at $\theta/(1 - \alpha)$. In turn, this growth in output per worker results in an upward shift in the sy curve. Therefore, over time, equilibrium moves upward and rightward along a straight line (Figure 3-3).

Figure 3-3: Steady State in Neoclassical Model over Time

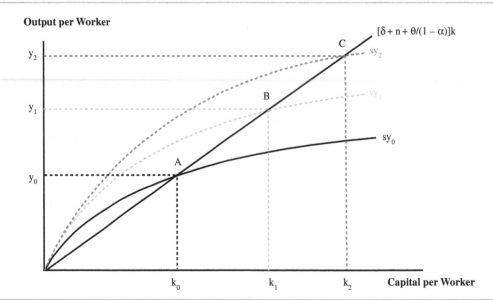

- Over time, TFP grows at θ, so y grows at $\theta/(1 - \alpha)$.
- Since y is increasing, the sy curve moves upwards over time (from sy_0 to sy_1 to sy_2).
- In each successive period, the point of intersection between the investment per worker curve and the required investment line moves upward and rightward along a straight line (from Point A to Point B to Point C).
- The capital-labor ratio (k) increases from k_0 to k_1 to k_2. It grows at the rate $[\theta/(1 - \alpha)]$.
- Output per worker (y) increases from y_0 to y_1 to y_2. It also grows at the rate $[\theta/(1 - \alpha)]$.
- Even though there are diminishing marginal returns to capital, the marginal product of capital remains constant over time ($MP_K = \alpha Y/K = r$). This is because the growth in TFP (at rate θ) offsets the impact of diminishing marginal returns

LESSON 4: NEOCLASSICAL GROWTH THEORY (PART II) AND ENDOGENOUS GROWTH THEORY

LOS 14i: Compare classical growth theory, neoclassical growth theory, and endogenous growth theory. Vol 1, pp 637–652

LOS 14k: Describe the economic rationale for governments to provide incentives to private investment in technology and knowledge. Vol 1, pg 651

Now we are in a position to evaluate the impact of changes in any of the parameters that we have discussed so far:

Saving rate (s): An increase in the saving rate increases investment per worker (represented by an upward shift in the sy curve from s_0y to s_1y on Figure 4-1). The investment per worker curve now intersects the required investment line at Point B, where the capital labor ratio is higher (k_1 vs. k_0)

and output per worker is also higher (y_1 vs. y_0). Note that even though an increase in the saving rate has increased the *levels* of k and y in the new steady state, it has no impact on the *growth rates* of k and y. They continue to grow at their steady state rates of growth $\theta/(1 - \alpha)$, while total output (Y) continues to grow at $\theta/(1 - \alpha) + n$.

Figure 4-1: Impact of Increase in Saving Rate on the Steady State

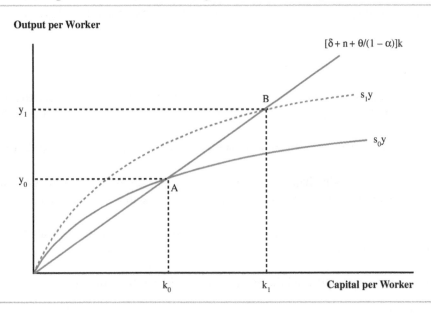

Labor force growth (n): An increase in labor force growth (from n_0 to n_1) increases the slope of the required investment line (see Figure 4-2). Equilibrium moves from Point A to Point B with a lower capital-labor ratio (k_1 vs. k_0) and a lower output per worker (y_1 vs. y_0) at the new steady state.

Figure 4-2: Impact of Increase in Labor Force Growth on the Steady State

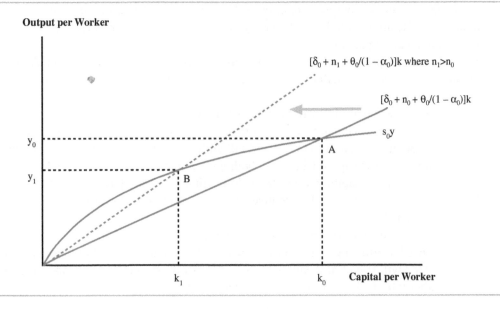

Depreciation rate (δ): An increase in depreciation has the same impact as an increase in labor force growth. The slope of the required investment line increases, and new steady state equilibrium is reached where the capital-labor ratio and output per worker are lower.

Growth in TFP (θ): An increase in the growth rate of TFP results in an increase in the slope of the required investment line. This results in a decline in the capital-labor ratio and output per worker. This impact is similar to that of an increase in labor force growth and an increase in the depreciation rate. However, raising the growth rate of TFP implies that output per worker and capital per worker will grow faster (since they both grow at $\theta/(1-\alpha)$ and θ is now higher). Overall, the economy would grow at a steeper trajectory in the future (due to higher future growth in output per worker) but start from a lower level of output per worker than if TFP growth were slower.

To summarize:

- Changes in (1) the savings rate, (2) labor force growth rate, and/or (3) depreciation rate impact the level of output per worker but do not have a long-term impact on the growth rate of output per worker.
- Only a change in TFP has a permanent impact on the growth rate of output per worker.

So far, we have only described what happens once the economy is on the steady state growth path. Now we discuss what happens if the economy is not currently in the steady state.

If the economy is not currently on the steady state growth path, it can experience faster or slower growth relative to the steady state.

The growth rates of output per capita and the capital-labor ratio can be expressed as:

> You do not need to learn to derive these equations, nor do you need to commit them to memory, but make sure you understand the takeaways that follow.

$$\frac{\Delta y}{y} = \left(\frac{\theta}{(1-\alpha)}\right) + \alpha s\left(\frac{Y}{K} - \Psi\right)$$

$$\frac{\Delta k}{k} = \left(\frac{\theta}{(1-\alpha)}\right) + s\left(\frac{Y}{K} - \Psi\right)$$

- In the steady state, the output-capital ratio (Y/K) equals Ψ. Therefore, the second terms in the formulae above equal 0 so the growth rates of output per capita ($\Delta y/y$) and capital-labor ratio ($\Delta k/k$) equal $\theta/(1-\alpha)$.
- Whenever the output-capital ratio (Y/K) is greater than Ψ (to the right of Point A on Figure 4-3), $[(Y/K) - \Psi]$ will be positive. $s[(Y/K) - \Psi]$ will be greater than $\alpha s[(Y/K) - \Psi]$ as α is less than 1.
  - This means that $\Delta k/k$ will be greater than $\Delta y/y$.
  - Since k is growing at a faster rate than y, and y/k equals Y/K, we conclude that the output-capital ratio (Y/K) will fall until it equals Ψ. Going forward, output per capita and the capital labor ratio both grow at the steady state rate $\theta/(1-\alpha)$.
- Whenever the output-capital ratio (Y/K) is lower than Ψ (to the left of Point A on Figure 4-3), $[(Y/K) - \Psi]$ will be negative. $s[(Y/K) - \Psi]$ will be lower than $\alpha s[(Y/K) - \Psi]$ as α is less than 1.
  - This means that $\Delta k/k$ will be lower than $\Delta y/y$.
  - Since k is growing at a lower rate than y, we conclude that the output-capital ratio (Y/K) will rise until it equals Ψ. Going forward, output per capita and the capital labor ratio both grow at the steady state rate $\theta/(1-\alpha)$.

Figure 4-3: Dynamics in the Neoclassical Model

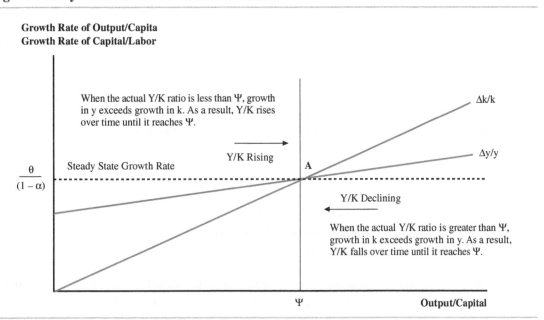

What you **need** to take away from the preceding analysis is that in the neoclassical model:

Capital deepening (or capital accumulation) affects the level of output, but not the growth rate in the long run. Regardless of the initial capital-labor ratio and the initial level of productivity, the economy will move to a point of steady state growth (as illustrated in Figure 4-3). In the long run, output grows at a constant rate $\theta/(1 - \alpha) + n$, and output per capita grows at a constant rate $\theta/(1 - \alpha)$.

When countries first begin to accumulate capital, they witness growth that is above the steady state rate of growth. Over the long run however, this rapid pace of growth will slow down. In developing countries, capital-labor ratios are relatively low so MP of capital is relatively high. If these countries can stimulate savings and investment, they can grow at a faster rate than developed countries. This suggests that eventually there should be a convergence of per capita incomes between developed and developing countries.

In the long term, economies cannot rely solely on capital deepening for sustainable growth. In fact, if the capital-labor ratio grows too quickly, capital becomes less productive and growth slows down as opposed to accelerating.

Because of diminishing marginal returns to capital, the only way to sustain GDP per capita growth in the long run is through growth in TFP, which results in an upward shift in the production function.

An increase in rate of saving and investment will temporarily raise the rate of growth in the economy. Over time, the growth rate will revert to the steady state growth rate. However, countries with higher rates of saving and investment will have a higher per capita output, a higher capital-labor ratio, and a higher level of labor productivity.

Criticisms of the Neoclassical Model

- Studies have found that growth in TFP explains a significant portion of economic growth. Under neoclassical theory, TFP is determined outside the model (it is an exogenous variable) so the theory provides no explanation for the determinants of technological progress or how TFP changes over time.
- Economists have found that savings rates and growth rates are positively related across countries. Neoclassical theory asserts that the steady state rate of economic growth is unrelated to the rate of saving and investment. Under neoclassical theory, long-run growth is determined by growth in TFP and labor, while higher rates of saving and investment only have a temporary impact on growth.

Endogenous Growth Theory

Endogenous growth theory focuses on explaining technological progress (which has proven to be the primary determinant of economic growth in the long run) as opposed to neoclassical growth theory (which treats technological progress as an exogenous variable).

> R&D is defined as investment in new knowledge that improves the production process.

Endogenous theory broadens the definition of capital to include human and knowledge capital and R&D. As a result, savings can be used to pay for labor, physical capital or knowledge and human capital and R&D. However, there is an important difference between spending on physical capital and spending on R&D. Investment in physical capital increases output, while investment in R&D results in ideas.

> Recall that in neoclassical theory, the production function is a curved line that eventually flattens out.

The theory asserts that not only do these ideas have a positive impact on the company that comes up with them, but that they have positive externalities and spillover effects as they can be copied by competitors as well. Overall, R&D results in increasing returns to scale across the entire economy as companies benefit from the private spending of their competitors. Therefore, the economy does not reach a steady growth rate (as predicted by the neoclassical model). Instead, saving and investment can generate self-sustaining growth at a permanently higher rate as the positive externalities associated with R&D prevent diminishing marginal returns to capital from setting in. The production function in the endogenous growth model is an upward-sloping straight line given by:

$$y_e = f(k_e) = ck_e$$

Output per worker (y_e) is proportional to the stock of capital per worker (k_e), while c is the constant marginal product of capital.

Takeaways from endogenous growth theory

- Since there are no diminishing marginal returns to capital from the perspective of the economy as a whole, an increase in the savings rate would permanently increase the rate of economic growth.
- Since R&D entails positive externalities, there may be a market failure in the sense that there would be underproduction of R&D from the societal perspective. Therefore, there may be a strong case for government intervention to increase investment in capital in the economy.

- If the government encourages investment in physical capital, there would be capital deepening, which (as neoclassical theory predicts) would only result in a temporary surge in growth. Even if the high rate of investment is sustained, growth will eventually decline. Note that the benefit of this approach by the government is that there would be a high probability of success as the policy does not require investment in unproven technologies.
- However, if the government encourages investment in R&D and knowledge and human capital, growth is likely to be permanently enhanced if the investment is successful in improving efficiency and generating the desired positive externalities. However, note that while the impact of this policy is likely more powerful, success is also more uncertain.

- Due to the constant (or sometimes even increasing) returns associated with investment in knowledge capital and R&D, developed countries can continue to grow faster than developing countries. As a result, there is no reason for incomes to converge over time (as predicted by the neoclassical model).

LESSON 5: THE CONVERGENCE DEBATE AND GROWTH IN AN OPEN ECONOMY

LOS 14j: Explain and evaluate convergence hypotheses. Vol 1, pp 652–656

The Convergence Debate

Convergence means that countries with low per capita incomes should grow at a faster rate than countries with high per capita incomes, such that over time, per capita income differences will be eliminated.

- Absolute convergence means that regardless of their particular characteristics, output per capita in developing countries will eventually reach the level of developed countries.
    - Neoclassical theory asserts that since all countries have access to the same technology, per capita income in all countries will eventually *grow* at the same rate (at the steady state rate). Therefore, the model predicts convergence in per capita growth rates across countries. Note that it does not assert that the *level* of per capita income will be the same across countries regardless of their underlying characteristics, so it does not imply absolute convergence.
- Conditional convergence means that convergence in output per capita is dependent (or conditional) upon countries having the same savings rates, population growth rates, and production functions.
    - Neoclassical theory predicts that if these conditions hold, countries will converge to the same level of per capita output. Looking at Figure 3-2, these countries would have the same k* and therefore, the same steady state.
        - If they have different capital-labor ratios, their growth rates will differ temporarily during the transition to the steady state, but eventually converge (as illustrated in Figure 4-3).
        - If they have different saving rates and different population growth rates, they will have different steady state values for k* and different steady state values for per capita income. Their growth rates of per capita output will still converge [to $\theta/(1 - \alpha)$].

In contrast to the neoclassical model, the endogenous growth model does not assert that convergence will occur. Developed countries can stay ahead of developing countries in terms of growth by maintaining a high rate of investment in knowledge and human capital and R&D.

Studies have shown that some of the poorer countries are in fact diverging rather than converging towards the income levels of developed countries. This phenomenon is explained by club convergence. Countries with similar structural characteristics (e.g., production technologies, preferences, government policies, etc.) form a club. Within the club, countries with the lowest per capita incomes grow at the fastest rates, while countries outside the club fall further behind. Note that membership of the club is based on the economy exhibiting certain desirable structural characteristics, not on income levels. Poor countries can join the club by making appropriate institutional changes; otherwise they risk falling into a nonconvergence trap.

Convergence between developing and developed countries can occur from two sources:

- Capital deepening: Developing countries tend to operate at relatively low capital-labor ratios so the marginal productivity of capital in those countries is still relatively high. On the other hand, developed countries tend to operate at high capital-labor ratios, where marginal productivity of capital is relatively low. Therefore, developing countries can catch up to their developed peers simply through capital accumulation.
- By importing technologies from developed countries, developing countries can achieve faster economic growth and converge to the income levels of advanced economies.

If the convergence hypothesis is correct, we would expect an inverse relationship between countries' initial levels of per capita GDP and their growth rates in per capita GDP. Stated differently, poor countries should exhibit a higher growth rate than rich countries. A study of growth rates of 33 countries found that almost two-thirds of the countries that had a lower standard of living than the United States in 1950 grew at a faster rate than the United States during the 1950 to 2010 period. However, there were some countries that fell further behind. Therefore, we can conclude that there is some support for the convergence hypothesis. However, the evidence suggests that developing appropriate legal, political, and economic institutions (and becoming part of the convergence club) is also important for developing countries to grow. In addition, trade policy is an important factor (discussed in the next LOS).

LOS 14l: Describe the expected impact of removing trade barriers on capital investment and profits, employment and wages, and growth in the economies involved. Vol 1, pp 656–664

Growth in an Open Economy

Opening up the economy to trade and financial flows has the following advantages:

- Investment is not constrained by domestic savings as the country can finance investments with foreign savings.
- Productivity improves as the country can focus on industries in which it has a comparative advantage.
- Domestic producers can exploit economies of scale as they attain access to larger overseas markets.
- TFP improves as countries are able to import latest technologies.
- Faced with competition from foreign producers, domestic companies strive to produce better products and improve productivity.

Convergence (as predicted by the neoclassical model) should occur more quickly if there is free trade and no restrictions on capital flows. Generally speaking, developing countries have lower capital-labor ratios than developed countries. This implies that the marginal product of capital (and the real interest rate) is higher in developing countries. With free movement of capital across borders, global savers will shift capital from developed countries to developing countries. The resulting capital accumulation in developing countries will result in higher productivity growth leading to convergence of per capita incomes.

Capital inflows will temporarily help developing countries grow at a rate higher than steady state growth rate. Over time, more and more capital investment will lead to diminishing marginal returns to capital, slowing down growth until it reaches the steady state rate. In the neoclassical model, there is no permanent increase in the rate of growth in an economy after the reallocation of world savings. Both the developed and developing countries grow at a steady state rate of growth.

In contrast, endogenous growth models predict that opening up economies will lead to a permanent increase in the rate of economic growth. This can be explained through the following:

- Selection effect: Foreign competition forces less efficient domestic companies to exit the industry and more efficient companies to innovate, increasing the efficiency of the overall national economy.
- Scale effect: Producers are better able to exploit economies of scale with access to large overseas markets.
- Backwardness effect: Less advanced countries or sectors are able to catch up with the more advanced countries or sectors as a result of knowledge spillovers.

Despite the benefits of open markets highlighted by both the neoclassical and endogenous growth models, developing countries have pursued two contrasting strategies in the pursuit of economic development over the last 50 years:

- Inward-oriented policies: Also known as import substitution policies, these policies attempt to develop domestic industries by restricting imports, even if they are less costly. Studies have shown that countries that pursued inward-oriented policies witnessed slower economic growth and little convergence.
- Outward-oriented policies: These policies attempt to integrate domestic industries with those of the global economy through trade. Exports are deemed key drivers of growth. Studies have shown that countries that pursued outward-oriented policies benefited from improved standards of living and convergence with developed countries.

READING 15: ECONOMICS OF REGULATION

LESSON 1: ECONOMICS OF REGULATION

LOS 15a: Describe classifications of regulations and regulators. Vol 1, pp 680–683

A regulatory framework develops a set of rules and standards of conduct. Regulation affects individual businesses and the overall economy. Regulation can be classified as:

- Statutes: Laws enacted by legislative bodies.
- Administrative regulations: Rules issued by government agencies and other regulators.
- Judicial law: Interpretations of courts.

Regulations can come from government agencies or independent regulators. Independent regulators get their regulatory authority through recognition from a government body or agency. Note that independent regulators do not receive government funding so they are politically independent.

Independent regulators include self-regulatory organizations (SROs). These are private entities that represent their members and regulate them as well. While they may be immune from political pressure, SROs are subject to pressure from their members, which can give rise to conflicts of interest. Not all SROs are independent regulators however. Those that are granted authority by government bodies obviously serve as independent regulators, but there are others that get their regulating authority from their members. These members agree to comply with the SROs rules and standards and to enforce them. Note that this authority does not have the force of law.

Regulatory authorities may sometimes reference the work of outside bodies (e.g., accounting standard-setting bodies like FASB and IASB, and credit rating agencies like Moody's and S&P) in their regulations. However, they still retain the legal authority to enforce any regulation that references the work of these bodies.

LOS 15b: Describe uses of self-regulation in financial markets. Vol 1, pp 680–683

As mentioned earlier, SROs may face pressure from their members. Therefore, SROs that are given regulatory authority can face conflicts of interest. However, SROs under the supervision of regulatory agencies have been able to effectively meet the objectives of regulation.

In the U.S., the Securities and Exchange Commission (SEC) regulates the financial markets. The SEC allocates some regulatory authority to specific SROs. One such SRO is FINRA, whose mission is to protect investors by ensuring fairness of capital markets.

Outside the United States SROs are rarely or never recognized as regulatory authorities. Concerns over the effectiveness of SROs arise from (1) their corporate governance and (2) management of their conflicts of interest.

Reasons for Reliance on Self-Regulation
- Increases overall level of regulatory resources.
- Uses knowledge and expertise of industry professionals.
- Enables the regulator to focus on other priorities while relying on the SRO for frontline supervision of members and markets.

Reasons for Decreased Reliance on Self-Regulation
- Privatization of securities exchanges.
- Intense competition.
- Uncertainty regarding effectiveness of self-regulation.
- Internationalization.
- Strengthening of government regulators.
- Trend toward consolidation of financial regulators.
- "Cooperative regulation."
- Pressure to increase efficiency and lower costs.

LOS 15c: Describe the economic rationale for regulatory intervention.
Vol 1, pp 683–684

Regulatory intervention becomes essential due to the presence of informational frictions and externalities.

Informational friction results in the following issues:

- Adverse selection, where some market participants have access to information that is unavailable to others.
- Moral hazard occurs in a situation where one party will have a tendency to take risks because the costs that could be incurred will not be felt by the party taking the risk.

Regulation for overcoming informational frictions focuses on establishing rights and responsibilities of entities to ensure that no entity is treated unfairly.

Externalities in the context of regulation refer to the provision of public goods. Public goods give rise to the free-rider problem, as consumption of a public good by a person does not preclude another person from also consuming it. Examples of public goods include national defense and street lighting. Due to the positive externalities associated with these goods, regulation is necessary to ensure that society produces the optimal quantity of these goods.

LOS 15d: Describe regulatory interdependencies and their effects. Vol 1, pp 684–686

The regulatory capture theory argues that regulation can often actually advance the interests of the regulated (e.g., by restricting potential competition and coordinating the strategies of rivals). The theory is based on the premise that regulatory bodies are usually headed by individuals hailing from the industry itself as those individuals are already very familiar with the industry and are, therefore, in the best position to supervise its activities. The argument is that their long association with the industry renders them incapable of making impartial decisions.

Regulatory differences across jurisdictions can result in shift in location and the behavior of entities due to regulatory competition and regulatory arbitrage.

- **Regulatory competition** refers to competition between regulators to provide a regulatory environment designed to attract certain entities.
- **Regulatory arbitrage** refers to practices whereby firms capitalize on loopholes in regulatory systems in order to circumvent unfavorable regulation. It includes cases where companies shop around for locations that allow certain behavior rather than changing their own behavior.

Different countries may have common regulatory issues, but regulators in different countries may have different perspectives or face different trade-offs when addressing specific issues. This can lead to differences in regulatory treatments, encouraging companies to pursue regulatory arbitrage. For example, in the aftermath of the global financial crisis of 2008 many European and Asian countries were slower than the United States to respond and implement derivatives reforms. As a result, there were concerns that U.S. markets would suffer from (arguably unduly restrictive) regulation of U.S.-based financial institutions.

There have been similar problems in coordinating efforts to deal with global warming and pollution on a global scale. Since regulations limiting greenhouse gas emission are not applied consistently by all countries, polluters have the option to simply relocate to developing countries where regulations are not as restrictive.

Further, there can sometimes be conflicts between different regulatory bodies within the same country, leading to a regulatory framework that seems inconsistent.

LOS 15e: Describe tools of regulatory intervention in markets. Vol 1, pp 686–691

Regulatory Tools

Regulatory tools available to authorities include:

Price mechanisms (taxes and subsidies): Taxes are imposed to discourage certain behaviors (e.g., taxes on cigarettes to deter smoking), while subsidies are imposed to encourage certain behavior (e.g., subsidies for farmers on certain crops to increase domestic production).

Regulatory mandates and restrictions on behaviors: Governments can mandate certain activities (e.g., minimum capital requirements for banks) or restrict certain activities (e.g., insider trading).

Provision of public goods and financing for private projects: Governments can provide public goods (e.g., national defense, transportation infrastructure) or provide loans to individuals and businesses for specific activities that the government wants to promote. The extent of government provision of public goods and financing for private projects depends on the structure of the government, its philosophy, and the country's GDP.

Generally, it is feasible to consider more than one regulatory approach in a specific situation. An example can be found in the case of trade restrictions on corporate insiders where both regulator-level and corporate-level restriction can be used. An example of a regulatory action would be a requirement for corporate insiders to disclose trades, while an example of corporate action would be a blackout period during which insiders are banned from trading the company's stock. The appropriate action depends on the individual facts and circumstances and specific context of the case.

Effective regulation also requires that regulators should have the ability to impose sanctions on violators. Sanction on violators of securities regulations or regulations on business can be imposed on the violating company or the individual violator (or both). Company sanctions are appropriate when the company has caused harm to others. However, in the case of accounting fraud, sanctions on the company would entail imposing sanction on shareholders, who have already been victims of the wrongdoing. In this case, a more compelling argument can be made for penalizing the individual perpetrators.

However, it is usually difficult to prosecute or achieve settlements with individual violators. This is because (1) it is difficult to identify the individuals who were directly at fault, (2) individuals have strong incentives to fight to protect their reputation and livelihood, and (3) individuals are usually able to fight using corporate resources because of indemnification provisions in their employment contracts.

LOS 15f: Explain purposes in regulating commerce and financial markets.
Vol 1, pp 691–694

Regulation of Commerce

Governments play an important role in promoting commerce at the local, national, regional, and global levels. They are responsible for establishing a legal framework for contracting and setting standards, which is an important part of creating an environment where business can prosper.

- Government regulation plays an important role in various aspects of business such as protecting workers' and employers' rights and responsibilities, and consumer's health and safety.
- Governments set the legal standards for the recognition and protection of different types of intellectual property.
- Other examples of government regulations covering commerce include company laws, tax laws, bankruptcy laws, and banking laws.
- Governments take the steps they deem necessary to support and protect domestic business interests against unfair competition (e.g., by imposing anti-dumping duties).

Regulation of Financial Markets

Failures in the financial system can lead to financial losses to specific parties, an overall loss of confidence in the financial system, and disruption of commerce. This makes regulation of securities markets and financial institutions very important.

Regulation of Securities Markets

Securities regulation is generally aimed at protecting investors, creating confidence in markets, and enhancing capital formation. Various aspects of securities regulation include:

- Securities registration requirements to develop investor confidence. For example, disclosure requirements on companies to allow investors to value financial assets and make well-informed investing decisions. The disclosure framework includes financial reporting requirements and accounting standards.
- Regulations geared towards mitigating the principal-agent problem. Examples of such regulations include soft dollar standards, execution requirements on broker/dealers, and corporate governance issues.
- Protecting the interests of retail investors. This focus on smaller investors explains the relatively lax coverage of hedge fund and private equity fund investors who tend to be "qualified."

Regulation of Financial Institutions

Regulation of financial institutions focuses on protecting consumers and investors, ensuring the safety and soundness of financial institutions, promoting the smooth operation of the payments system, and maintaining availability to credit. Financial regulation also aims to tackle concerns relating to the overall economy such as price stability, unemployment, and economic growth.

Prudential supervision refers to regulation and monitoring of the safety and soundness of financial institutions for promoting financial stability, reducing system-wide risks, and protecting customers of financial institutions. This aspect of financial regulation is critical because a failure of a financial institution can have far-reaching consequences on the overall economy.

Sometimes, regulators may set up funds to provide against losses and require that premiums be paid into these funds. For example, in the United States the FDIC insures the money deposited in bank accounts. Note that such activities have some implicit costs, such as the moral hazard situation created due to insurance coverage, which may encourage banks to take greater risks.

The financial crisis of 2008 highlighted two negative externalities that have recently been tackled by financial regulation. These are:

- Systematic risk: The risk of failure of the financial system.
- Financial contagion: A situation in which financial shocks spread from their place of origin to other countries (i.e., when faltering economies affect healthier ones).

Increased globalization has led to increased concerns about contagion and regulatory competition.

LOS 15g: Describe anticompetitive behaviors targeted by antitrust laws globally and evaluate the antitrust risk associated with a given business strategy. Vol 1, pp 691–694

As mentioned earlier, government regulation of commerce includes taking steps to protect domestic businesses from foreign competition. In the domestic arena however, governments aim to promote competition (or alternatively, prevent anticompetitive practices). For example, regulatory approval is required for mergers and acquisitions of large companies. In evaluating mergers and acquisitions regulators evaluate whether the merger will lead to monopolization of the market. Competition and antitrust laws also prohibit other types of anticompetitive behavior. Examples of such behavior include exclusive dealings and refusals to deal, price discrimination, and predatory pricing.

Large companies that operate in multiple markets need to simultaneously satisfy regulators from several countries when faced with antitrust issues. For example, over the last decade, Microsoft has faced antitrust litigation in the United States and Europe over its attempts to monopolize the browser market by bundling its browser with the Windows operating system. Competing firms may also use competition laws as a part of their business strategy to catch up to rivals. An example of such a challenge is Microsoft's challenge in Europe that Google is unfairly impeding competition in the search engine market.

For analysts, it is important to evaluate whether or not an announced merger or acquisition would be blocked by regulators on antitrust grounds.

LOS 15h: Describe benefits and costs of regulation. Vol 1, pp 696–698

Cost-Benefit Analysis of Regulation

Benefits of regulation have been described in earlier sections, so our focus here is on evaluating the costs of regulation.

- **Regulatory burden** refers to the costs of regulation for the regulated entity. It can be viewed as the private costs of regulation or government burden.
- **Net regulatory burden** results from subtracting private benefits of regulation from private costs.

When conducting cost-benefit analysis, analysts should consider direct and indirect costs of regulation. An example of direct costs of regulation is the cost of hiring compliance attorneys, while indirect costs would refer to the way in which economic decisions and behavior are changed due to the regulation. Further, there may be "unintended" costs associated with regulations. These costs may be also be direct (e.g., more compliance lawyers needed than originally anticipated) or indirect. It is important for regulators to assess the unintended consequences of potential regulations as they can result in high unanticipated costs.

It is easier to assess the costs and benefits of regulations on a retrospective basis than on a prospective basis, as costs and benefits can be measured more reliably after the fact. In order to encourage regulators to conduct retrospective analysis and assess the impact of previous regulations on an ongoing basis, there have been calls for sunset provisions. These provisions require regulators to conduct a new cost-benefit analysis before the regulation is renewed.

LOS 15i: Evaluate how a specific regulation affects an industry, company, or security. Vol 1, pp 698–703

It is important for analysts to monitor issues of concern to regulators and to assess the implications of potential regulations. Some regulations may benefit certain market sectors or industries (e.g., by increasing barriers to entry), while others may cause certain industries to shrink (e.g., heavy taxation on cigarette consumption). Regulations are usually more likely to benefit the regulated if regulators are "captive" to the industries they regulate.

Sometimes, regulations can result in increased inefficiency in the market. For example, the response of policy makers to the financial crisis (by granting them bailouts) has led many market participants to anticipate that major financial institutions are likely to be supported by the government in times of crises in the future. As a result, credit spreads may no longer accurately represent the risks of financial sector companies. Further, these companies may now be willing to assume greater risks.

Regulation also plays a significant role when it comes to protecting the environment, property rights, and the interests of employees. Therefore, it is important for analysts to assess the type of regulation that an industry or business is susceptible to. For example, compared to capital-intensive industries, labor-intensive industries are more susceptible to changes in regulations relating to labor conditions and rights, while pharmaceutical companies are more susceptible to regulations relating to intellectual property rights.

STUDY SESSION 5: FINANCIAL REPORTING AND ANALYSIS: INTERCORPORATE INVESTMENTS, POST-EMPLOYMENT AND SHARE-BASED COMPENSATION, AND MULTINATIONAL OPERATIONS

LESSON 1: INTERCORPORATE INVESTMENTS—AN INTRODUCTION

Investments in Financial Assets

Intercorporate investments (investments in other companies) can have a significant impact on the investing company's financial performance (income statement) and financial position (balance sheet). A company may invest in debt and equity instruments issued by other companies to diversify its asset base, enter new markets, or improve profitability.

When it comes to accounting standards the govern classification, measurement and accounting of intercorporate investments, the IASB and FASB have made significant progress in attaining convergence. This has improved the relevance, transparency and comparability of financial statements across companies. Some differences remain, but there are generally adequate disclosures to allow analysts to adjust for those differences.

LESSON 2: INVESTMENTS IN FINANCIAL ASSETS

LOS 16a: Describe the classfication, measurement, and disclosure under International Financial Reporting Standards (IFRS) for (1) investments in financial assets, (2) investments in associates, (3) joint ventures, (4) business combinations, and (5) special purpose and variable interest entities. Vol 2, pp 9–56

LOS 16b: Distinguish between IFRS and U.S. GAAP in the classification, measurement, and disclosure of investments in financial assets, investments in associates, joint ventures, business combinations, and special purpose and variable interest entities. Vol 2, pp 9–56

Investments in marketable debt and equity securities can be categorized as:

- Investments in financial assets, in which the investor has no significant influence or control over operations of the investee. Generally speaking, there is a lack of significant influence if the investor holds less than 20% equity interest in the investee.
- Investments in associates, in which the investor can exert significant influence, but not control, over the investee. Generally speaking, there is significant influence (but not control) if the investor holds between a 20% and 50% equity interest in the investee.
- Business combinations (including investments in subsidiaries), in which the investor has control over the investee. Generally speaking, an equity interest exceeding 50% indicates control over the investee.
- Joint ventures, in which control is shared by two or more entities.

Note that the classification of an investment is based on the degree of influence or control, not purely on the percentage holdings listed above.

Table 2-1 summarizes the accounting treatments for various types of corporate investments under **IFRS**.

Table 2-1: Summary of Accounting Treatment for Investments

<table>
<tr><td></td><td></td><td>In Financial Assets</td><td>In Associates</td><td>Business Combinations</td><td>In Joint Ventures</td></tr>
<tr><td rowspan="2">U.S. GAAP categorizes intercorporate investments similarly, but not identically.</td><td>Influence</td><td>Not significant</td><td>Significant</td><td>Controlling</td><td>Shared Control</td></tr>
<tr><td>Typical percentage interest</td><td>Usually < 20%</td><td>Usually 20%–50%</td><td>Usually > 50%</td><td>Varies</td></tr>
<tr><td></td><td>Current Financial Reporting Treatment (prior to IFRS 9 taking effect)</td><td>Classified as
• Held-to-maturity
• Available-for-sale
• Fair value through profit or loss (held for trading or designated as fair value)
• Loans and receivables</td><td>Equity method</td><td>Consolidation</td><td>IFRS: Equity method or proportionate consolidation</td></tr>
<tr><td></td><td>New Financial Reporting Treatment (post IFRS 9 taking effect)</td><td>Classified as
• Fair value through profit or loss
• Fair value through other comprehensive income
• Amortized cost</td><td>Equity method</td><td>Consolidation</td><td>IFRS: Equity method</td></tr>
</table>

Investments in Financial Assets: Standard IAS 39 (as of December 2012)

Investments in financial assets are considered passive as the investor does not exert significant influence or control over the investee. The accounting treatment of investments in financial assets is similar under IFRS and U.S. GAAP.

Under **IFRS**, financial assets may be classified as:

1. Held-to-maturity.
2. Available-for-sale.
3. Fair value through profit or loss; which includes
   • Held-for-trading, and
   • Designated as fair value through profit or loss.
4. Loans and receivables.

Generally speaking:

- Investments in financial assets are initially recognized at fair value.
- Dividend and interest income from all financial assets (regardless of categorization) is reported on the income statement.
- The reporting of subsequent changes in fair value depends on the classification of the investment.

Held-to-Maturity (HTM) Investments

HTM investments are investments in financial assets with fixed or determinable payments and fixed maturities (debt securities) that the investor has a positive intent and ability to hold till maturity. HTM investments cannot be reclassified or sold prior to maturity except in unusual circumstances. Reclassification/sale of HTM investments can result in the investor being precluded from classifying investments under the HTM category going forward.

> HTM investments are exceptions to the general requirement (under IFRS and U.S. GAAP) that financial assets be subsequently recognized at fair value.

Under **IFRS**, financial assets classified as HTM are *initially* recognized on the balance sheet at **fair value**, while under **U.S. GAAP**, HTM securities are *initially* recognized at **initial price paid**. Generally speaking, initial fair value equals initial price paid, so the treatment is essentially the same under the two sets of standards.

Under both **IFRS** and **U.S. GAAP**, HTM securities are *subsequently* (at each reporting date) reported at **amortized cost** using the **effective interest method** (unless objective evidence of impairment exists).

> Note that transaction costs are included in initial fair value for investments that are not classified as fair value through profit or loss.

- Interest income and realized gains/losses are recognized in the income statement.
- Unrealized gains/losses (due to changes in fair value) are ignored.

We studied the effective interest method of accounting for financing liabilities in detail at Level I. Just to recap, under the effective interest method:

- Any difference between the fair value and par value of the security is amortized over its term.
  - When the par value *exceeds* fair value, the securities trade at a discount. This occurs when the effective interest rate is *greater* than the stated interest (coupon) rate.
  - When the par value is *lower* than fair value, the securities trade at a premium. This occurs when the effective interest rate is *lower* than the stated interest (coupon) rate.
  - Amortization of the discount/premium results in changes in the carrying value of the securities (as it converges towards par) each year.

Fair Value through Profit or Loss (IFRS)

Under IFRS, investments classified as fair value through profit or loss include (1) securities held for trading and (2) those designated by management as carried at fair value. U.S. GAAP is similar.

- Investments are initially recognized at fair value.

Held-for-trading (HFT) investments include debt and equity securities that are bought with the intention of selling them in the near term. Under both IFRS and U.S. GAAP:

- HFT investments are *initially* recognized at *fair value,* and *remeasured* at each reporting date to reflect *current fair value.*
- Realized gains/losses (upon sale), unrealized gains/losses (due to changes in fair value), interest income, and dividend income are all reported in profit or loss.

Under both, IFRS and U.S. GAAP, investment that can be classified as available-for-sale (AFS) or HTM can also be initially designated at fair value. The accounting treatment of these designated at fair value investments is similar to that of held-for-trading investments.

- Investments are initially recognized at fair value.
- At each subsequent reporting date, investments are remeasured at fair value.
- Unrealized gains/losses, realized gains/losses, interest income, and dividend income are all reported in profit or loss.

Available-for-Sale (AFS) Investments

AFS investments are debt and equity securities that are not classified as held-to-maturity or at fair value through profit or loss.

Under **IFRS**:

- AFS investments are initially recognized at fair value, and remeasured at each reporting date to reflect fair value.
- All unrealized gains/losses (except for gains/losses on AFS **debt** securities arising from exchange rate movements) are recognized (net of taxes) in equity under other comprehensive income. When they are sold, these (now realized) gains/losses are reversed out of other comprehensive income and reported in profit or loss as a reclassification adjustment.
- Unrealized gains/losses on AFS **debt** securities resulting from exchange rate movements are recognized on the income statement.
- Realized gains/losses, interest income, and dividend income, are also recognized on the income statement.

The accounting treatment of AFS securities is the same under **U.S. GAAP**, except that **all unrealized gains/losses** (including those on AFS debt securities caused by exchange rate movements) are reported in other comprehensive income.

Loans and Receivables

Loans and receivables are defined as nonderivative financial assets with fixed or determinable payments.

- **IFRS** has a specific definition (it does not rely on legal form) for loans and receivables. Items that meet the definition are carried at amortized cost unless they are designated as (1) fair value through profit or loss or (2) available-for-sale.
- **U.S. GAAP** relies on legal form for the classification of debt securities. Loans and receivables that meet the definition of debt securities are classified as HFT, AFS, or HTM, with HFT and AFS securities being measured at fair value.

Reclassification of Investments

Under **IFRS**:

- Reclassification of securities into and out of the "designated at fair value" category is generally prohibited.
- Reclassification out of the "held-for-trading" category is restricted.
- HTM (debt) securities can be reclassified as AFS securities if there is a change in intention or ability to hold the asset until maturity.
  - When HTM securities are reclassified as AFS securities, they are remeasured at fair value and any differences between fair value and carrying amount (amortized cost) are recognized in other comprehensive income.
  - As mentioned earlier, once a company has reclassified HTM securities, it may be prohibited from using the HTM classification for other existing debt securities and new purchases.
- Debt securities initially classified as AFS can be reclassified as HTM securities if there is a change in intention or ability to hold the asset until maturity.
  - When AFS debt securities are reclassified as HTM securities, their fair value at time of reclassification becomes their (new) amortized cost and any unrealized gains/losses previously recognized in other comprehensive income are amortized to profit or loss over the security's remaining life using the effective interest method.
  - Differences between the new amortized cost and par (maturity) value are also amortized over the remaining term of the securities using the effective interest method.
- Debt instruments may be reclassified from HFT or AFS to loans and receivables if (1) the definition is met and (2) the company expects to hold them for the forseeable future.
- An investment classified as AFS may be measured at **cost** if there is no reliable measure of fair value and no evidence of impairment.
  - Note that once a reliable fair value estimate becomes available, the asset must be remeasured at fair value and any changes in value must be recognized in other comprehensive income.

U.S. GAAP generally allows reclassifications of securities between all categories when justified, with fair values being determined at the transfer date. However, if HTM securities are reclassified, the company may be precluded from using the HTM category for other investments.

The treatment of unrealized gains/losses on the transfer date depends on security's initial classification.

- For HFT securities that are being reclassified as AFS securities, any unrealized gains/losses (differences between carrying value and current fair value) have already been recognized in profit and loss.
- When securities are reclassified as HFT securities, any unrealized gains/losses are recognized immediately in profit and loss.
  - When AFS securities are reclassified as HFT, the cumulative amount of unrealized gains/losses previously recognized in other comprehensive income is recognized in profit and loss on the date of transfer.
- When HTM securities are reclassified as AFS, unrealized gains/losses (differences between fair value and amortized cost) at the date of the transfer are reported in other comprehensive income.

- When AFS debt securities are reclassified as HTM, the cumulative amount of unrealized gains/losses that have been recognized in other comprehensive income are amortized over the security's remaining life as an adjustment of yield (interest income) in the same manner as a premium or discount.

Impairments

There are some key differences in the approaches taken by IFRS and U.S. GAAP in (1) determining whether a financial asset is impaired and (2) in measuring and reporting the impairment loss.

Under **IFRS**, at the end of each reporting period, all financial assets that are not carried at fair value must be assessed for impairment, and any current impairment must be recognized in profit or loss immediately. Securities classified as fair value through profit or loss (which includes those designated at fair value through profit or loss and those held for trading) are reported at fair value so any impairment losses have already been recognized in profit or loss.

A **debt** security is considered impaired if at least one loss event (which has an impact on its estimated future cash flows that can be reliably estimated) has occurred. Examples of loss events that cause impairment include (1) the issuer facing financial difficulty and (2) default or delinquency in interest or principal payments.

Note that a credit rating downgrade or the absence of an active market for the security do not provide evidence of impairment. Further, losses expected from **future** events are not recognized no matter how probable they may be.

An **equity** security is considered impaired if:

- There has been a substantial and extended decline in the fair value of the security below its cost.
- There have been significant changes in the technology, market, and/or legal environment that have had an adverse impact on the investee, and indicate that the initial cost of the investment may not be recovered.

For (1) HTM (debt) securities and (2) loans and receivables that have become impaired, the impairment loss is calculated as the difference between the security's carrying value and the present value of its expected future cash flows discounted at the initial effective interest rate.

- The carrying amount of the security is reduced either directly or indirectly through an allowance account.
- The impairment loss is recognized in profit or loss.
- Reversals of previously recognized impairment losses are allowed.
- A reversal of a previously recognized impairment charge results in an increase in the carrying value of the asset and an increase in net income.

For AFS securities that have become impaired, the cumulative loss recognized in other comprehensive income (as the security is remeasured at fair value at each successive reporting date) is transferred from other comprehensive income to the income statement as a reclassification adjustment.

- Reversal of impairment losses is only allowed for AFS debt securities, not for AFS equity securities.
- The amount of reversal is recognized in profit or loss.

Under **U.S. GAAP**, AFS and HTM securities must be assessed for impairment at each balance sheet date. A security is considered impaired if the decline in its value is "other than temporary." See Example 2-1.

For debt securities, impairment means that the investor will be unable to collect all amounts owed according to contractual terms at acquisition.

- If the decline in fair value is deemed other than temporary, the cost basis of the securities is written down to their fair value, which then becomes the new cost basis.
- The impairment loss is treated as a realized loss on the income statement.

For AFS debt and equity securities:

- If the decline in fair value is deemed other than temporary, the cost basis of the securities is written down to their fair value, which then becomes the new cost basis.
- The impairment loss is treated as a realized loss on the income statement.
- However, the new cost basis cannot be increased if there is a subsequent increase in fair value (i.e., reversals of impairment losses are not allowed).
- Subsequent increases in fair value (and decreases of other than temporary) are treated as unrealized gains and included in other comprehensive income.

Example 2-1: Accounting for Investments in Financial Assets

On January 1, 2010, Alpha invested $240,000 in debt securities of Beta. The securities carry a coupon rate of 7% payable annually on par value of $200,000. On December 31, 2010, the fair value of the securities is $270,000.

1. Given that the market interest rate in effect when the bonds were purchased was 5%, how would Alpha account for the investment on December 31, 2010, if it designated the investment as:
   a. Held-to-maturity.
   b. Held-for-trading.
   c. Available-for-sale.
   d. Designated at fair value.
2. What gain would Alpha recognize in each of the above investment classifications if it sold the securities on January 1, 2011, for $273,000?

Solution:

1. The investment's amortized cost at year end may be calculated as the carrying amount at the beginning of the year adjusted for the amortization of premium. The amount of premium amortized in each period equals the excess of the coupon payment over interest expense.

   Carrying value at the beginning of 2010 = $240,000
   Coupon payment received for 2010 = $200,000 × 0.07 = $14,000
   Interest income (effective interest method) for 2010 = $240,000 × 0.05 = $12,000
   Amortization of premium during 2010 = 14,000 − 12,000 = $2,000
   Therefore, investment's carrying value at the end of 2010 = 240,000 − 2,000 = $238,000

> You may want to review the analysis of financing liabilities from Level I to understand the amortization of bond premium/discount under the effective interest method.

	Income Statement	Balance Sheet	Shareholders' Equity
Held-to-maturity	Interest income = $12,000	Reported at amortized cost = $238,000	No effect
Held-for-trading	Interest income = $12,000 Unrealized gain = $32,000 (= 270,000 − 238,000)	Reported at fair value = $270,000	No effect
Available-for-sale	Interest income = $12,000	Reported at fair value = $270,000	Unrealized gain of $32,000 is reported net of taxes under other comprehensive income.
Designated at fair value	Interest income = $12,000 Unrealized gain = $32,000	Reported at fair value = $270,000	No effect

2. The gain recognized in the income statement during 2011 for each of the investment classifications is calculated as:

Held-to-maturity: Selling price − Carrying value (amortized cost)
= 273,000 − 238,000 = $35,000

Held-for-trading: Selling price − Carrying value (fair value at the end of 2010)
= 273,000 − 270,000 = $3,000

Available-for sale: Selling price − Carrying value (fair value at the end of 2010)
+ Unrealized gain for 2010*
= (273,000 − 270,000) + 32,000* = $35,000

* The unrealized gain is transferred from other comprehensive income to the income statement as a reclassification adjustment.

Investments in Financial Assets: IFRS 9 (As of December 2012)

The IASB has issued the first phase of their project dealing with classification and measurement of financial instruments by including relevant chapters in IFRS 9, which will take effect on January 1, 2015, but can be adopted early. When all phases of the project are complete this standard is expected to replace IAS 39.

Although the FASB has not finalized its standards, it appears that there will be significant (but not complete) convergence with IFRS.

Classification and Measurement of Financial Assets under IAS 9

All financial assets are measured at fair value when initially acquired. Subsequently, financial assets are measured at either fair value or amortized cost.

Debt instruments that meet the following two criteria are generally measured at amortized cost.

- The financial assets are being held to collect contractual cash flows (known as the business model test); and
- The contractual cash flows are solely payments of principal and interest on principal (known as the cash flow characteristic test).

Note that management may still choose to classify those debt instruments (that meet the above criteria) as fair value through profit or loss to avoid an "accounting mismatch." An accounting mismatch is an inconsistency resulting from different measurement bases for assets and liabilities.

Equity instruments are measured at fair value through profit or loss (FVPL) or at fair value through other comprehensive income (FVOCI).

- Equity investments **held-for-trading** must be measured at fair value through profit or loss (FVPL).
- Other equity investments can be measured at FVPL or FVOCI, but the choice is irrevocable.
- The terms available-for-sale and held-to-maturity no longer appear in IFRS 9.

Financial assets that are **derivatives** are measured at fair value through profit or loss (except for hedging instruments). See Figure 2-1.

Figure 2-1: Financial Assets Classification and Measurement Model, IFRS 9[1]

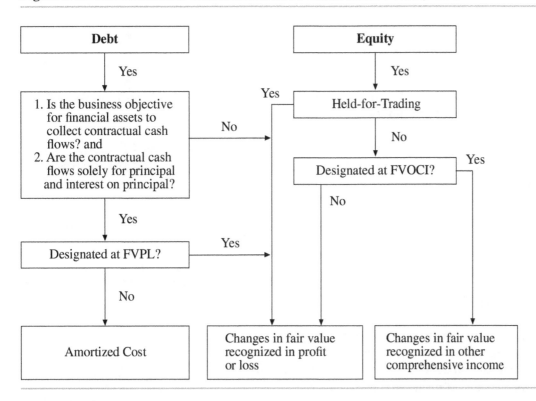

1 - Exhibit 4, Volume 2, CFA Program Curriculum 2017

Reclassification of Investments

Under the new standards:

- Reclassification of **equity** instruments is not permitted (the initial classification as FVPL and FVOCI is irrevocable).
- Reclassification of **debt** instruments from FVPL to amortized cost (or vice versa) is only permitted if the objective for holding the assets (business model) has changed in a way that significantly affects operations.
  - When reclassification is deemed appropriate, there is no restatement of prior periods at the reclassification date.
  - If the financial asset is reclassified from amortized cost to FVPL, the asset is measured at fair value with gain or loss recognized in profit or loss.
  - If the financial asset is reclassified from FVPL to amortized cost, the fair value at the reclassification date becomes the carrying amount.

Analysis of Investments in Financial Assets

Convergence between IFRS and U.S. GAAP standards for the classification, measurement, and reporting of investments in financial assets has made it easier for analysts to make comparisons across companies. Analysts typically assess the performance of a company's operating and investing activities separately.

- Analysis of operating performance should exclude items related to investing activities (e.g., interest income, dividends, realized and unrealized gains/losses).
- Nonoperating assets should be excluded from the calculation of return on operating assets.
- Use of market values of financial assets is encouraged when assessing performance ratios. Both IFRS and U.S. GAAP require disclosure of the fair value of all classes of financial assets.

LESSON 3: INVESTMENTS IN ASSOCIATES AND JOINT VENTURES

LOS 16a: Describe the classification, measurement, and disclosure under International Financial Reporting Standards (IFRS) for investments in associates and joint ventures. Vol 2, pp 9–56

LOS 16b: Distinguish between IFRS and U.S. GAAP in the classification, measurement, and disclosure of investments in associates and joint ventures. Vol 2, pp 9–56

Investments in Associates

An investor may exert significant influence over the investee despite owning less than a 20% ownership stake in the investee if any of these indicators are present.

Associates are corporate investments over which the investor exercises significant influence, but not control (usually demonstrated by an ownership stake between 20% and 50%). Other indicators of significant influence include:

- Representation on the board of directors;
- Participation in the policy-making process;
- Material transactions between the investor and the investee;
- Interchange of managerial personnel; or
- Technological dependency.

Equity Method of Accounting

Under both IFRS and U.S. GAAP, investments in associates are accounted for using the equity method.

Under the equity method:

- The investment is initially recognized on the investor's **balance sheet** at cost (within a single line item) under noncurrent assets.
  - The investor's proportionate share of investee earnings increases the carrying amount of the investment, while its proportionate share of losses and dividends decreases the carrying value of the investment.
- The investor's proportionate share of investee earnings is reported within a single line item on its **income statement**.
  - Note that dividend payments have no impact on the amount reported on the income statement.

If the value of the investment falls to zero (e.g., due to losses), use of the equity method to account for the investment is discontinued. Use of the equity method may only be resumed if the investee subsequently reports profits and the investor's share of profits exceeds the losses not reported by it since abandonment of the equity method. See Example 3-1.

Example 3-1: Equity Method

Alpha purchased a 20% interest in Beta for $500,000 on January 1, 2009. The following table lists income reported and dividends paid by Beta for 2009 and 2010. Alpha uses the equity method to account for its investment in Beta.

	Income	Dividends
2009	$350,000	$100,000
2010	$500,000	$150,000
Total	**$850,000**	**$250,000**

1. Determine the amount related to its investment in Beta that appears on Alpha's balance sheet for 2010.
2. Determine the amount of investment income from Beta recognized on Alpha's income statement for 2009 and 2010.

Solution:

1. The value of the investment in Beta that appears on Alpha's 2010 balance sheet is calculated as the initial cost plus Alpha's proportionate share in Beta's net income (for 2009 and 2010) minus its proportionate share in dividends declared by Beta (for 2009 and 2010).

Initial cost	$500,000
Add: Share of Beta's 2009 income (20% of 350,000)	70,000
Less: Share of dividends declared by Beta for (20% of 100,000)	(20,000)
Value of Investment in Beta (end 2009)	**550,000**
Add: Share of Beta's 2010 income (20% of 500,000)	100,000
Less: Share of dividends declared by Beta for (20% of 150,000)	(30,000)
Value of investment in Beta (end 2010)	**$620,000**

This value can also be calculated as initial cost plus Alpha's proportionate share of Beta's cumulative undistributed earnings since the date of investment.

Value of investment in Beta (end 2010) = 500,000 + [20% × (850,000 − 250,000)]
= **$620,000**

2. The amount recognized as investment income from Beta in Alpha's income statement simply equals Alpha's proportionate share in Beta's earnings.

Equity income for 2009: 20% of 350,000 = **$70,000**
Equity income for 2010: 20% of 500,000 = **$100,000**

Note that the equity method provides a more objective basis for reporting investment income compared to the treatment of investments in financial assets. This is because the investor may be able to influence the timing of dividend distributions.

Excess of Purchase Price over Book Value and Amortization of Excess Purchase Price

In Example 3-1, we implicitly assumed that the purchase price was equal to the value of the purchased equity in the book value of Beta's net assets. If the amount paid by the investor to purchase shares in the investee is greater than the book value of those shares (i.e., the value of the investor's proportionate share in the investee's net identifiable tangible and intangible assets):

- The investor first allocates the excess amount to its proportionate share in specific assets whose fair value exceeds book value.
  - Amounts allocated to inventory are expensed.
  - Amounts allocated to depreciable or amortizable assets are capitalized and subsequently expensed (depreciated or amortized) over an appropriate period of time.
  - Amounts allocated to land and other assets or liabilities that are not amortized continue to be reported at fair value as of the date of investment.
- Any remaining excess (after being allocated to specific identifiable assets) is treated as goodwill, which is not amortized but reviewed periodically for impairment. The investor continues to recognize goodwill as part of the carrying amount of the investment.

Note that the excess of fair value over book value is not reflected in the investee's balance sheet, nor are the necessary periodic charges made on the investee's income statement. The **investor** directly records the impact of these charges on the carrying amount of the investment on its balance sheet and on its share of investee profits recognized on the income statement. See Example 3-2.

Example 3-2: Equity Method Investments with Goodwill

On January 1, 2010, Prime Manufacturers acquired a 25% equity interest in Alton Corp. for $700,000. The following information regarding Alton's assets and liabilities on the date of acquisition is provided:

	Book Value ($)	Fair Value ($)
Current assets	220,000	220,000
Plant and equipment	1,300,000	1,500,000
Land	900,000	1,050,000
Total assets	2,420,000	2,770,000
Liabilities	750,000	750,000
Net assets	**1,670,000**	**2,020,000**

Plant and equipment are depreciated on a straight-line basis to zero over a term of 10 years.

Prime uses the equity method to account for its investment in Alton. Alton reports net income of $250,000 for 2010 and pays dividends of $100,000. Calculate the following:

1. Goodwill included in the purchase price.
2. The amount of equity income to be reported on Prime's income statement for 2010.
3. The value of its investment in Alton recognized by Prime on its balance sheet for 2010.

Solution:

1. Purchase price	$700,000
Proportionate share in book value of Alton's net assets	(417,500)
$(= 25\% \times 1,670,000)$	
Excess purchase price	282,500
Less: Attributable to plant and equipment	(50,000)
$[= 25\% \times (1,500,000 - 1,300,000)]$	
Less: Attributable to land	(37,500)
$[= 25\% \times (1,050,000 - 900,000)]$	
Goodwill (residual)	**$195,000**
2. Proportionate share in Alton's 2010 earnings	$62,500
$(= 25\% \times \$250,000)$	
Less: Amortization of excess purchase price	
Attributable to plant and equipment $(= 50,000 / 10)$	5,000
Equity income	**$57,500**

3.	Purchase price	$700,000
	Add: Proportionate share in net income (= 25% × 250,000)	62,500
	Less: Dividends received (= 25% × 100,000)	(25,000)
	Less: Amortization of excess purchase price	
	Attributable to plant and equipment (= 50,000 / 10)	(5,000)
	Investment balance at December 31, 2010	**$732,500**

Note that land is not a depreciable asset so it will continue to be reported based on its fair value as of the date of investment. Further, note that goodwill is included in the carrying amount of the investment (it is not recognized separately). The investment balance/carrying amount ($732,500) incorporates the purchase price ($700,000), which includes goodwill of $195,000.

Fair Value Option

Both U.S. GAAP and IFRS (with certain restrictions) now offer investors the option to account for their equity method investments using fair values. Under both standards, the decision to apply the fair value method must be made at the time of initial recognition and is irrevocable. When the fair value method is applied:

- Unrealized gains/losses arising from changes in fair value as well as interest and dividends received are included in the investor's income.
- The investment account on the investor's balance sheet does not reflect the investor's proportionate share in the investee's earnings, dividends, or other distributions.
- The excess of cost over the fair value of the investee's identifiable net assets is not amortized.
- Goodwill is not created.

Impairment

Under both IFRS and U.S. GAAP, equity method investments should be reviewed periodically for impairment. Since goodwill is included in the carrying amount of the investment (i.e., it is not separately recognized) under the equity method, it is not tested for impairment separately.

> Note that for investments accounted for using the equity method, there is a **total** fair value of impairment test. You will see later that for business combinations, there is a **disaggregated** goodwill impairment test.

- Under IFRS, an impairment loss is recognized if there is objective evidence of a loss event and the recoverable amount of the investment is less than the carrying amount.
  - Recoverable amount is the higher of "value in use" and "net selling price."
- Under U.S. GAAP, an impairment loss is recognized if the fair value of the investment is less than the carrying amount and the decline is deemed to be permanent.
- Impairment results in a decrease in net income and reduces the investment's carrying amount on the balance sheet.
- Reversal of an impairment loss is not allowed under IFRS or U.S. GAAP.

Transactions with Associates

Profits from transactions between the investor and the investee must be deferred until they are confirmed through use or sale to a third party. This is because the investing company has significant influence over the terms of transactions with associates. See Example 3-3.

- Sales from investee to investor are known as upstream sales. The profits on these sales are recognized on the investee's income statement, so a proportionate share of these profits is also included in the investor's income statement. Until these profits are confirmed, the investor must reduce its equity income by the amount of its **proportionate share** in profits from upstream sales. The investor may recognize these profits once they are confirmed.
- Sales from investor to investee are known as downstream sales. Associated profits are recognized on the investor's income statement. The investor's **proportionate share** in unconfirmed profits from sales made to the investee must be eliminated from the investor's equity income.

Example 3-3: Equity Method with Transactions with Associates

In Example 2-3, we calculated equity income on Prime's (the investor's) income statement for 2010 to be $57,500 and the value of the investment in Alton on Prime's balance sheet for 2010 to be $732,500. Suppose that the following transactions also took place.

1. $12,000 of profit from an upstream sale from Alton to Prime during 2010 was still in Prime's inventory at the end of 2010 as the goods had not been sold to an outside party yet.
2. Prime made downstream sales of $100,000 worth of goods to Alton for $160,000. During 2010, Alton sold goods worth $140,000 to outside parties, while the remaining $20,000 worth of goods was sold in 2011.

Calculate the amount of equity income reported on Prime's income statement for 2010 and the value of the investment in Alton on Prime's 2010 balance sheet after incorporating the effects of the above transactions.

Solution:

1. **Upstream sale:**

   Unrealized profit = $12,000
   Prime's **proportionate share** in the unrealized profit = 25% × 12,000 = $3,000

2. **Downstream sale:**

   Prime's profit on sales to Alton = 160,000 − 100,000 = $60,000
   Alton sells 87.5% (= 140,000/160,000 × 100) of goods purchased from Prime during 2010, while 12.5% remains unsold.
   Therefore, total unrealized profit = 12.5% × 60,000 = $7,500

   Prime's **proportionate share** of unrealized profit = 25% × 7,500 = $1,875

Therefore:

Revised equity income for 2010 = 57,500 – 3,000 – 1,875 = $52,625
Revised carrying value of investment for 2010 = 732,500 – 3,000 – 1,875 = $727,625

In 2011, when unconfirmed sales for 2010 (worth $20,000) are actually confirmed, related profits that were not realized during 2010 (worth $1,875) are realized. These profits contribute to equity income for 2011.

Analysis of Investments in Associates

- Analysts should evaluate the appropriateness of the use of the equity method for accounting for investment in an associate. For example:
  - In a situation where an investing company owns a 30% equity interest in an associate, but **does not** exert significant influence on the investee, the investing company may prefer the equity method so that it can report associated income on its financial statements.
  - In a situation where an investing company owns a 19% equity interest in an associate, but **does** exert significant influence on the investee, the investing company may prefer not to use the equity method to avoid recognition of its proportionate share of investee losses on its financial statements.
- The investment is presented on the investor's balance sheet as a single-line item. This affects the leverage ratios reported by the investor as the investor's proportionate share in assets and liabilities of the investee are not reported separately on its financial statements.
- Since the investor's proportionate share in investee earnings is reported on its income statement, but its proportionate share in investee revenues is not, the net profit margin may be overstated.
- The equity method assumes that its proportionate share in each dollar earned by the associate is available to the investor, even if earnings are not distributed as dividends. Analysts should therefore consider any restrictions on dividend payments.

Joint Ventures

A joint venture is a venture undertaken and controlled by two or more parties. They can be organized in a variety of different forms (e.g., jointly controlled operations and jointly controlled assets) and structures (e.g., partnerships, limited liability companies, and unincorporated associations). IFRS identifies the following characteristics of joint ventures:

- A contractual agreement exists between two or more venturers; and
- The contractual arrangement establishes joint control.

Both **IFRS** and **U.S. GAAP** now require the use of the equity method to account for joint ventures.

LESSON 4: INVESTMENTS IN BUSINESS COMBINATIONS

LOS 16a: Describe the classification, measurement, and disclosure under International Financial Reporting Standards (IFRS) for business combinations. Vol 2, pp 9–56

LOS 16b: Distinguish between IFRS and U.S. GAAP in the classification, measurement, and disclosure of business combinations. Vol 2, pp 9–56

Business Combinations

A business combination refers to the combination of two or more entities into a larger economic entity.

- IFRS does not differentiate between business combinations based on the structure of the surviving entity.
- U.S. GAAP categorizes business combinations based on the structure after the combination. (See Table 4-1.)
  - Mergers: The acquirer absorbs all the assets of the acquired company. The acquired company ceases to exist and the acquirer is the only surviving entity.
  - Acquisitions: Both the entities continue to exist, and are connected through a parent-subsidiary relationship.
    - Each entity maintains separate financial statements.
    - The acquirer is required to present consolidated financial statements for each reporting period.
    - If the acquiring company acquires less than 100% equity interest, it must also report noncontrolling (minority) interests.
  - Consolidation: A new entity is formed that absorbs both the predecessor companies, which cease to exist.

Table 4-1: Types of Business Combinations

Combination	Description
Merger	Company A + Company B = Company A
Acquisition	Company A + Company B = (Company A + Company B)
Consolidation	Company A + Company B = Company C

In the past, business combinations could be accounted for using either the purchase method or the uniting- or pooling-of-interests method.

Pooling-of-Interests Method (U.S. GAAP) / Uniting-of-Interests Method (IFRS)

Under this method, the two firms are combined using their historical **book values**, and their operating results are restated as if they had always operated as a single entity. Further, ownership interests are continued and former accounting bases are maintained. Fair values are not used in accounting for a business combination under this method, and the actual price paid for the acquisition is not evident on the financial statements.

Purchase Method

Under the purchase method, the combination is accounted for as a purchase of net assets (tangible and intangible assets minus liabilities), where net assets are recorded at **fair values**. Since the value of depreciable assets is higher under this method (compared to the pooling/uniting-of-interests method), the additional depreciation expense results in lower reported income and lower total asset turnover. Therefore, managers would prefer the pooling/uniting-of-interests method.

U.S. GAAP and IFRS now prohibit use of the pooling (uniting) of interests method and require the acquisition method (which has replaced the purchase method). This reporting consistency makes it easier for analysts to evaluate how the operations of the acquirer and acquiree will combine and to examine the effects of the transaction on the combined entity's subsequent performance.

Acquisition Method for Business Combinations

Under the acquisition method:

- All the assets, liabilities, revenues, and expenses of the acquiree are combined with those of the parent.
    - All identifiable tangible and intangible assets and liabilities of the acquired entity are measured at fair value.
    - The acquirer must also recognize any assets and liabilities that the acquiree has not recognized on its financial statements. For example, identifiable intangible assets such as brand names and patents that the acquiree had developed internally would now be recognized by the acquirer.
- The acquirer must recognize any contingent liability assumed in the acquisition if (1) it is a present obligation that arises from past events, and (2) it can be measured reliably. Costs that the acquirer expects (but is not obliged) to incur, however, are not recognized as liabilities, but are expensed in future periods as they are incurred.
- The acquirer must recognize an indemnification asset if the acquiree contractually indemnifies the acquirer for (1) the outcome of a contingency, (2) an uncertainty related to a specific asset or liability of the acquiree, or (3) against losses above a specified amount on a liability arising from a particular contingency.
- If the purchase price is less than the fair value of the subsidiary's net assets, it is referred to as a bargain acquisition. Both IFRS and U.S. GAAP require the difference between the fair value of the acquired net assets and the purchase price to be recognized immediately as a gain in profit or loss.
- Transactions between the acquirer and acquiree are eliminated.
- The acquiree's shareholders' equity accounts are ignored.

See Example 4-1.

Example 4-1: Acquisition Method

Pyramid Inc. acquired a 100% equity interest in Sam Corp. by issuing 1 million shares of common stock. The par value of each share was $1, while the market price of each share at the time of the transaction was $10. The following information relates to the two companies just before the transaction:

	Pyramid Inc.	Sam Corp.	
	Book Value ($ '000)	Book Value ($ '000)	Fair Value ($ '000)
Cash and receivables	12,500	450	450
Inventory	11,000	1,500	3,500
Net PP&E	25,500	2,800	4,000
Total assets	**49,000**	**4,750**	**7,950**
Current payables	7,500	800	800
Long-term debt	15,000	2,500	2,000
Total liabilities	**22,500**	**3,300**	**2,800**
Net assets	**26,500**	**1,450**	**5,150**
Capital stock ($1 par)	5,500	300	
Additional paid-in capital	7,000	400	
Retained earnings	14,000	750	
Total shareholders' equity	**26,500**	**1,450**	

Based on the acquisition method, calculate the amounts presented on the post-combination balance sheet. Assume that Sam has no identifiable intangible assets.

Solution:

Under both IFRS and U.S. GAAP, the purchase price equals the fair value of shares issued by Pyramid to finance the acquisition. Since the purchase price ($10 million) exceeds the book value of Sam's net assets ($1.45 million), the excess is allocated to identifiable assets and liabilities to reflect their fair values and the remainder is recognized as goodwill.

Excess purchase price = Cost of acquisition − BV of net assets acquired
= ($10 × 1,000,000) − $1,450,000 = **$8,550,000**

Excess purchase price	**$8,550,000**
Allocated to identifiable net assets:	
Inventory	2,000,000
PP&E	1,200,000
Long-term debt	500,000
Allocated to goodwill	4,850,000
Total	**8,550,000**

For the consolidated balance sheet, assets and liabilities are combined using book values of Pyramid's assets and liabilities and fair values of Sam's assets and liabilities. Further, only Pyramid's retained earnings are carried to the combined entity.

Consolidated Balance Sheet

	$ ('000)
Cash and receivables (= 12,500 + 450)	12,950
Inventory (= 11,000 + 3,500)	14,500
PP&E (= 25,500 + 4,000)	29,500
Goodwill	4,850
Total assets	**61,800**
Current payables (= 7,500 + 800)	8,300
Long-term debt (= 15,000 + 2,000)	17,000
Total liabilities	**25,300**
Capital stock ($1 par) (= 5,500 + 1,000)	6,500
Additional paid-in capital (= 7,000 + 9,000)	16,000
Retained earnings	14,000
Total equity	**36,500**
Total liabilities and shareholders' equity	**61,800**

Calculations:

Capital stock = Parent's capital stock + Par value of shares issued
$$= 5,500,000 + 1,000,000 = \$6,500,000$$

Additional paid-in capital = Parent's additional paid-in capital + (Market value of shares issued − Par value of shares issued)
$$= 7,000,000 + [(1,000,000 \times 10) - (1,000,000 \times 1)] = \$16,000,000$$

IMPORTANT: At the date of acquisition, only the acquirer's retained earnings are carried over to the combined entity. The acquiree's earnings and retained earnings are only included on the consolidated income statement in post-acquisition periods.

Also note that in post-acquisition periods, amortization and depreciation will be based on the historical cost of Pyramid's assets and the fair value (as of the acquisition date) of Sam's assets. So under the acquisition method, as Sam's inventory is sold COGS would be $2,000,000 higher, and depreciation on PP&E would be $1,200,000 higher over the life of assets compared to under the pooling-of-interests method (where companies are combined using book values).

Business Combinations with Less Than 100% Acquisition

Note that in such an arrangement, the parent and the subsidiary prepare their own financial statements, but the parent also prepares **consolidated** financial statements for each reporting period.

If a parent controls a subsidiary, but owns less than a 100% equity interest in the company, it must also create a noncontrolling interest account on the consolidated balance sheet and income statement to reflect the proportionate share in the net assets and net income of the subsidiary that belongs to minority shareholders (i.e., shareholders other than the parent).

- Noncontrolling interests on the consolidated balance sheet (presented in the equity section) reflects minority shareholders' proportionate share in the net assets of the subsidiary.

- Noncontrolling interests on the income statement (deducted from consolidated net income) reflects minority shareholders' proportionate share in the net income of the subsidiary.

Measuring Goodwill and Noncontrolling (Minority) Interests

U.S. GAAP requires the use of the full goodwill method, in which goodwill equals the excess of the **total fair value of the subsidiary** over the **fair value of its identifiable net assets**.

IFRS permits both the full goodwill method and the partial goodwill method. Under the partial goodwill method, goodwill equals the excess of the **purchase price** over the **fair value of the parent's proportionate share of the subsidiary's identifiable net assets**. See Example 4-2.

- If the full goodwill method is used, the noncontrolling interest is measured based on its **proportionate share of the subsidiary's fair value**.
- If the partial goodwill method is used, the noncontrolling interest is measured based on its **proportionate share of the fair value of the subsidiary's identifiable net assets**.
- The income statement is exactly the same under the full and partial goodwill methods.

> Note that when preparing consolidated accounts when the parent does not own 100% of the subsidiary (upstream and downstream), intercompany transactions must be eliminated.

Example 4-2: Goodwill and Noncontrolling Interests

On January 1, 2010, Pluto Inc. acquired a 90% equity interest in Saturn Inc. in exchange for $450,000 worth of Pluto stock. The fair market value of Saturn on the date of acquisition was $500,000. The following information is available about the two companies immediately prior to the transaction:

	Pluto	Saturn	
	Book Value ($)	Book Value ($)	Fair Value ($)
Cash and receivables	50,000	20,000	20,000
Inventory	130,000	95,000	95,000
Net PP&E	250,000	110,000	160,000
Total assets	**430,000**	**225,000**	**275,000**
Payables	60,000	25,000	25,000
Long-term debt	100,000	60,000	60,000
Total liabilities	**160,000**	**85,000**	**85,000**
Net assets	**270,000**	**140,000**	**190,000**
Capital stock	90,000	50,000	
Retained earnings	180,000	90,000	
Total shareholders' equity	**270,000**	**140,000**	

---

1. Calculate the value of goodwill and noncontrolling interest at the acquisition date under the full goodwill method.
2. Calculate the value of goodwill and noncontrolling interest at the acquisition date under the partial goodwill method.
3. Compare the post-combination balance sheets under the full goodwill and partial goodwill methods.

Solution:

1. **Full Goodwill Method**

   Goodwill equals the excess of the total fair value of the subsidiary over the fair value of its identifiable net assets.

   > Subsidiary's fair value = $500,000
   > Fair value of subsidiary's identifiable net assets = $190,000
   > Goodwill = 500,000 − 190,000 = $310,000

   The noncontrolling interest is measured based on its proportionate share of the subsidiary's fair value.

   > Noncontrolling interest (NCI) = Percentage of NCI × Subsidiary's fair value
   > = 10% × $500,000 = $50,000

2. **Partial Goodwill Method**

   Goodwill equals the excess of the purchase price over the fair value of the parent's proportionate share of the subsidiary's identifiable net assets.

   > Acquisition price = $450,000
   > Fair value of proportionate share of acquired net assets = 90% × $190,000
   > = $171,000
   > Goodwill = 450,000 − 171,000 = $279,000

   The noncontrolling interest is measured based on its proportionate share of the fair value of the subsidiary's identifiable net assets.

   > NCI = Percentage of NCI × Fair value of subsidiary's identifiable net assets
   > = 10% × $190,000 = $19,000

3. **Post-combination Balance Sheets:**

Consolidated Balance Sheet

	Full Goodwill ($)	Partial Goodwill ($)
Cash and receivables	70,000	70,000
Inventory	225,000	225,000
PP&E	410,000	410,000
Goodwill	310,000	279,000
Total assets	**1,015,000**	**984,000**
Payables	85,000	85,000
Long-term debt	160,000	160,000
Total liabilities	**245,000**	**245,000**
Noncontrolling interests	50,000	19,000
Capital stock (= 90,000 + 450,000)	540,000	540,000
Retained earnings	180,000	180,000
Total equity	**770,000**	**739,000**
Total liabilities and shareholders' equity	**1,015,000**	**984,000**

The full goodwill method results in *higher* total assets and equity compared to the partial goodwill method.

As far as the income statement is concerned, net income to the parent's shareholders will be the same regardless of whether the full goodwill or partial goodwill method is employed to value goodwill and noncontrolling interests on the balance sheet. On the income statement, the noncontrolling interests will share the burden of the additional depreciation (that arises from the $50,000 increase in PP&E). Since depreciation expense is the same under both methods, net income and retained earnings ($180,000) on the consolidated balance sheet are the same under both methods.

Note that although net income is the same, return on assets and return on equity will be *lower* if the full goodwill method is used because it results in higher assets and higher equity than the partial goodwill method. Also understand that over time, the value of the subsidiary will change due to (1) changes in equity or (2) net income. Therefore, the value of noncontrolling interest on the consolidated balance sheet will also change.

Impairment of Goodwill

Since goodwill is an intangible asset with an **indefinite** life, it is not amortized. However, goodwill must be tested for impairment at least annually or more frequently if events and circumstances indicate that it may be impaired. Once an impairment charge has been made against goodwill, it cannot subsequently be reversed.

Under **IFRS** (see Example 4-3):

- At the time of acquisition, the total amount of goodwill recognized is allocated to each of the acquirer's **cash-generating units** that will benefit from the synergies expected from the business combination.
- There is a one-step approach: Goodwill is deemed impaired if the recoverable amount of the cash-generating unit is lower than its carrying amount (including goodwill).
- The impairment loss equals the difference between carrying value and recoverable amount of the unit.
- The impairment loss is first applied to the goodwill of the cash-generating unit. Once this has been reduced to zero, the remaining amount of the loss is allocated to all the other assets in the unit on a pro rata basis.

Under **U.S. GAAP** (see Example 4-4):

- At the time of acquisition, the total amount of goodwill recognized is allocated to each of the acquirer's **reporting units**.
- There is a two-step approach to goodwill impairment testing.
  - Test for impairment: If the carrying value of the reporting unit (including goodwill) exceeds its fair value, goodwill is deemed to be impaired.
  - Measurement of impairment loss: The impairment loss equals the difference between the implied fair value of the reporting unit's goodwill (implied goodwill) and its carrying amount.
    - Implied goodwill equals the fair value of the unit minus the fair value of the net assets of the unit.
- The impairment loss is applied to the goodwill allocated to the reporting unit. After the reporting unit's goodwill has been eliminated, no adjustments are made to the carrying amounts of the unit's other assets or liabilities.

Under both IFRS and U.S. GAAP, the impairment loss is recognized as a separate line item on the consolidated income statement.

Example 4-3: Impairment of Goodwill under IFRS

An analyst obtains the following information regarding a cash-generating unit of Mercury Inc.:

Carrying value of unit (including recognized goodwill of $600,000) = $2,600,000
Recoverable amount of unit = $2,200,000
Fair value of identifiable net assets of unit = $1,900,000

Calculate the impairment loss recognized under IFRS.

Solution:

Impairment loss = Carrying value of unit − Recoverable amount of unit
Impairment loss = 2,600,000 − 2,200,000 = $400,000

Note that if the recoverable amount of the cash-generating unit had been $1,900,000 instead of $2,200,000, the impairment loss would have been $700,000. This would first be absorbed by goodwill allocated to the unit ($600,000) and the remaining amount of the impairment ($700,000 − $600,000 = $100,000) would then be allocated on a pro rata basis to other assets within the unit.

Example 4-4: Impairment of Goodwill under U.S. GAAP

An analyst obtains the following information regarding a reporting unit of Mercury Inc.:

Carrying value of unit (including recognized goodwill of $600,000) = $2,500,000
Fair value of unit = $2,100,000
Fair value of identifiable net assets of unit = $1,900,000

Calculate the impairment loss recognized under U.S. GAAP.

Solution:

Step 1: Determine whether goodwill is impaired:

Since the carrying value ($2.5m) of the reporting unit exceeds its fair value ($2.1m), impairment exists.

Step 2: Measure the impairment loss:

Implied goodwill = Fair value of unit − Fair value of identifiable net assets of the unit
Implied goodwill = 2,100,000 − 1,900,000 = $200,000

Impairment loss = Recognized goodwill − Implied goodwill
Impairment loss = 600,000 − 200,000 = $400,000

If the fair value of the unit was $1,200,000 instead of $2,100,000, the implied goodwill would equal negative $700,000. In this case, the maximum amount of the impairment loss recognized would be capped at the carrying amount of goodwill ($600,000).

LESSON 5: INVESTMENTS IN SPES/VIES

LOS 16a: Describe the classification, measurement, and disclosure under International Financial Reporting Standards (IFRS) for special purpose and variable interest entities. Vol 2, pp 9–56

LOS 16b: distinguish between IFRS and U.S. GAAP in the classification, measurement, and disclosure of special purpose and variable interest entities. Vol 2, pp 9–56

Variable Interest Entities (U.S. GAAP) and Special Purpose Entities (IFRS)

Special Purpose Entities (SPEs) are established to meet specific objectives of the sponsoring company. They are structured in a manner that allows the sponsoring company to retain financial control over the SPE's assets and/or operating activities, while third parties hold the majority of the voting interest in the SPE. Typically, these third parties funded their investments in the SPE with debt that was (directly or indirectly) guaranteed by the sponsoring company.

In the past, such an arrangement enabled sponsoring companies to avoid consolidation of SPEs on their financial statements due to a lack of "control" (i.e., ownership of a majority voting interest) of the SPE. As a result, sponsoring companies were able to:

- Avoid disclosures of guarantees relating to the debt of the SPE made by the sponsoring company.
- Transfer assets and liabilities from their own balance sheets to the SPE and record revenues and gains related to these transactions.
- Avoid recognition of assets and liabilities of the SPE on their financial statements.

Consequently, reported financial performance (as presented by unconsolidated financial statements) of sponsoring companies was economically misleading as it indicated improved asset turnover, higher profitability, and lower levels of operating and financial leverage. Enron provides an excellent example of the use of off-balance sheet financing to improve reported financial performance. The company's subsequent collapse was (in part) related to the guarantees it provided on the debt of the SPEs that it had created.

IFRS and U.S. GAAP now require sponsoring companies to prepare consolidated financial statements that account for arrangements where parties other than the holders of majority voting rights exercise financial control over another entity. Further, standards relating to measurement, reporting, and disclosure of guarantees have been revised. For example, under U.S. GAAP, the primary beneficiary of a VIE must consolidate it as its subsidiary regardless of how much of an equity investment it has in the VIE.

- The primary beneficiary (which is often the sponsor) is defined as the entity that is (1) expected to absorb the majority of the VIE's expected losses, (2) receive the majority of the VIE's residual returns, or (3) both.
- If one entity will absorb a majority of the VIE's expected losses while another entity will receive a majority of the VIE's expected profits, the entity absorbing a majority of the losses must consolidate the VIE.
- If there are noncontrolling interests in the VIE, these would also be shown in the consolidated balance sheet and consolidated income statement of the primary beneficiary.

Securitization of Assets

SPEs are often set up to securitize receivables held by the sponsor. The SPE issues debt to finance the purchase of these receivables from the sponsor, and interest and principal payments to debt holders are made from the cash flow generated from the pool of receivables.

The motivation for the sponsor to sell its accounts receivable to the SPE is to accelerate inflows of cash. However, an important aspect of the arrangement is whether the SPE's debt holders have recourse to the sponsor if sufficient cash is not generated from the pool of receivables. In this case, the transaction is basically just like taking a loan and collateralizing it with the receivables. If the receivables are not entirely realized, the loss is borne by the sponsor.

When the receivables are first sold by the sponsor, accounts receivable decrease, and the cash received contributes to CFO. However, if the risk of nonrealization is still borne by the sponsor (e.g., through a debt guarantee), an analyst must adjust accounts receivable and current liabilities upward. Further, the cash inflow previously classified as CFO must be reclassified as CFF to reflect the fact that the transaction is effectively merely a collateralized borrowing. See Example 5-1.

Adjusted Values Upon Reclassification of Sale of Receivables:

CFO	Lower
CFF	Higher
Total cash flow	Same
Current assets	Higher
Current liabilities	Higher
Current ratio *(Assuming it was greater than 1)*	Lower

Example 5-1: Securitization of Receivables

Violet Inc. wants to raise $75 million in capital by borrowing against its financial receivables. The company's finance director presents the following two options to senior management:

Option 1: Borrow directly against accounts receivables.
Option 2: Create a special purpose entity (SPE) with an initial investment of $10 million, have the SPE borrow $75 million, and then use the funds to purchase $85 million of Violet's receivables.

The following information is also available:

Balance Sheet	2010 ($)
Cash	40,000,000
Accounts receivable	85,000,000
Other assets	35,000,000
Total assets	**160,000,000**
Current liabilities	30,000,000
Noncurrent liabilities	35,000,000
Total liabilities	**65,000,000**
Shareholders' equity	95,000,000
Total liabilities and shareholders' equity	**160,000,000**

Selected financial ratios:

Current ratio = 4.17
Long-term debt-to-equity ratio = 0.37
Equity to total assets = 0.59

Prepare Violet's balance sheet as it would appear after it raises the required amount under either alternative.

Solution:

Option 1: Borrow Directly Against the Receivables

Violet's cash and noncurrent liabilities will increase by $75 million.

Balance Sheet	2010 ($)
Cash	115,000,000
Accounts receivable	85,000,000
Other assets	35,000,000
Total assets	**235,000,000**
Current liabilities	30,000,000
Noncurrent liabilities	110,000,000
Total liabilities	**140,000,000**
Shareholders' equity	95,000,000
Total liabilities and shareholders' equity	**235,000,000**

Selected financial ratios:

Current ratio = 6.67
Long-term debt-to-equity ratio = 1.16
Equity to total assets = 0.40

Relative to its original balance sheet, if Violet borrows directly against the receivables:

- It reports higher total assets and higher total liabilities.
- Therefore, the equity to total assets ratio is lower (worse).
- Profitability ratios (e.g., return on assets and return on total capital) are lower (worse).
- The long-term debt-to-equity ratio is higher (worsens).
- The current ratio is higher (improves).

Option 2: Establish an SPE

Violet's accounts receivable will decrease by $85 million and cash will increase by $75 million (calculated as proceeds from sale of receivables, $85 million, minus the amount invested in the SPE, $10 million). The investment in the SPE is listed under assets on the balance sheet.

Balance Sheet (Unconsolidated)	2010 ($)
Cash	115,000,000
Accounts receivable	0
Investment in SPE	10,000,000
Other assets	35,000,000
Total assets	**160,000,000**
Current liabilities	30,000,000
Noncurrent liabilities	35,000,000
Total liabilities	**65,000,000**
Shareholders' equity	95,000,000
Total liabilities and shareholders' equity	**160,000,000**

Selected financial ratios:

Current ratio = 3.83
Long-term debt-to-equity ratio = 0.37
Equity to total assets = 0.59

Relative to its original balance sheet, if Violet establishes an SPE to raise the funds **and does not consolidate the SPE's financial statements with its own:**

- Total assets and liabilities remain unchanged.
- Therefore, the company's long-term debt-to-equity ratio and the equity to total assets ratio are unaffected.
- The increase in cash ($75 million) is lower than the decrease in accounts receivable ($85 million), which reduces current assets. Therefore, the current ratio is lower (worse).

If Violet consolidates the financial statements of the SPE, its balance sheet would look like this:

Consolidated Balance Sheet	2010 ($)
Cash	115,000,000
Accounts receivable (= 85m)	85,000,000
Other assets	35,000,000
Total assets*	**235,000,000**
Current liabilities	30,000,000
Noncurrent liabilities = (35m + 75m)	110,000,000
Total liabilities	**140,000,000**
Shareholders' equity	95,000,000
Total liabilities and equity	**235,000,000**

*Investment in SPE ($10m) that is presented on the unconsolidated balance sheet is not presented on the consolidated balance sheet.

Selected financial ratios:

Current ratio = 6.67
Long-term debt-to-equity ratio = 1.16
Equity to total assets = 0.40

If Violet were required (by accounting standards) to consolidate the SPE's financial statements with its own, its financial ratios would be the same as those calculated under Option 1.

The table below summarizes financial statement ratios based on reported financials under the different options:

| | | | With an SPE | |
| | | Direct | | |
Selected Ratios	Original	Borrowing	Unconsolidated	Consolidated
Current ratio	4.17	6.67	3.83	6.67
Long-term debt to equity	0.37	1.16	0.37	1.16
Equity to total assets	0.59	0.40	0.59	0.40

The important thing to note is that if Violet were able to raise funds via the establishment of an SPE and not be required to present consolidated financial statements, it would report a lower (better) debt-equity ratio (0.37) and higher (better) equity-total assets ratio (0.59) compared to a direct borrowing (1.16 and 0.40, respectively). However, if accounting standards were to require consolidation of SPEs, Violet's presented financial position would be the same regardless of whether it raises the funds through an SPE or by borrowing directly (D-E = 1.16; A-E = 0.40).

Additional Issues in Business Combinations

- IFRS and U.S. GAAP differ on the treatment of contingent assets and liabilities.
  - Under **IFRS**, contingent assets are not recognized, while contingent liabilities are recognized (given that their fair values can be measured reliably) separately during the cost allocation process.
  - Under **U.S. GAAP**, contractual contingent assets and liabilities are recognized at their fair values at the time of acquisition. Further, noncontractual contingent assets and liabilities may also be recognized if it is "more likely than not" that they meet the definition of an asset or liability at the acquisition date.
- A parent may agree to pay additional amounts to the subsidiary's shareholders if the combined entity achieves certain performance targets. This is referred to as contingent consideration.
  - Under both IFRS and U.S. GAAP, contingent consideration should initially be measured at fair value and be classified as a financial liability or equity.
  - Subsequent changes in the fair value of these liabilities (and assets in case of U.S. GAAP) are recognized in the consolidated income statement.
  - Contingent consideration classified as equity is not remeasured under both IFRS and U.S. GAAP. Any settlements are accounted for within equity.

- Under both IFRS and U.S. GAAP, in-process research and development (R&D) acquired in a business combination is recognized as a separate intangible asset at fair value. In subsequent periods, IPR&D is amortized.
- Under both IFRS and U.S. GAAP, restructuring costs associated with a business combination are expensed in the period in which they are incurred (they are not included in the acquisition price).

LOS 16c: Analyze how different methods used to account for intercorporate investments affect financial statements and ratios. Vol 2, pp 9–56

To summarize:

Under the equity method, the investment is presented on the investor's balance sheet as a single-line item. Further, the investor's share in investee's earnings is reported as a single-line item on the investor's income statement. Nonrecognition of the investee's debt results in lower leverage ratios, while nonrecognition of the investee's revenues results in higher profit margins.

Under the acquisition method, the fair value of the subsidiary's assets, liabilities, income, and expenses are combined in their full amounts with those of the acquirer. As a result, the acquisition method results in higher assets, liabilities, revenues, and expenses than the equity method. However, net income is the same under both methods.

Within the acquisition method, the full goodwill method results in *higher* total assets and equity compared to the partial goodwill method. Therefore, return on assets and return on equity will be *lower* if the full goodwill method is used. Note that retained earnings and net income are same under both methods, but shareholders' equity is different (due to different noncontrolling interests).

Usually, the equity method provides more favorable results than the acquisition method. See Table 5-1.

Table 5-1: Impact of Different Accounting Methods on Financial Ratios

	Equity Method	Acquisition Method
Leverage	Better (lower) as liabilities are lower and equity is the same	Worse (higher) as liabilities are higher and equity is the same
Net Profit Margin	Better (higher) as sales are lower and net income is the same	Worse (lower) as sales are higher and net income is the same
ROE	Better (higher) as equity is lower and net income is the same	Worse (lower) as equity is higher and net income is the same
ROA	Better (higher) as net income is the same and assets are lower	Worse (lower) as net income is the same and assets are higher

READING 17: EMPLOYEE COMPENSATION: POST-EMPLOYMENT AND SHARE-BASED

LESSON 1: TYPES OF POST-EMPLOYMENT BENEFIT PLANS AND MEASURING A DEFINED BENEFIT PENSION PLAN'S OBLIGATIONS

LOS 17a: Describe the types of post-employment benefit plans and implications for financial reports. Vol 2, pp 72–75

Companies can offer several types of benefits to their employees (e.g., pension plans, health care plans, medical insurance, etc.). Some of these benefits are paid to employees while they are working for the company, while many are paid out in the future once employees retire. The objective of accounting for employee benefits is to recognize the costs associated with providing these benefits in the sponsoring company's financial statements during the term of employees' service to the company. Estimating the value of future benefits requires several assumptions, and these assumptions have a significant impact on the company's reported financial performance and financial position. Further, differences in assumptions reduce comparability across companies.

Pension plans (as well as other post-employment benefits) can be classified as defined contribution plans or defined benefit plans.

Defined Contribution Pension Plans

Under a defined contribution (DC) pension plan, the employer contributes specific (agreed-upon) amounts to an employee's pension plan. Typically, an individual account is set up for each participating employee. Once the employer has made the agreed-upon contribution (generally in the same period during which the employee provides the service) **it has no obligation to make payments beyond the specified amount**.

- Investments are typically made through a financial intermediary (an investment management company or an insurance company).
- The employee and employer can both contribute to the plan.
- Any gains and losses related to the investments are borne by the employee. Therefore, the risk that plan assets will not be sufficient to meet future requirements is borne by the **employee**.

Since the employer has no obligations beyond specified periodic contributions, accounting for DC plans is relatively straightforward.

- Periodic payments that must be made by the employer to the pension plan are treated as an expense.
- Payments that are made reduce cash (assets). If payments remain due as on the balance sheet date, these obligations are classified as current liabilities.

Defined-Benefit Pension Plans

Under a defined-benefit (DB) pension plan, the employer promises to pay a defined amount of pension **in the future**. The employee works in the current period in exchange for a pension to be paid after retirement. This pension (to be paid after retirement), along with her current salary, comprises the employee's total compensation. The promised annual pension payment is typically defined based on the employee's age, years of service, and salary.

Under both IFRS and U.S. GAAP, all plans for pensions and other post-employment benefits, if not explicitly structured as DC plans, are classified as DB plans.

For example, a company may promise to make an annual pension payment to an employee every year after retirement until her death based on the following formula:

$$\text{Annual pension payment} = 1\% \text{ of final salary at retirement} \times \text{No. of years of service}$$

...Equation 1

Given that an employee worked for 20 years and her final salary at time of retirement is $150,000, she would receive $30,000 (calculated as 0.01 × 150,000 × 20) from the company each year after retirement until her death under the terms of this DB pension plan.

In order to account for the obligations that arise from a DB plan, the employer (sponsor) must estimate the value of future payments that it would owe its employees upon their retirement. This exercise involves making numerous assumptions (e.g., employee turnover, average retirement age, and life expectancy) as we will learn in the sections that follow. It is important for analysts to assess the reasonableness of these assumptions and to be able to evaluate their impact on the company's financial statements.

DB plans are usually funded through a separate legal entity, typically a pension trust.

> Since the employer is obligated to make promised pension payments regardless of whether the plan assets generate sufficient returns to provide the benefits, many companies are reducing the use of DB pension plans.

- The employer makes periodic contributions to the plan and manages the assets with the aim of generating an adequate total return on plan assets in order to make pension payments as they come due.
- Since the employer is obligated to pay a defined benefit in the future, the investment risk is borne by the **employer**.
- The difference between the fair value of assets in the pension trust and the present value of estimated future payments (estimated liability) is known as the funded status of the plan.
  - If the fair value of assets in the pension trust is greater than the present value of the estimated liability, the plan is said to be **overfunded**. In this case, the company has a **net pension asset**.
  - If the fair value of assets in the pension trust is lower than the present value of the estimated liability, the plan is said to be **underfunded**. In this case, the company has a **net pension liability**.

Going forward, we will use the terms *net pension liability/asset* and *funded status* interchangeably.

Other Post-Employment Benefits (OPB)

> OPBs are known as unfunded plans as the employer is not required to make periodic contributions to, or hold assets in, a trust to fund associated obligations.
>
> DB plans are known as funded plans because employers are required to make periodic contributions to, and hold assets in, a trust to finance associated future obligations.

These are similar to DB pension plans in that the employer promises to pay benefits to employees in the future. Examples of other post-retirement benefits include health care insurance and life insurance premium payments for retired employees. Accounting for OPB can be even more complex than accounting for DB pension plans as there is a need to estimate future increases in costs (e.g., health care) over a relatively long time horizon.

OPBs differ from DB pension plans in that employers are not required by law to fund an OPB plan in advance to the same degree as they are required to fund DB pension plans. Therefore, employers recognize an expense on the income statement as OPB benefits are earned, but cash flows are not affected until benefits are actually paid to employees.

Table 1-1 summarizes the features of the different types of post-employment benefits.

Table 1-1: Types of Post-Employment Benefits[1]

Type of Benefit	Amount of Post-Employment Benefit to Employee	Obligation of Sponsoring Company	Sponsoring Company's Pre-funding of Its Future Obligation
Defined-contribution pension plan	Amount of future benefit is not defined. Actual future benefit will depend on investment performance of plan assets. Investment risk is borne by employee.	Amount of the company's obligation (contribution) is defined in each period. The contribution, if any, is typically made on a periodic basis with no additional future obligation.	Not applicable.
Defined-benefit pension plan	Amount of future benefit is defined, based on the plan's formula (often a function of length of service and final year's compensation). Investment risk is borne by company.	Amount of the future obligation, based on the plan's formula, must be estimated in the current period.	Companies typically pre-fund the DB plans by contributing funds to a pension trust. Regulatory requirements to pre-fund vary by country.
Other post-employment benefits (e.g., retirees' health care)	Amount of future benefit depends on plan specifications and type of benefit.	Eventual benefits are specified. The amount of the future obligation must be estimated in the current period.	Companies typically do not pre-fund other post-employment benefit obligations.

LOS 17b: Explain and calculate measures of a defined-benefit pension obligation (i.e., present value of the defined-benefit obligation and projected benefit obligation) and net pension liability (or asset). Vol 2, pp 75–88

In this reading (just as in the curriculum reading) we will use IFRS as the basis for discussion. Instances where U.S. GAAP significantly differs are discussed.

The net pension liability (asset) is calculated as pension obligation minus the fair value of plan assets. In the following two sections, we illustrate factors that influence (1) the value of the pension obligation and (2) the fair value of plan assets.

---

1 - Exhibit 1, Volume 2, CFA Program Curriculum 2017

Measuring a Defined Benefit Pension Plan's Obligations

Under both IFRS and U.S. GAAP, a company's pension obligation is measured as the **present value** of all future benefits that its employees are entitled to (or have "earned") for services provided to the company to date. Pension obligation is referred to as the present value of the defined benefit obligation (PV of DBO) under IFRS, and the projected benefit obligation (PBO) under U.S. GAAP.[2] We will use the term "pension obligation" to refer to PVDBO and PBO for the remainder of this reading. Note that PVDBO and PBO account for future compensation levels and increases in compensation.

Computing the pension obligation requires a company to make several estimates including:

- Future compensation increases and levels as they directly influence the dollar amount of the annual pension payment owed to an employee upon retirement. For example, if an employee's annual pension payment is based on her final salary at retirement (as in Equation 1), the higher her final salary, the greater the annual amount that the company owes her during retirement, the higher the value of total benefits earned, and the higher the pension obligation (PV of those benefits).
- The discount rate, which is used to determine the present value of pension payments that must be paid in the future. The greater the discount rate, the lower the pension obligation (present value of promised future payments).
- The probability that some employees will not satisfy the plan's vesting requirements. Vesting refers to a provision in pension plans whereby an employee is only entitled to future benefits if she meets certain criteria (e.g., a minimum number of years of service to the company).
  - If the employee leaves the company before satisfying these requirements, she would be entitled to none or only a portion of the benefits earned to date.
  - If the employee leaves the company after satisfying these requirements, she would be entitled to receive all the benefits earned to date.

The impact of these and other actuarial assumptions on a company's financial statements will become clear when we go through a comprehensive example (Example 1-1). Before we move into that example, we define certain items that directly influence the amount of a company's pension obligation.

- Current service costs refer to the increase in the pension obligation (PV of promised benefits) as a result of an employee's service in the current period. For example, consider the annual pension payment calculated through Equation 1. This payment is directly related to the employee's number of years of service. Each additional year of service increases the **amount** of the annual pension payment that the company would owe to the employee upon her retirement, and hence also increase the **total present value** of promised payments (i.e., the pension obligation).

---

2 - U.S. GAAP identifies two additional measures of pension obligation:
  - Accumulated benefit obligation (ABO): This is the present value of all future benefits earned by employees ignoring increases in compensation in the future.
  - Vested benefit obligation (VBO): This is the amount of ABO that has already been vested and therefore, is not contingent upon continued service.
  Generally speaking: VBO < ABO < PBO.

- Interest expense. A company does not make pension payments to employees until they retire (which is why the pension obligation reflects the present value of promised payments). With the passage of time, interest accrues on these unpaid amounts to increase the pension obligation. This accrued interest, or increase in the value of the obligation due to the passage of time, is classified as interest expense.
- Past service costs (PSC) refer to the increase in the pension obligation from retroactive benefits given to employees for years of service provided before the date of adoption, amendment, or curtailment of the plan.
- Changes in actuarial assumptions (e.g., discount rate, rate of future compensation increases, life expectancy of employees, etc.) result in changes in the estimated pension obligation.
  - A change in actuarial assumptions that increases the pension obligation gives rise to an actuarial loss.
  - A change in actuarial assumptions that decreases the pension obligation gives rise to an actuarial gain.
- Benefits paid by the company to employees decrease the pension obligation as they reduce the amount owed by the company to employees.

> An increase in liabilities reflects a loss/expense for the company, while a decrease in liabilities represents a gain.

To summarize, a company's pension obligation will *increase* as a result of:

- Current service costs.
- Interest costs.
- Past service costs.
- Actuarial losses.

A company's pension obligation will *decrease* as a result of:

- Actuarial gains.
- Benefits paid.

> Settlement and curtailment gains reduce the pension liability, while settlement and curtailment losses increase the liability.
>
> A curtailment occurs when there is a significant reduction by the company (1) in the number of employees covered by the plan or (2) in benefits.
>
> A settlement refers to a situation when the employer sells off a part or the whole of its operation.
>
> Settlements and curtailments are not important at all for our purposes. The curriculum only briefly mentions them.

Therefore, the beginning and ending balances of the pension obligation may be reconciled as follows:

> **Pension obligation at the beginning of the period**
>   + Current service costs
>   + Interest costs
>   + Past service costs
>   + Actuarial losses
>   – Actuarial gains
>   – Benefits paid
> **Pension obligation at the end of the period**

IFRS uses the projected unit credit method to measure the DB obligation. Under this method, (illustrated in Example 1-1), each year of service entitles the employee to an additional unit of benefit. Current service costs reflect the present value of this additional unit of benefit earned by an employee for her service to the company over the reporting period.

Example 1-1: Calculation of Pension Obligation for an Individual Employee

Jupiter Corp. establishes a DB pension plan for its only employee. The employee has a current salary of $75,000/year and is expected to work for five more years before retiring. The discount rate and the compensation growth rate assumed by the company are 7% and 4.5%, respectively.

Under the terms of the pension plan, each year during her retirement until her death, Jupiter will pay the employee a pension payment of 1% of her final salary at retirement for each year of service beyond the date of establishment of the plan. On the day that the plan is established, the employee is also given credit for 20 years of past service with immediate vesting. The company expects the employee to live for 15 years after retirement.

Given that there are no changes in actuarial assumptions, all compensation increases are awarded on the first day of the service year, and no additional adjustments are made to reflect the possibility that the employee may leave the company at an earlier date, calculate Jupiter's closing pension obligation for each of the 5 years until the employee actually retires using the projected unit credit method.

Solution:

Based on the employee's current salary ($75,000) and the assumed annual compensation growth rate (4.5%), we can calculate her final year's salary at retirement as:

$$\text{Final year's salary} = \text{Current salary} \times [(1 + \text{Annual compensation increase})^{\text{years until retirement}}]$$
$$= 75,000 \times (1 + 0.045)^4 = \boxed{\$89,438.90}$$

Now that we know the final year's salary, we can compute the annual pension payment that the company expects to pay the employee for 15 years during her retirement:

$$\text{Estimated annual payment} = (\text{Estimated final salary} \times \text{Benefit formula}) \times \text{Years of service}$$
$$= (89,438.90 \times 1\%) \times (5 + 20) = \$22,359.72$$

> We use 25 years of service (instead of 5) to determine the annual pension payment because the plan grants the employee 20 years of credit for past service with immediate vesting. If there were no such clause, the estimated annual pension payment would be $4,471.95 (based on just 5 years of service).

Next, we compute the present value (at a discount rate of 7%) of the 15 annual pension payments that the company expects to pay, **as of the employee's retirement date**:

$$N = 15; \text{ I/Y} = 7; \text{ PMT} = 22,359.72; \text{ FV} = 0; \text{ CPT PV} \rightarrow \textbf{PV} = \textbf{\$203,650.44}$$

Finally, we compute the annual unit credit (benefit) per service year. This is calculated as the value of pension obligation as of the retirement date divided by the number of years of service (25).

$$\text{Annual unit credit} = \text{Value at retirement / Years of service}$$
$$= 203,650.44 / 25 = \boxed{\$8,146.02}$$

The annual unit credit tells us that for each year of service, the employee earns $8,146.02 worth of future benefits.

Table 1-2 illustrates the calculation of closing pension obligation for each of the 5 years until the employee retires. All calculations are illustrated below the table.

Table 1-2: Calculation of Pension Obligation

Year	1	2	3	4	5
Estimated annual salary	75,000.00	78,375.00	81,901.88	85,587.46	89,438.90
Benefits attributed to:					
Prior years	162,920.35	171,066.37	179,212.39	187,358.41	195,504.42
Current year	8,146.02	8,146.02	8,146.02	8,146.02	8,146.02
Total benefits earned	**171,066.37**	**179,212.39**	**187,358.41**	**195,504.42**	**203,650.44**
Opening pension obligation	*116,159.96	130,505.72	146,290.69	163,646.09	182,714.41
Interest cost	8,131.20	9,135.40	10,240.35	11,455.23	12,790.01
Current service costs	6,214.56	6,649.58	7,115.05	7,613.10	8,146.02
Closing pension obligation	**130,505.72**	**146,290.69**	**163,646.09**	**182,714.41**	**203,650.44**

*The Year 1 amount of opening pension obligation ($116,159.96) would be classified as past service costs (PSC) because there was no previous recognition of these obligations and there is immediate vesting. Recall that PSC refer to increase in the pension obligation from retroactive benefits given to employees for years of service provided before the date of adoption or amendment of the plan.

Calculations:

Benefit attributed to prior years = Annual unit credit × No. of years of past service

     For Year 1: 8,146.02 × 20 = $162,920.35
     For Year 2: 8,146.02 × 21 = $171,066.37

Benefit attributed to current year = Annual unit credit = $8,146.02

The opening pension obligation for a period equals the closing pension obligation for the previous period. Think of it as the **present value, as of the beginning of the current period, of all pension benefits earned in prior years:**

Opening pension obligation = Benefits earned in prior years / [(1 + Discount rate)$^{\text{years until retirement}}$]

     For Year 1: 162,920.35 / (1.07)^5 = $116,159.96
     For Year 2: 171,066.37 / (1.07)^4 = $130,505.72

Interest costs refer to the increase in the present value of promised payments (or the increase in the pension obligation) due to the passage of time:

     Interest cost = Opening pension obligation × Discount rate
     Year 1: 116,159.96 × 7% = $8,131.20
     Year 2: 130,505.72 × 7% = $9,135.40

Current service costs equals the present value, as of the end of the current period, of the annual unit credit earned by the employee for her service in the current period:

Current service costs = Annual unit credit / [(1 + Discount rate)$^{\text{years until retirement}}$]
Year 1: 8,146.02 / (1.07)^4 = \$6,214.56
Year 2: 8,146.02 / (1.07)^3 = \$6,649.58

The closing pension obligation equals the opening pension obligation plus interest costs plus current service costs. It can also be calculated as the present value of benefits earned in prior years plus the current year:

Closing pension obligation = Total benefits earned to date / [(1 + Discount rate)$^{\text{years until retirement}}$]
For Year 1: 171,066.37 / (1.07)^4 = \$130,505.72
For Year 2: 179,212.39 / (1.07)^3 = \$146,290.69

Closing pension obligation = Opening pension obligation + Interest costs + Current service costs
For Year 1: 116,159.96 + 8,131.20 + 6,214.56 = \$130,505.72
For Year 2: 130,505.72 + 9,135.40 + 6,649.58 = \$146,290.69

Measuring a Defined-Benefit Pension Plan's Assets

As mentioned earlier, DB pension plans are required to be funded. The employer must make periodic contributions to the pension trust and is responsible for ensuring that plan assets are sufficient to pay promised future benefits.

The fair value of **assets** held in the pension trust (plan) will *increase* as a result of:

- A positive actual dollar return earned on plan assets; and
- Contributions made by the employer to the plan.

On the other hand, the fair value of plan assets will *decrease* as a result of:

- Benefits paid to employees.

Note that benefits paid to employees result in a decrease in (1) pension obligation as well as (2) the fair value of plan assets. Therefore, benefits paid have no net effect on the net pension liability (asset).

Therefore, the beginning and ending balances of the fair value of plan assets may be reconciled as follows:

Fair value of plan assets at the beginning of the period
+ Actual return on plan assets
+ Contributions made by the employer to the plan
− Benefits paid to employees
Fair value of plan assets at the end of the period

Balance Sheet Presentation of Defined-Benefit Pension Plans

Under both IFRS and U.S. GAAP, the defined-benefit liability (or asset) reported on the balance sheet equals the pension plan's funded status (FS). The funded status equals the difference between the fair value of plan assets (FVPA) and pension obligation (PO), so it represents a net amount.

Funded status = Fair value of plan assets − Pension obligation

- If the pension obligation is greater than the fair value of plan assets, the plan is said to be **underfunded**, and a net pension liability equal to the negative difference is recognized on the balance sheet.

- If the pension obligation is less than the fair value of plan assets, the plan is said to be **overfunded**, and a net pension asset equal to the positive difference is recognized on the balance sheet.
  - Note that the amount of net pension asset reported is subject to a **ceiling** equal to the present value of future economic benefits, such as refunds from the plan or reductions of future contributions.

It is very important for you to understand that the funded status represents the net pension asset:
- If pension obligation > fair value of plan assets:
  Plan is underfunded → Negative funded status → Net pension liability.
- If pension obligation < fair value of plan assets:
  Plan is overfunded → Positive funded status → Net pension asset.

Disclosures in the notes offer additional information on the net pension asset/liability reported on the balance sheet. The effects of incorporating the information contained in these disclosures into financial analysis are discussed later in the reading.

> Refunds and reductions in future contributions reflect overfunding of the plan. Companies may be able to withdraw funds or reduce future contributions to the plan as a result of overfunding.

Example 1-2: Determining the Amount to Be Reported on the Balance Sheet

The information below relates to the DB pension plan of two hypothetical companies as of December 31, 2010:

Company	Pension Obligation	Fair Value of Plan Assets
A	$8,612	$6,775
B	$3,163	$3,775

Further, for Company B, the present value of available future refunds and reductions in future contributions is $125.

Calculate the amount that each company would report as net pension asset or liability on its 2010 balance sheet.

Solution:

Company A's plan is underfunded by $8,612 − $6,775 = $1,837. Therefore, it will report a net pension liability of $1,837 on its 2010 balance sheet.

Company B's plan is overfunded by $3,775 − $3,163 = $612. Since the company has a surplus, the amount of net pension asset that it can report on its balance sheet is the lower of (1) the surplus, and (2) the present value of future economic benefits, such as refunds and reductions in contributions to the plan (asset ceiling). In this case, the asset ceiling is given as $125, so the amount of net pension asset that Company B will report on its 2010 balance sheet would be limited to $125.

LESSON 2: COMPONENTS OF PERIODIC PENSION COST: IFRS VERSUS U.S.GAAP

LOS 17c: Describe the components of a company's defined-benefit pension costs. Vol 2, pp 75–81

Before you begin this section, it is absolutely essential that you recognize the difference between periodic pension cost and periodic pension expense (especially since the CFA Program curriculum does not adequately emphasize the difference between the two).

- Periodic pension cost is the total cost related to a company's DB pension plan for a given period. Various components of this total cost (as you will soon see) can be recognized on the profit and loss (P&L) or in other comprehensive income (OCI) under IFRS and U.S. GAAP.
- Periodic pension expense refers to the components of periodic pension cost that are recognized on the P&L (not OCI).

PERIODIC PENSION COST

Please note that we have spent a LOT more time on this section (calculating periodic pension cost) than the curriculum reading has. This is because (in our opinion) understanding the components of periodic pension cost is essential to attain a complete understanding of the underlying concepts, and unfortunately the curriculum does not do a good job on this.

Calculating Periodic Pension Cost

There are two approaches to calculate periodic pension cost. Further, for a particular company over a given period, periodic pension cost would come to the same amount whether it subscribes to IFRS or to U.S. GAAP when preparing its financial statements.

Approach 1: Adjusting the Change in Net Pension Liability (Asset) for Employer Contributions

The periodic cost of a company's DB pension plan equals the change in the net pension liability/ asset excluding the effects of employer contributions to the plan.

Net periodic pension cost = Ending net pension liability − Beginning net pension liability
+ Employer contributions

- An increase in net pension liability or a decrease in net pension asset over the reporting period entails a pension-related cost for the company.
- A decrease in net pension liability or an increase in net pension asset over the reporting period results in a pension-related benefit for the company.

To understand why we add employer contributions to the change in the funded status when computing periodic pension cost, assume that a company has just established a DB pension plan. At inception, the net pension liability equals $0 (pension obligation = $0; fair value of plan assets = $0). Over Year 1, service costs equal $200 so the pension obligation rises to $200 at the end of the year.

- If the employer makes no contributions to the plan over the year, the net pension liability would increase to $200 (pension obligation = $200; fair value of plan assets = $0). The increase in the net pension liability (from $0 to $200) represents the periodic pension cost ($200).
- If the employer contributes $200 to the plan, the net pension liability would remain unchanged at $0 (pension obligation = $200; fair value of plan assets = $200). In this situation, even though the net pension liability has remained the same, the periodic pension cost equals $200 (equal to employer contributions over the year).
- If the employer contributes $250 to the plan, it would recognize a net pension **asset** of $50 at the end of the year (pension obligation = $200; fair value of plan assets = $250). The change in the net pension liability would be –$50. Adding employer contributions over the year ($250) to the **negative** change in the net pension liability will give us a periodic pension cost of $200.

> Service costs amount to $200 and since there are no interest costs (as pension obligation at the beginning of the period was 0 so no interest accrues during Year 1) periodic pension cost should equal $200. This is how periodic pension cost will be computed under Approach 2.

The bottom line is that periodic pension cost has nothing to do with the amount of funds contributed by the sponsor into the plan over the reporting period. If employer contributions were higher, the ending net pension liability would automatically be lower. Periodic pension cost is only affected by the economic expenses that affect the pension obligation adjusted for the actual return on plan assets (as you will see in Approach 2). Therefore, in order to compute periodic pension cost, the ending net pension liability must be computed based on plan assets reduced by the amount of employer contributions over the reporting period.

> This paragraph (especially the last sentence) about excluding employer contributions will become clear in Example 2-1.

VERY Important: *Please note that the curriculum in one instance uses a (seemingly) different formula to compute periodic pension cost. That formula, along with the associated footnote (Footnote 10), will only confuse you. Every year candidates face an issue here, but the CFA Institute refuses to change the way it presents this formula. Please just stick to our formula and thought process and you will be fine for the exam.*

Approach 2: Aggregating Periodic Components of Cost

The components of periodic pension cost are basically items that result in changes in the (net pension liability) other than employer contributions. Changes in the net pension liability come from (1) changes in the pension obligation and/or (2) changes in the fair value of plan assets.

Changes in the pension obligation are caused by:

- Economic expenses for the period. These include:
  ○ Current service costs
  ○ Interest costs
  ○ Past service costs
  ○ Actuarial losses (gains)
- Benefits paid to employees.

Note that actuarial gains and benefits paid to employees *reduce* the pension obligation.

Changes in the fair value of plan assets are caused by:

- The actual return on plan assets.
- Benefits paid to employees.
- Employer contributions.

Note that:

- Benefits paid to employees reduce the pension obligation and the fair value of plan assets, so they have no impact on the overall funded status.
- We have already shown that employer contributions have nothing to do with periodic pension cost.
- Therefore, the periodic pension cost of a company's DB pension plan equals the increase in the pension obligation (excluding the impact of benefits paid to employees) minus actual earnings on plan assets.

$$\text{Periodic pension cost} = \text{Current service costs} + \text{Interest costs} + \text{Past service costs}$$
$$+ \text{Actuarial losses} - \text{Actuarial gains} - \text{Actual return on plan assets}$$

Basically, this formula aggregates all sources of change in a plan's net pension liability over the year except for employer contributions.

Essentially, what we are trying to say is:

Periodic pension cost = Ending net pension liability − Beginning funded status + Employer contributions.

Periodic pension cost = Change in net pension liability + Employer contributions … **Approach 1**

Change in net pension liability = Change in pension obligation − Change in fair value of plan assets

> Don't get lost in all the fancy colors and the intimidating formulas. Try to work through the math here and then move into Example 2-1. If you understand Example 2-1, and the text in the box next to Example 2-1 makes sense, you are good to go.

Change in pension obligation = Current service costs + Interest costs + Past service costs
+ Actuarial losses − Actuarial gains − Benefits paid

Change in fair value of plan assets = Actual return on plan assets + Employer contributions
− Benefits paid

Change in net pension liability = (Current service costs + Interest costs + Past service costs
+ Actuarial losses − Actuarial gains − Benefits paid)
− (Actual return on plan assets + Employer contributions
− Benefits paid)

Change in net pension liability = Current service costs + Interest costs + Past service costs
+ Actuarial losses − Actuarial gains − ~~Benefits paid~~ − Actual
return on plan assets − Employer contributions + ~~Benefits paid~~

Periodic pension cost = Change in net pension liability + Employer contributions
= (Current service costs + Interest costs + Past service costs
+ Actuarial losses − Actuarial gains − Actual return on plan assets
− ~~Employer contributions~~) + ~~Employer contributions~~

$$\text{Periodic pension cost} = \text{Current service costs} + \text{Interest costs} + \text{Past service costs}$$
$$+ \text{Actuarial losses} - \text{Actuarial gains} - \text{Actual return on plan assets}$$
$$\text{… Approach 2}$$

To summarize, periodic pension cost may be calculated using either of the following two methods:

1. By adding the positive change in the net pension liability over the period (increase in net pension liability) to contributions made by the company; or
2. By summing all economic expenses that affect the pension obligation (other than benefits paid), and deducting the actual return on plan assets.

As Example 2-1 illustrates, both these approaches will yield the same value for periodic pension cost.

Example 2-1: Calculating Periodic Pension Cost

An analyst gathers the following information regarding a company's pension plan:

Reconciliation of Beginning and Ending Pension Obligation

Beginning pension obligation	$2,225
+ Current service costs	$845
+ Interest cost	$120
+ Past service costs	$635
− Benefits paid	$170
Ending pension obligation	**$3,655**

Reconciliation of Beginning and Ending Fair Value of Plan Assets

Beginning fair value of plan assets	$1,850
+ Actual return on plan assets	$250
+ Employer contributions	$580
− Benefits paid	$170
Ending fair value of plan assets	**$2,510**

Compute periodic pension cost given that there are no actuarial gains or losses for the period.

Solution:

Method 1:

Ending net pension liability = 3,655 − 2,510 = $1,145 (a positive value indicates a net pension liability)
Beginning net pension liability = 2,225 − 1,850 = $375
Change in net pension liability over the period = 1,145 − 375 = $770

An increase in the net pension liability over the year represents a cost for the company. Contributions made by the company to the pension plan are also expenses as far as the company is concerned.

Periodic pension cost = Increase in net pension liability + Employer contributions
= 770 + 580 = **$1,350**

Method 2:

Periodic pension cost = Service costs + Interest cost + Past service costs
− Actual return on plan assets
= 845 + 120 + 635 − 250 = **$1,350**

Think of it this way. The positive change in the net pension liability over the period would be greater were it not for employer contributions to the plan (which increased the value of plan assets by $580).

The increase in the net pension liability, after adjusting plan assets for contributions made by the employer, reflects total periodic pension cost.

Periodic Pension Cost Under IFRS and U.S. GAAP

Note that in some cases, certain pension costs may qualify for being capitalized and included as part of the cost of certain assets (e.g., inventories). These capitalized pension costs are then included in P&L as a part of COGS when inventories are later sold. Our focus in this reading however, remains on amounts not capitalized.

While total periodic pension cost is the same under IFRS and U.S. GAAP, the manner in which total pension cost is divided between the P&L and other comprehensive income (OCI) is different under the two sets of standards.

Under **IFRS**, periodic pension cost is divided into three components. Two of them are recognized in P&L, while one is recognized in OCI.

1. Service costs: Both current and past service costs are recognized as an expense on the P&L under IFRS.
2. Net interest expense/income: Net interest expense/income is also recognized on the P&L under IFRS. This amount is calculated as:

    Net interest expense (income) = Net pension liability (asset) × Discount rate
    $$= \text{(Pension obligation − Fair value of plan assets)} \times r$$
    $$= \text{Pension obligation} \times r - \text{Fair value of plan assets} \times r$$

    Note that the discount rate, r, is the rate used to determine the pension obligation (present value of benefits earned).
    *   Net interest expense represents the financing cost of deferring payments related to the plan.
    *   Net interest income represents the financing income from prepaying amounts related to the plan.
3. Remeasurement: This component of periodic pension cost is recognized in OCI under IFRS. Further, remeasurement amounts are **not subsequently amortized** into P&L. Remeasurement of the net pension liability (asset) includes:
    *   Actuarial gains and losses.
    *   The difference between the actual return on plan assets and the return on plan assets (based on the discount rate, r) that has already been accounted for in the calculation of net interest expense/income.
        *   Actual return on plan assets − (Fair value of plan assets × r)

Before contrasting the division of periodic pension cost under IFRS with its division under U.S. GAAP, let's prove that the three components of periodic pension cost under IFRS add up to the same amount as periodic pension cost as calculated under Approach 2—that is, summing all economic expenses that affect the pension obligation (other than benefits paid) and deducting the actual return on plan assets.

Periodic pension cost = Current service costs + Interest costs + Past service costs + Actuarial losses − Actuarial gains − Actual return on plan assets … **Approach 2**

Periodic pension cost (IFRS) = Service costs + Net interest expense/income − Remeasurement

- Service costs = Current service costs + Past service costs
- Net interest income/expense = Pension obligation × r − Fair value of plan assets × r
- Remeasurement = Actuarial gains (losses)
  + [Actual return on plan assets − (Fair value of plan assets × r)]

Periodic pension cost (IFRS) = (Current service costs + Past service costs) +
(Pension obligation × r − Fair value of plan assets × r) −
{Actuarial gains (losses) + [Actual return on plan assets − (Fair
value of plan assets × r)]}

Pension obligation × r equals interest costs. **Therefore:**

Periodic pension cost (IFRS) = Current service costs + Past service costs + Interest costs
− ~~Fair value of plan assets × r~~ − Actuarial gains (losses)
− Actual return on plan assets + ~~Fair value of plan assets × r~~

> Periodic pension cost (IFRS) = Current service costs + Interest costs + Past service costs
> + Actuarial losses − Actuarial gains − Actual return on plan
> assets
>
> … **Approach 2**

Contrasting U.S. GAAP Treatment of Periodic Pension Cost with IFRS Treatment

Under U.S. GAAP:

- Service costs are recognized in P&L. However, past service costs are reported in OCI in the period during which the change that gave rise to the costs occurred. In subsequent years, these past service costs are amortized to P&L over the average service lives of affected employees. Recall that under IFRS, past service costs were also recognized on the P&L as *pension expense* for the period.
- Periodic pension expense includes interest expense on pension obligations (which increases pension cost) and returns on plan assets (which decrease pension cost). However, unlike IFRS:
  - These two components are not presented in a single net amount. Recall that the second component of pension cost under IFRS (i.e., net interest expense/income), represented a single net amount.
  - The return on plan assets is calculated based on an assumed expected return on plan assets. The difference between the actual return and the expected return on plan assets is *another* source (in addition to changes in assumptions that determine the value of the pension obligation—e.g., discount rate and life expectancy) of actuarial gains and losses under U.S. GAAP.

Note that earlier in the Reading, we said that actuarial gains and losses have an impact on the pension obligation and the funded status. However, this **additional** source of actuarial gains and losses under U.S. GAAP (from differences between actual and expected returns on plan assets) does not have an impact on the plan's funded status.

- All actuarial gains and losses can be reported either in P&L or in OCI. Typically, companies report actuarial gains and losses in OCI and recognize gains and losses in P&L by applying the corridor method. Recall that under IFRS, actuarial gains and losses are a part of the remeasurement component, which is never amortized into P&L from OCI.

Under the corridor method, if the net cumulative amount of unrecognized actuarial gains and losses at the beginning of the reporting period exceeds 10% of the greater of (1) the defined benefit obligation or (2) the fair value of plan assets, then the *excess* is amortized over the expected average remaining working lives of the employees participating in the plan and included as a component of periodic *pension expense* on the P&L. Example 2-2 illustrates the corridor method.

> Companies may use a faster recognition method provided that they apply the method to both gains and losses consistently in all the periods presented.

Example 2-2: The Corridor Method of Amortizing Actuarial Gains and Losses

The following information relates to Alpha Corp., which follows U.S. GAAP:

  Beginning balance of defined benefit obligation = $3,750,000
  Beginning balance of fair value of plan assets = $4,200,000
  Beginning balance of cumulative unrecognized actuarial losses = $450,000
  Expected average remaining working lives of plan employees = 10 years

Estimate the amount of unrecognized actuarial losses that should be recognized in P&L for the current period.

Solution:

Under the corridor method, amortization of unrecognized actuarial gains and losses sets in when the cumulative amount of unrecognized actuarial G/Ls exceeds 10% of the greater of (1) defined benefit obligations and (2) the fair value of plan assets. In the given scenario, the beginning balance of the fair value of plan assets ($4.2m) exceeds pension obligation ($3.75m). Therefore, the corridor is calculated as 10% of the fair value of plan assets:

  Corridor = $4,200,000 \times 10\% = \$420,000$

Since the beginning balance of cumulative unrecognized actuarial losses ($450,000) exceeds the corridor ($420,000), the *excess* will be amortized over the expected average remaining working lives of plan employees (10 years). Therefore, the amount recognized in *pension expense* on the current period P&L is calculated as:

  $(\$450,000 - \$420,000) / 10 = \$3,000$

Now, just as we did for IFRS earlier in the reading, we are going to prove that the components of periodic pension cost under U.S. GAAP add up to the amount calculated for periodic pension cost under Approach 2:

Periodic pension cost = Current service costs + Interest costs + Past service costs + Actuarial losses − Actuarial gains − Actual return on plan assets ... Approach 2

Periodic pension cost (U.S. GAAP) = Current service costs + Past service costs + Interest costs + Actuarial losses − Actuarial gains − Expected return on plan assets

Actuarial gains and losses under U.S. GAAP include the impact of changes in various assumptions on the pension obligation **and** the difference between the actual and expected return on plan assets. If the actual return on plan assets exceeds (is less than) the expected return, it gives rise to an actuarial gain (loss).

Periodic pension cost (U.S. GAAP) = Current service costs + Past service costs + Interest costs + Actuarial losses (gains) other than those arising from differences between the expected and actual return on plan assets − (Actual return on plan assets − Expected return on plan assets) − Expected return on plan assets

Periodic pension cost (U.S. GAAP) = Current service costs + Past service costs + Interest costs + Actuarial losses (gains) other than those arising from differences between the expected and actual return on plan assets − Actual return on plan assets + ~~Expected return on plan assets~~ − ~~Expected return on plan assets~~

Periodic pension cost (U.S. GAAP) = Current service costs + Past service costs + Interest costs + Actuarial losses − Actuarial gains − Actual return on plan assets

... Approach 2

So now we have proved that under both IFRS and U.S. GAAP, periodic pension cost equals the change in the net pension liability over the period plus employer contributions over the period (Approach 1 = Approach 2). However, the recognition of periodic pension cost across the P&L and OCI is different across the two sets of standards. These differences have been listed earlier, and are summarized in Table 2-1.

Table 2-1: Components of a Company's Defined-Benefit Pension Periodic Costs[3]

IFRS Component	IFRS Recognition	U.S. GAAP Component	U.S. GAAP Recognition
Service costs	Recognized in P&L.	Current service costs Past service costs	Recognized in P&L. Recognized in OCI and subsequently amortized to P&L over the service life of employees.
Net interest income/ expense	Recognized in P&L as the following amount: Net pension liability or asset × interest rate[(a)]	Interest expense on pension obligation Expected return on plan assets	Recognized in P&L. Recognized in P&L as the following amount: Plan assets × expected return.
Remeasurements: Net return on plan assets and actuarial gains and losses	Recognized in OCI and <u>not</u> subsequently amortized to P&L.	Actuarial gains and losses including differences between the actual and expected returns on plan assets	Recognized immediately in P&L or, more commonly, recognized in OCI and subsequently amortized to P&L using the corridor or faster recognition method.[(b)]
	• Net return on plan **assets** = Actual return − (Plan assets × Interest rate).		• Difference between expected and actual return on assets = Actual return − (Plan assets × Expected return).
	• Actuarial gains and losses = Changes in a company's pension obligation arising from changes in actuarial assumptions.		• Actuarial gains and losses = Changes in a company's pension obligation arising from changes in actuarial assumptions.

(a) The interest rate used is equal to the discount rate used to measure the pension liability (the yield on high-quality corporate bonds).

(b) If the cumulative amount of unrecognized actuarial gains and losses exceeds 10% of the greater of the value of the plan assets or of the present value of the DB obligation (under U.S. GAAP, the projected benefit obligation), the difference must be amortized over the service lives of the employees.

3 - Exhibit 2, Volume 2, CFA Program Curriculum 2017

Reporting the Periodic Pension Cost

We mentioned earlier that certain pension costs may be capitalized. For those pension costs that are not capitalized:

- **IFRS** only differentiates between components included in P&L and in OCI. It does not specify where exactly the various components of pension cost must be presented.
- **U.S. GAAP** also differentiates between components included in P&L and in OCI. Further, it requires all components of pension expense recognized in P&L to be aggregated and presented within one net line item on the income statement.

Note that both IFRS and U.S. GAAP require total periodic pension cost to be disclosed in the notes to the financial statements.

LESSON 3: EFFECTS OF CHANGES IN KEY ASSUMPTIONS

LOS 17d: Explain and calculate the effect of a defined benefit plan's assumptions on the defined benefit obligation and periodic pension cost.
Vol 2, pp 87–88

Effects of Changes in Key Assumptions

We have already mentioned that a company's pension obligation is computed based on several estimates and assumptions (e.g., rate of future compensation increases, employee turnover, length of service, employee life expectancy post-retirement, the discount rate, etc.). A change in any of these assumptions will have an impact on (1) the net pension liability recognized on the balance sheet and (2) periodic pension cost.

The Discount Rate

The assumed discount rate is used to calculate:

- The present value of DB payments (pension obligation).
- Current service costs (PV of annual unit credit).
- Interest expense (under U.S. GAAP) as r × beginning pension obligation.
- Net interest expense/income (under IFRS) to be recognized on the P&L
  - Net interest expense/income is calculated as (r × pension obligation – r × Fair value of plan assets)
- Remeasurement (under IFRS) to be recognized in OCI.
  - The second component of remeasurement is calculated as:
    Actual return on plan assets – r × Fair value of plan assets

An increase in the assumed discount rate:

For mature plans (where time to retirement is short) an increase in the discount rate may lead to an increase in interest expense.

In extremely rare cases, the higher interest expense may offset the impact of lower service costs, and pension cost may actually increase.

- Decreases the opening pension obligation (as the PV of promised payments decreases).
- Typically decreases total periodic pension cost.
  - For interest expense (r × beginning pension obligation):
    - On one hand, a higher discount rate *increases* the interest component of pension expense (r).
    - On the other hand, a higher discount rate *decreases* the beginning pension obligation.
    - The effect of the decrease in the opening obligation usually outweighs the effect of the increase in the discount rate so interest expense typically *falls*.
  - Current service costs *decline* as the PV of annual unit credit falls with the increase in the discount rate.
- Typically decreases the closing pension obligation.

Compensation Growth Rate

If the pension formula is based on the final year's salary, an increase in the assumed rate of growth in compensation:

- Increases the pension obligation.
- Increases periodic pension cost.

A higher compensation growth rate increases the total value of payments owed to employees after retirement (benefits earned). This increases annual unit credit, which results in an increase in the pension obligation, service costs and interest costs.

Expected Return on Plan Assets

The curriculum does not emphasize the difference between periodic pension cost and periodic pension expense. A higher expected return on plan assets would reduce pension expense, but should have no impact on total periodic pension cost.

Under U.S. GAAP, the expected return on plan assets reduces the periodic *pension expense*. An increase in the assumed expected return on plan assets:

- Has no impact on a company's net pension liability (funded status) reported on the balance sheet. The funded status is calculated based on the actual fair value of plan assets, which is not influenced by the expected rate of return assumption.
- Decreases the company's *pension expense* (under U.S. GAAP). Note that total periodic pension cost is not affected by a change in the expected return on plan assets. An increase in the expected return reduces *pension expense* on the P&L, but this is offset by a higher pension cost recognized in OCI (as an actuarial loss).

Expected Life Expectancy

If, under the terms of the plan, the sponsoring company must make pension payments to employees until their death, an increase in assumed life expectancy will result in an increase in the annual unit credit and the pension obligation. Further, service costs and interest costs will also increase so periodic pension cost will rise.

Table 3-1 summarizes the impact of changes in key assumptions on net pension liability and periodic pension cost, and Examples 3-1 and 3-2 show the effects of changes in key assumptions.

Table 3-1: Impact of Key Assumptions on Net Pension Liability and Periodic Pension Cost

Assumption	Impact of Assumption on Net Pension Liability (Asset)	Impact of Assumption on Periodic Pension Cost and Pension Expense
Higher discount rate	Lower obligation	Pension cost and pension expense will both typically be lower because of lower opening obligation and lower service costs
Higher rate of compensation increase	Higher obligation	Higher service and interest costs will increase periodic pension cost and pension expense
Higher expected return on plan assets	No effect, because fair value of plan assets are used on balance sheet	Not applicable for IFRS No effect on periodic pension cost under U.S. GAAP Lower periodic pension expense under U.S. GAAP

Example 3-1: Effects of Changes in Key Assumptions

Based on Example 1-1, estimate the impact of a 1% increase in the assumed discount rate (from 7% to 8%) on:

1. Closing pension obligation in Year 1;
2. Pension cost in Year 1.

Solution:

1. If the assumed discount rate increases from 7% to 8%, the employee's estimated final salary ($89,438.90) and annual payments after retirement ($22,359.72) remain unchanged, but the present value of these promised payments as of the retirement date decreases.

    PV of pension payments as of retirement date:

    N = 15; I/Y = 8; PMT = 22,359.72; FV = 0; CPT PV → **PV = $191,387.58**

    Therefore, annual unit credit decreases:

    Annual unit credit = 191,387.58 / (20+5) = **$7,655.50**

Year	1	Calculations
Benefits attributed to:		
Prior years	153,110.00	$= 7,655.50 \times 20$
Current year	7,655.50	$= 7,655.50$
Total benefits earned	**160,765.50**	
Opening pension obligation	104,204.09	$= 153,110/(1.08)^5$
Add: Interest cost	8,336.33	$= 104,204.09 \times 0.08$
Add: Current service costs	5,627.02	$= 7,655.50/(1.08)^4$
Closing pension obligation	**118,167.44**	

Notice in this example that interest expense actually increased despite the decrease in beginning pension obligation. However, overall pension costs declined as the decline in service costs outweighed the increase in interest expense.

The company's closing pension obligation has **decreased** from $130,505.72 to $118,167.44.

2. Year 1 pension cost (current service costs plus interest cost) **decreases** from $14,345.76 (calculated as $8,131.20 + $6,214.56) to $13,963.35 (calculated as $8,336.33 + $5,627.02).

Example 3-2: Effects of Changes in Key Assumptions

Using the information provided in Example 1-1, what is the effect of a 100 bp increase (from 4.5% to 5.5%) in the assumed annual compensation increase on Year 1 closing pension obligation?

Solution:

Based on the change in the assumed rate of compensation increase, we must recalculate the estimated final salary at retirement, the annual pension payment, the value (as of the retirement date) of estimated future payments, and the annual unit credit.

$$\text{Estimated final salary} = \$75,000 \times (1 + 0.055)^4 = \$92,911.85$$

$$\text{Estimated annual pension payment} = \$92,911.85 \times 0.01 \times 25 = \$23,227.96$$

The present value of 15 pension payments (as of retirement date) is calculated as:

N = 15; I/Y = 7; PMT = **23,227.96**; FV = 0; CPT PV; PV → $211,558.28

Annual unit credit = 211,558.28 / 25 = **$8,462.33**

Year	1	Calculations
Benefits attributed to:		
Prior years	169,246.63	$8,462.33 \times 20$
Current year	8,462.33	$= 8,462.33$
Total benefits earned	**177,708.96**	
Opening pension obligation	120,670.51	$= 169,246.63/(1.07)^5$
Add: Interest cost	8,446.94	$= 120,670.51 \times 0.07$
Add: Current service costs	6,655.87	$= 8,462.33/(1.07)^4$
Closing pension obligation	**135,573.32**	

The company's closing pension obligation has **increased** from $130,505.72 to $135,573.32.

LESSON 4: DISCLOSURES OF PENSION AND OTHER POST-EMPLOYMENT BENEFITS, AND CASH FLOW RELATED INFORMATION

LOS 17e: Explain and calculate how adjusting for items of pension and other post-employment benefits that are reported in the notes to the financial statements affects financial statements and ratios. Vol 2, pp 88–98

LOS 17f: Interpret pension plan note disclosures including cash flow related information. Vol 2, pp 88–98

Disclosures of Pension and Other Post-Employment Benefits

When comparing financial results of different companies using ratios, analysts should consider the impact of pensions and other post-employment benefits on the financial statements. Comparisons across companies can be affected by:

- Differences in key assumptions.
- Amounts reported on the balance sheet at net amounts (net pension liability or asset). Adjustments to incorporate gross amounts would impact financial ratios.
- Noncomparability of periodic pension *expense*. Pension expense may not be comparable as IFRS and U.S. GAAP differ with regards to how periodic pension costs can be recognized on the P&L vs. OCI.
- Differences across IFRS and U.S. GAAP regarding the reporting of components of pension expense on the income statement. Recall that under IFRS, companies may report the different components of pension expense within different line items on the income statement. On the other hand, under U.S. GAAP, companies are required to aggregate all components of pension expense and report the net amount within a single line item on the income statement under operating expenses.
- Differences across IFRS and U.S. GAAP regarding the classification of pension contributions on the cash flow statement. Under IFRS, a portion of contributions may be treated as financing cash flows rather than operating cash flows. Under U.S. GAAP, all contributions are treated as operating cash flows.

Assumptions

Companies disclose their assumptions about discount rates, expected compensation increases, medical expense inflation rates, and (for U.S. GAAP companies) expected return on plan assets. Analysts should examine these assumptions over time and across companies to assess whether a company is becoming increasingly conservative or aggressive in accounting for its DB obligations. A company could employ aggressive pension-related assumptions to improve reported financial performance by assuming:

- A higher discount rate.
- A lower compensation growth rate.
- A higher expected rate of return on plan assets.

Note that if a company assumes a higher discount rate than its peers when accounting for its DB obligations, it does not necessarily mean that the company is being relatively aggressive in its accounting practices. This is because the appropriate discount rate depends on the timing of the company's pension obligations (i.e., the relative maturity of its DB plan), which could be different from its peers. It is also possible that the company may be operating in a different country (with higher interest rates) than its peers.

Further, analysts should confirm that a company's pension-related assumptions are internally consistent. For example, the assumed discount rate and compensation growth rate should reflect a consistent view of inflation. A relatively high discount rate and a relatively low compensation growth rate would be inconsistent because high discount rates are associated with high-inflation environments, while a low compensation growth rate implies low inflation.

Finally, analysts should also evaluate the reasonableness of the assumed expected return on plan assets (made by U.S. GAAP companies) in light of the plan's target asset allocation (which companies are required to disclose). A higher expected return on plan assets is consistent with a greater proportion of plan assets being allocated to relatively risky investments.

Accounting for other post-employment benefits also requires companies to make several assumptions. For example, in order to estimate the medical obligation and associated periodic cost for post-employment health care plans, companies must make assumptions regarding the health care inflation rate, life expectancy, and so on. Typically, companies assume that the health care inflation rate will eventually taper off towards a lower, constant ultimate health care trend rate (see Example 4-1). All other things constant, each of the following assumptions will lead to an increase in the company's medical obligation and associated periodic cost:

> Note that most post-employment health care plans are unfunded. Therefore, the expected rate of return on plan assets is irrelevant.

- A higher health care inflation rate.
- A higher ultimate health care trend rate.
- A longer time to reach the ultimate health care trend rate.

Example 4-1: Comparisons about Trends in Health Care Costs

An analyst is evaluating the assumptions made by two companies (Company A and Company B) relating to their post-employment health care plans. The table below shows the companies' assumptions about health care costs and health care plan-related amounts:

	Assumptions about Health Care Costs			Amounts Reported for Other Post-Employment Benefits ($ Millions)	
	Initial Health Care Trend Rate	Ultimate Health Care Trend Rate	Year Ultimate Trend Rate Is Attained	Accumulated Benefit Obligation (Year-End 2009)	Periodic Cost for Benefits (for 2009)
Company A	8%	5%	2018	$2,542	$125
Company B	6%	5%	2017	$5,358	$285

The table below shows the effects of a 100bp increase or decrease in the assumed health care cost trend rates on 2009 accumulated post-employment benefit obligations and periodic costs.

	1 Percentage Point Increase	1 Percentage Point Decrease
Company A	Obligation: +$240 million Cost: +$15 million	Obligation: −$212 million Cost: −$12 million
Company B	Obligation: +$502 million Cost: +$47 million	Obligation: −$462 million Cost: −$42 million

Based on the information above, answer the following questions:

1. Which company's assumptions regarding health care costs appear less conservative?
2. What would be the effect of adjusting the less conservative company's post-employment benefit obligation and periodic post-employment benefit costs for a 1% increase in health care cost trend rates? Would this make the two companies more comparable?
3. Compute the change in each company's D/E ratio assuming a 1% increase in the health care cost trend rate. Assume that there are no taxes. Total liabilities and total equity as on the end of 2009 for the two companies are given below:

As of December 31, 2009	Company A	Company B
Total liabilities	$14,487	$44,394
Total equity	$5,765	$7,518

Solution:

1. Company B's assumptions about the trend in health care costs appear less conservative as they result in lower health care costs. This is because Company B assumes:
   - A lower initial health care cost increase of 6%, which is significantly lower than the initial health care cost increase assumed by Company A (8%).
   - That the rate of health care cost increases will level off at 5% (the ultimate health care trend rate) sooner (in 2017) than Company A (in 2018).
2. The sensitivity disclosures indicate that a 1% increase in the assumed health care cost trend rate would increase Company B's accumulated post-employment benefit obligation by $502 million and its periodic cost by $47 million. However, this adjustment is not enough to make the two companies comparable. The size of the adjustments to post-employment benefit obligation and periodic cost must be multiplied by 2 to reflect the 2 percentage point difference in the companies' assumed health care cost trend rates (Company A: 8%; Company B: 6%). Note that this adjustment would only be an approximation because the sensitivity of benefit obligations and periodic costs to changes in the assumed health care cost trend rate would not be exactly linear. Also note that the differences in the companies' assumed health care trend rates may be justifiable based on their respective locations (i.e., Company B may be located in a country with lower inflation than Company A).
3. The D/E ratio before and after adjusting for a 1% increase in the health care cost trend rate are calculated below:

   Company A:
   D/E (reported) = $14,487 / $5,765 = 2.51
   D/E (after adjustment) = ($14,487 + $240) / ($5,765 − $240) = 2.67

   Company B:
   D/E (reported) = $44,394 / $7,518 = 5.91
   D/E (after adjustment) = ($44,394 + $502) / $7,518 − $502) = 6.40

   A 1% increase in the health care cost trend rate:
   - Increases Company A's D/E ratio by 6.3% (from 2.51 to 2.67)
   - Increases Company B's D/E ratio by 8.3% (from 5.91 to 6.40)

Net Pension Liability (Asset)

We learned previously that under both IFRS and U.S. GAAP, the DB pension plan-related amount reported on the balance sheet is a net amount (net pension liability or net pension asset). Analysts should examine the notes to the financial statements and (1) add the gross amount of plan assets to the company's total assets and (2) add the gross amount of pension obligation to the company's total liabilities to reflect the underlying economic assets and liabilities of the sponsor. Analysts should compare the gross amount of pension obligation to the sponsoring company's (1) total assets (including gross plan assets), (2) shareholders' equity, and (3) earnings. The larger the ratio of gross plan obligations to any of these items, the greater the financial impact that a small change in pension liability will have on the sponsoring company's overall financial position.

Periodic Pension Costs Recognized in P&L versus OCI

Total periodic pension cost recognized under IFRS and U.S. GAAP is the same. However, the two sets of standards differ in their provisions regarding which components are recognized in P&L and which ones are recognized in OCI. These differences are important for analysts when evaluating companies that use different sets of standards.

- Under IFRS, current and past service costs are recognized in P&L. Under U.S. GAAP, the P&L only reflects current service costs (and amortization of any past service costs).
- Under IFRS, pension expense on the P&L incorporates a return on plan assets equal to the discount rate (used for measuring the pension obligation) times the value of plan assets. Under U.S. GAAP, pension expense on the P&L incorporates a return on plan assets equal to an estimated rate of return on plan assets times the value of plan assets.
- Under IFRS, the P&L would never show amortization of pension-related amounts previously recognized in OCI. Under U.S. GAAP, the P&L would reflect amortization of any past service costs, and may reflect amortization of actuarial gains and losses if they were initially recorded in OCI and if the "corridor" has been exceeded.

An analyst comparing the financial statements of a company that follows IFRS to one that follows U.S. GAAP would have to make adjustments to reported amounts to achieve comparability. To make a U.S. GAAP-following company's P&L comparable to the P&L of a company following IFRS, she would:

- Include past service costs on the P&L as pension expense.
- Exclude the effects of amortization of past service costs arising in previous periods.
- Exclude the effects of amortization of unrecognized actuarial gains and losses arising in previous periods.
- Incorporate the effects of the expected return on plan assets based on the discount rate (rather than the expected rate).

Alternatively, she could use total periodic pension cost as the basis for comparison by focusing on comprehensive income (which includes net income and other comprehensive income).

Classification of Periodic Pension Costs Recognized in P&L

Periodic pension costs recognized on the P&L are referred to as pension expense, which is generally treated as an operating expense. Conceptually however, the components of pension expense can be classified as operating and/or nonoperating. For example:

These classification issues also apply to OPB costs.

- Only current service costs should be treated as operating expenses.
- Interest expense should be treated as a nonoperating expense.
- The return on plan assets should be treated as nonoperating income.

Analysts should make the following adjustments to reflect a company's operating performance more accurately on the income statement:

1. Add back the entire amount of pension costs recognized on the P&L (pension expense) to operating income.
2. Subtract service costs before determining operating profit.
3. Add the interest component of pension expense to the company's interest expense.
4. Add the return on plan assets to nonoperating income.

The first two adjustments combined effectively exclude (1) amortization of past service costs, (2) amortization of actuarial gains and losses, (3) interest expense, and (4) return on plan assets from operating income.

Further, analysts may also make adjustments to reflect the actual return on plan assets. Recall that:

- Under IFRS, net interest expense/income on the P&L incorporates a return on plan assets based on the discount rate. The difference between this return and the actual return is a part of remeasurement, which is included in OCI.
- Under U.S. GAAP, pension expense incorporates a return on plan assets based on an expected rate of return assumption. The difference between the actual and expected return is a source of actuarial gains (losses), which are typically initially reported in OCI.

Note that adjusting the P&L to incorporate the actual return on plan assets introduces an element of volatility in net income. However, reclassification of interest expense has no impact on net income. See Example 4-2.

Example 4-2: Reclassifying Pension Expense

An analyst gathers the following information regarding a company:

Selected information from the income statement:

Operating profit	$550,000
Less: Interest expense	$125,000
Add: Other income	$70,000
Income before tax	**$495,000**

Selected information from notes to the financial statements:

Current service costs	$75,000
Add: Interest costs	$50,000
Less: Expected return on plan assets	$85,000
Total	**$40,000**

Difference between actual and expected return on plan assets = $5,000

Based on the information provided, reclassify the components of pension expense between operating and nonoperating items.

Solution:

We determine adjusted operating profit by adding back the total amount of pension expense recognized during the period ($40,000) to operating income and subtracting only current service costs ($75,000).

$$\text{Adjusted operating profit} = 550,000 + 40,000 - 75,000 = \$515,000$$

The interest component of pension expense ($50,000) is added to reported interest expense ($125,000).

$$\text{Adjusted interest expense} = 125,000 + 50,000 = \$175,000$$

The actual return on plan assets is added to other income ($70,000).

$$\text{Actual return on plan assets} = \text{Expected return} + (\text{Actual return} - \text{Expected return})$$
$$= \$85,000 + \$5,000 = \$90,000$$

$$\text{Adjusted other income} = 70,000 + 90,000 = \$160,000$$

Finally, income before taxes is computed as adjusted operating profit minus adjusted interest expense plus adjusted other income.

$$\text{Income before tax} = 515,000 - 175,000 + 160,000 = \$500,000$$

Cash Flow Information

For a funded plan, the impact of the plan on the sponsoring company's cash flows is the amount of contributions the company makes to fund the plan. For an unfunded plan, the impact of the plan on the sponsoring company's cash flows is the amount of benefits paid. Note that in both cases, these cash flows are usually classified as operating cash flows.

From an economic perspective however, classification of employer contributions to DB pension plans depends on how they relate to total pension costs for the period. Specifically:

- If a company's contribution to the plan over the period is greater than total pension cost for the period, the excess may be viewed as a reduction in the overall pension obligation.
  - Excess contributions are conceptually similar to making a principal payment on a loan in excess of the scheduled principal payment.
- If a company's contribution to the plan over the period is lower than total pension cost for the period, the shortfall results in an increase in the overall pension obligation.
  - A shortfall in contributions may be viewed as a source of financing.

If the amount of pension obligation is material, analysts may choose to reclassify the excess (shortfall) in contributions as a use (source) of cash from financing activities rather than operating activities. See Example 4-3.

Example 4-3: Adjusting Cash Flow

An analyst compiled the following information for XYZ Company's DB pension plan for 2009:

Total pension cost for 2009 = $1,350
Contributions made by the sponsor during 2009 = $580
Tax rate = 30%

How did the company's contributions to the plan during 2009 compare with total pension cost for the period? How would an analyst adjust cash from operating activities and financing activities?

Solution:

The company contributed $580 to its pension plan, which is $770 less than the total pension cost for the year. This $770 difference equals $539 [= $770 × (1 − 0.3)] on an after-tax basis.

Since the amount contributed by the sponsor to the plan over the year is lower than total pension cost for the year, the after-tax shortfall ($539) serves to increase the net pension liability. An analyst would therefore increase cash flow from financing activities by $539 and decrease cash flow from operating activities by $539.

LESSON 5: SHARE-BASED COMPENSATION

LOS 17g: Explain issues associated with accounting for share-based compensation. Vol 2, pp 98–105

LOS 17h: Explain how accounting for stock grants and stock options affects financial statements, and the importance of companies' assumptions in valuing these grants and options. Vol 2, pp 101–104

Employee compensation packages are usually composed of salary (for liquidity needs), bonuses (to provide short term performance incentives), nonmonetary benefits (to facilitate employees performing their jobs), and share-based compensation (to provide longer term incentives). Under both IFRS and U.S. GAAP, companies are required to disclose key elements of management compensation in their annual reports. Further, in the United States companies are required by the SEC to provide disclosures regarding management compensation on the proxy statement.

Share-based compensation is a form of deferred compensation and includes items such as stock, stock options, stock appreciation rights, and phantom shares.

Advantages
- Aligns employees' interests with those of shareholders.
- Does not typically require a cash outlay.

Disadvantages
- The employee may have limited influence on the company's market value, so share-based compensation may not necessarily provide the desired incentives.
- Increased ownership may make managers more risk-averse and conservative in their strategies.
- The option-like (asymmetrical) payoff may encourage management to take excessive risk.
- Leads to dilution of existing shareholders' ownership.

Accounting for cash compensation is straight-forward; compensation expense is recognized during the period in which employees are awarded the compensation. Accounting for share-based compensation, however, is more complicated.

- Both IFRS and U.S. GAAP require companies to **measure** share-based compensation expense based on the **fair value** of the compensation granted.
- Both IFRS and U.S. GAAP require companies to **disclose** the following regarding share-based compensation:
    - The nature and extent of share-based compensation for the period.
    - The basis for determining the fair value of share-based compensation over the period.
    - The effects of share-based compensation on the company's net income for the period and its financial position.
- As far as **accounting** for share-based compensation is concerned, the specifics depend on the type of compensation.

The various types of share-based compensation can be categorized as equity-settled compensation and cash-settled compensation.

- Equity-settled share-based compensation (e.g., stock grants and stock options) allow the employee to obtain direct ownership in the company.
- Cash-settled share-based compensation (e.g., stock appreciation rights and phantom stock) does not require the employee to hold shares in the company.

Stock Grants

Stock grants include outright stock grants, restricted stock grants, and performance shares.

- With outright stock grants, shares are granted to the employee without any conditions.
- Restricted stock grants require the employee to return the shares to the company if certain conditions are not met (e.g., if certain performance goals are not met).
- Performance shares are contingent on meeting performance goals, where performance is usually measured by accounting earnings or return on assets. Performance shares may provide incentives to management to manipulate reported earnings.

Compensation expense for stock grants is based on the fair value of shares, which typically equals their market value on the grant date. Compensation expense for stock grants is allocated over the employee's service period.

Stock Options

Under both IFRS and U.S. GAAP, compensation expense related to stock options is based on fair value, where fair value must be estimated using an appropriate valuation model. The market value of traded options on the company's stock cannot be used to measure the value of stock options-related compensation expense because stock options granted to employees are different from traded options.

Inputs to option valuation models include exercise price, stock price volatility, estimated life of stock options, estimated number of stock options that will be forfeited, dividend yield, and the risk-free rate. While some of these inputs (e.g., the exercise price) are known at the time that options are granted, others (e.g., stock price volatility and estimated life of stock options) are highly subjective and can change the estimated fair value and compensation expense significantly. Assumptions of *higher* stock price volatility, *longer* estimated life, *higher* risk-free interest rate, and a *lower* dividend yield *increase* the estimated fair value of employee stock options, *increasing* compensation expense.

Before moving on to accounting for stock options, we need to be familiar with the following terms:

- The grant date is the date when options are granted to employees.
- The vesting date is the date when employees can first exercise the stock options.
- The service period is the period between the grant date and the vesting date.
- The exercise date is the date when employees actually exercise the options and convert them to stock. If options go unexercised, they expire at a pre-determined future date (usually 5 or 10 years from the grant date).

Accounting for Compensation Expense Related to Stock Options
- If stock options vest immediately, the entire cost (fair value) of options awarded is recognized on the grant date (in the current period).
- If stock options vest after a specified service period, compensation expense is allocated over the service period.
- If vesting of stock options is conditional (e.g., upon a target share price being reached), compensation expense is recognized over the estimated service period.

As option expense is recognized over the relevant period, expenses increase and net income falls. Therefore, retained earnings also fall. The offsetting entry is an increase in paid-in-capital so total shareholders' equity remains unchanged. See Example 5-1.

Measurement of Compensation Expense Related to Stock Options
- If the number of shares and option price are known, compensation expense is measured at the grant date.
- If the fair value of options depends on events after the grant date, compensation expense is measured at the exercise date.

Example 5-1: Disclosures of Stock-Based Compensation

The following information is provided in the notes to the financial statements of Madrigal Inc. for 2011:

	2009	**2010**	**2011**
Total stock-based compensation expense	415 million	326 million	208 million
Total income tax benefit recognized for share-based compensation	65 million	81 million	98 million

Further, total unrecognized compensation cost relating to nonvested share-based compensation arrangements as of the end of 2011 equals $428 million. This cost is expected to be recognized over a weighted average period of 1.9 years.

Determine:

1. Total compensation expense relating to options already granted that will be recognized in future years as options vest.
2. Approximate compensation expense in 2012 and 2013 relating to options already granted.

Solution:

1. The unrecognized compensation expense relating to stock options already granted but not yet vested totals $428 million.
2. The options already granted are expected to vest over the next 1.9 years. Therefore, compensation expense related to stock options already granted will be approximately $225 million (= $428/1.9) in 2012 and $203 million (= $428 − $225) in 2013.

Stock Appreciation Rights (SARs)

With stock appreciation rights (SARs) an employee's compensation is tied to increases in the company's stock price, but the employee does not own the company's stock. Compensation expense for SARs is measured at fair value and allocated over the service life of the employee.

Advantages:
- The potential for risk aversion is limited as SARs holders have limited downside risk and unlimited upside potential.
- Ownership interests of existing shareholders are not diluted.

Disadvantage:
- SARs require a current period cash outflow.

Phantom Shares

With phantom share plans compensation is based on the performance of hypothetical stock rather than the company's actual stock. Phantom share plans can be used by private companies, by business units within a company, and by highly illiquid companies.

READING 18: MULTINATIONAL OPERATIONS

LESSON 1: DEFINING THE PRESENTATION CURRENCY, FUNCTIONAL CURRENCY, LOCAL CURRENCY, AND FOREIGN CURRENCY TRANSACTION EXPOSURE

LOS 18a: Distinguish among presentation (reporting) currency, functional currency, and local currency. Vol 2, pg 117

Most multinational companies engage in two types of foreign currency-related activities that require special accounting treatment.

1. They undertake transactions that are denominated in foreign currencies.
2. They invest in foreign subsidiaries that keep their accounts in foreign currencies.

To report these activities in their consolidated financial statements, multinationals must translate foreign currency amounts related to these activities into the currency in which they present their financial statements. Before moving into the details regarding currency translation, we define the following important terms:

- The **presentation currency (PC)** is the currency in which the parent company reports its financial statements. It is typically the currency of the country where the parent is located. For example, U.S. companies are required to present their financial results in USD, German companies in EUR, Japanese companies in JPY, and so on.
- The **functional currency (FC)** is the currency of the primary business environment in which an entity operates. It is usually the currency in which the entity primarily generates and expends cash.
- The **local currency (LC)** is the currency of the country where the subsidiary operates.

Since the local currency is generally the entity's functional currency as well, a multinational parent with subsidiaries in different countries around the world is likely to have a variety of different functional currencies.

LOS 18b: Describe foreign currency transaction exposure, including accounting for and disclosures about foreign currency transaction gains and losses. Vol 2, pp 118–129

LOS 18c: Analyze how changes in exchange rates affect the translated sales of the subsidiary and parent company. Vol 2, pp 118–129

A **foreign currency** is defined as any currency other than the entity's functional currency. Therefore, foreign currency transactions are those that are denominated in a currency other than the company's functional currency. Foreign currency transactions may involve:

- An import purchase or an export sale that is denominated in a foreign currency; or
- Borrowing or lending funds where the amount to be repaid or received is denominated in a foreign currency.

Each of these transactions gives rise to a foreign currency-denominated asset or a liability for the company.

Foreign Currency Transaction Exposure to Foreign Exchange Risk

Suppose that a U.S. company purchases (imports) goods worth €1m from a German company, and must pay for the goods in EUR within 90 days. By deferring payment, the U.S. company runs the risk that the EUR will appreciate versus the USD, in which case it would need to expend more USD to settle the €1m obligation. The U.S. company is said to have foreign currency transaction exposure.

- For an import purchase, foreign exchange transaction exposure for the importing company arises when it defers a payment that must be made in foreign currency. The importer faces the risk that the value of the foreign currency will increase between the purchase date and the settlement date. Appreciation of the foreign currency would mean that the importer will have to spend more units of domestic currency to purchase the required amount of foreign currency to settle the obligation.
- For an export sale, foreign exchange transaction exposure for the exporting company arises when it allows the purchaser to make the payment sometime after the purchase date and agrees to be paid in foreign currency. The exporter faces the risk that the value of the foreign currency will decrease between the date of sale and the settlement date. Depreciation of the foreign currency would mean that the exporter will receive a lower number of units of domestic currency upon converting the foreign currency amount when it is received.

An important thing for you to note is that all foreign currency transactions are recorded at the spot exchange rate on the transaction date. Foreign currency transaction risk only arises when the payment and settlement dates are different.

Both U.S. GAAP and IFRS require that changes in the value of a foreign currency asset/liability resulting from a foreign currency transaction be recognized as gains/losses on the income statement (see Example 1-1). The exact amount of gains/losses recognized depends on:

- Whether the company has an asset or a liability that is exposed to foreign exchange risk.
- Whether the foreign currency increases or decreases in value versus the domestic currency.

Example 1-1: Accounting for Foreign Currency Transactions

U.S.Co purchases goods from GermanCo for €200,000 on September 1, 2008, and agrees to make the payment in EUR in 60 days. U.S.Co's functional and presentation currency is the USD. Spot exchange rates between the EUR and USD are as follows:

- September 1, 2008: $/€ = 1.3805
- October 31, 2008: $/€ = 1.4025

Given that U.S.Co's accounting year ends on December 31, how will this foreign currency transaction affect the company's financial statements?

Solution:

U.S.Co prepares its accounts in USD. On the transaction date (September 1, 2008) it recognizes a liability of $276,100. This is because on the transaction date, U.S.Co could have settled the transaction by purchasing and delivering €200,000 to GermanCo at the then-current spot exchange rate (1.3805$/€). U.S.Co would have been able to purchase €200,000 for $276,100 (calculated as €200,000 × 1.3805$/€) on the transaction date.

Instead, U.S.Co settles the obligation 60 days after the transaction date. In the period between the transaction and settlement dates, the EUR has appreciated relative to the USD. U.S.Co actually ends up paying $280,500 (calculated as €200,000 × 1.4025$/€) to purchase €200,000 on October 31. By deferring the payment, U.S.Co incurs a loss of $4,400 (calculated as $280,500 − $276,100) on the transaction. This is a realized loss (as the company actually paid $4,400 more than the original obligation it recognized on its USD-denominated financial statements), which is reported on U.S.Co's 2008 income statement.

In Example 1-1, the transaction date and the settlement date occurred in the same reporting period (2008). If the balance sheet date occurs between the transaction date and settlement date:

- Foreign exchange gains/losses (based on changes in the exchange rate between the transaction date and the balance sheet date) are still recognized on the income statement (even though they have not been realized) for the period in which the transaction occurred.
- Once the transaction is settled, additional gains/losses are recognized (based on changes in the exchange rate from the balance sheet date till the settlement date) in the period during which the transaction was settled.
- Aggregating the foreign exchange gains/losses over the two accounting periods results in an amount that equals the actual realized gain/loss on the foreign exchange transaction (see Example 1-2).

Example 1-2: Accounting for Foreign Currency Transactions

U.S.Co exports goods worth £15,000 to U.K.Co on November 30, 2008, and agrees to be paid in GBP on January 31, 2009. U.S.Co's functional and presentation currency is the USD. Spot exchange rates between the GBP and USD are as follows:

- November 30, 2008: $/£ = 1.5054
- December 31, 2008: $/£ = 1.5386
- January 31, 2009: $/£ = 1.4975

Given that U.S.Co's accounting year ends on December 31 how will this foreign currency transaction affect its financial statements?

Solution:

On November 30, 2008, U.S.Co will recognize an asset (receivable) worth $22,581 (calculated as £15,000 × 1.5054$/£ = $22,581). This amount represents the USD value of the receivable based on the spot exchange rate on the transaction date.

The company's year-end is December 31, which falls between the transaction date and the settlement date. Therefore:

- On its 2008 financial statements, the company is required to recognize (unrealized) foreign exchange gains/losses based on the change in the USD-denominated value of the receivable due to changes in the exchange rate from the transaction date till the balance sheet date.
  - The value of the receivable rises to $23,079 (calculated as £15,000 × 1.5386$/£) on December 31, 2008.
  - Therefore, U.S.Co recognizes a profit of $23,079 − $22,581 = $498 on its income statement for 2008.
- Since the transaction is settled in 2009, the company is required to recognize on its financial statements for 2009, foreign exchange gains/losses based on the change in the USD-denominated value of the receivable due to changes in the exchange rate between the balance sheet date and the settlement date.
  - The value of the receivable falls to $22,462.50 (calculated as £15,000 × 1.4975$/£) on January 31, 2009.
  - Therefore, U.S.Co recognizes a loss of $23,079 − $22,462.50 = $616.50 on its income statement for 2009.
- The aggregate foreign currency gain (loss) recognized over the two accounting periods (2008–2009) by U.S.Co equals $498 − $616.50 = −$118.50.
  - The overall gain (loss) can also be calculated as the USD-denominated value of the receivable on the settlement date ($22,462.50) minus the USD-denominated value of the receivable on the transaction date ($22,581), which equals −$118.50.

Note that in Example 1-1:

- U.S.Co had a liability exposure (in the form of an account payable) to foreign exchange risk. As the foreign currency (EUR) *appreciated,* U.S.Co recognized a *loss* as the USD-denominated value of its *liability increased.*

Further, in Example 1-2:

- U.S.Co had an asset exposure (in the form of an account receivable) to foreign exchange risk. As the foreign currency (GBP) *appreciated* (from the transaction date until the balance sheet date) U.S.Co recognized a *gain* as the USD-denominated value of its *asset increased.*
- As the foreign currency (GBP) *depreciated* (from the balance sheet date till the settlement date) U.S.Co recognized a *loss* as the USD-denominated value of its *asset decreased.*

Table 1-1 summarizes how the nature of a company's exposure to exchange rate risk and the direction of change in the value of the foreign currency impact the foreign exchange gain or loss recognized by a company.

Table 1-1

Transaction	Type of Exposure	Foreign Currency	
		Strengthens	Weakens
Export sale	Asset (account receivable)	Gain	Loss
Import purchase	Liability (account payable)	Loss	Gain

Analytical Issues

Both IFRS and U.S. GAAP require foreign exchange transaction gains/losses to be recognized on the income statement, regardless of whether or not they have been realized. However, neither set of standards specifies where on the income statement these gains/losses must be presented. Companies usually report foreign exchange transaction gains/losses:

- As a component of other operating income/expense; or
- As a component of nonoperating income/expense.

This choice can have a substantial impact on the reported operating profit margin.

- If a foreign currency transaction gain is recognized as a part of operating income, the operating profit margin would be *higher* than it would be were the transaction gain recognized as a part of nonoperating income.
- If a foreign currency transaction loss is recognized as a part of operating expenses, the operating profit margin would be *lower* than it would be were the transaction loss recognized as a part of nonoperating expenses.
- Note that the placement of the foreign currency transaction gain/loss (under operating income/expense versus nonoperating income/expense) has no impact on the gross profit and net profit margins.

Another analytical issue relating to foreign currency transaction gains/losses is that, when the balance sheet date lies between the transaction and settlement dates, the eventual translation gain/loss recognized can be significantly different from the amount recognized initially. Notice (in Example 1-2) how the foreign currency transaction gain recognized in 2008 ($498) does not accurately reflect the loss that was ultimately realized in 2009 ($118.50).

Disclosures Relating to Foreign Currency Transaction Gains and Losses

IFRS and U.S. GAAP require disclosure of the **aggregate amount** of foreign currency transaction gains and losses included in net income for the period, but do not require disclosure of whether they are **classified** as operating or nonoperating income/expenses. Further, details regarding the exact line item in which these gains/losses are included is also not required.

LESSON 2: TRANSLATION OF FOREIGN CURRENCY FINANCIAL STATEMENTS: THE CURRENT RATE AND TEMPORAL METHODS

LOS 18d: Compare the current rate method and the temporal method, evaluate how each affects the parent company's balance sheet and income statement, and determine which method is appropriate in various scenarios. Vol 2, pp 130–271

LOS 18e: Calculate the translation effects and evaluate the translation of a subsidiary's balance sheet and income statement into the parent company's presentation currency. Vol 2, pp 130–172

LOS 18f: Analyze how the current rate method and the temporal method affect financial statements and ratios. Vol 2, pp 130–172

Translation of Foreign Currency Financial Statements

There are two approaches to translating foreign currency financial statements:

- The current rate method (also known as the all-current method) is used to translate financial statements presented in the functional currency (FC) into amounts expressed in the parent's presentation currency (PC).
- The temporal method (also known as remeasurement) is used to translate financial statements presented in local currency (LC) into amounts expressed in the functional currency (FC).

The translation method that applies to a particular situation depends on the entity's functional currency. A foreign entity's functional currency is defined as the currency of the primary economic environment in which the entity operates. The functional currency can either be the parent's presentation currency, or another currency (typically the currency of the country where the entity is located, local currency).

The functional currency is determined by management. According to the IFRS, management should consider the following factors in determining the functional currency:

U.S. GAAP offers similar guidance.

- The currency that influences sales prices for goods and services.
- The currency of the country whose competitive forces and regulations mainly determine the sales price of its goods and services.
- The currency that mainly influences labor, material, and other costs of providing goods and services.
- The currency in which funds from financing activities are generated.
- The currency in which receipts from operating activities are usually retained.

Once the functional currency is identified, the following rules are followed to determine which translation method is applicable:

- If the local currency is deemed to be the functional currency (LC = FC ≠ PC), the current rate method is used to translate foreign currency financial statements into the parent's presentation currency.
  - Such instances usually arise when the subsidiary is independent and its operating, investing, and financing activities are decentralized from the parent.

- If the presentation currency is deemed to be the functional currency (LC ≠ FC = PC), the temporal method is used to translate foreign currency financial statements into the parent's presentation currency.
  - ○ Such instances usually arise when the subsidiary and parent are well-integrated.
- If local currency, functional currency, and presentation currency are different (LC ≠ FC ≠ PC), then:
  - ○ The temporal method is used to convert local currency amounts into functional currency; and then
  - ○ The current rate method is used to convert functional currency amounts into presentation currency.

Figure 2-1 summarizes these rules:

Figure 2-1: Methods for Translating Foreign Currency Financial Statements of Subsidiaries

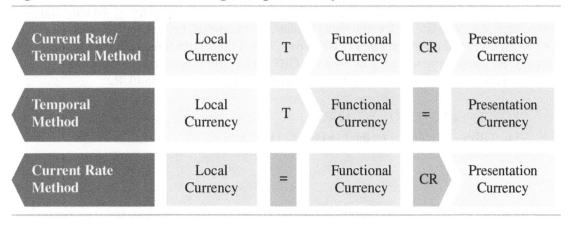

Before moving ahead, we need to be familiar with the following exchange rate definitions:

- The current rate is the exchange rate that exists on the balance sheet date.
- The average rate is the average exchange rate over the reporting period.
- The historical rate is the actual exchange rate that existed on the original transaction date.

The Current Rate Method

When the foreign entity's functional currency is different from the parent's presentation currency, the current rate method is used to translate the foreign entity's financial statements into the parent's presentation currency. For example, the current rate method will be applied when a Swiss subsidiary of a Japanese parent (that prepares its consolidated financial statements in JPY) uses CHF (the local currency) as its functional currency.

LC (CHF) = FC (CHF) ≠ PC (JPY)

LC, FC (CHF) → Current rate method → PC (JPY)

Translation Procedures

These translation procedures for the current rate and the temporal method will not make too much sense right now. Make sure you refer to the steps outlined here while going through Example 2-1, and then review Table 2-1 thoroughly to ensure that you understand the translation procedures.

- The income statement and statement of retained earnings are translated first, and then the balance sheet is translated.
- All income statement accounts are translated at the historical rate (which for practical purposes is assumed to equal the average rate).
- All balance sheet accounts (except common equity) are translated at the current rate.
- Capital stock is translated at the historical rate that existed on the date of capital contribution.
- Dividends are translated at the rate that applied when they were declared.
- The translation gain/loss for the period is the balancing amount. It is included in shareholders' equity under the cumulative translation adjustment (CTA).

The Temporal Method

When a foreign entity's functional currency is the parent's presentation currency, the temporal method is used to translate the foreign entity's financial statements. For example, consider a U.K.-based distribution company that is 100% owned by a French manufacturer. Being a U.K. company, the subsidiary must keep its books in GBP, so its GBP financial statements must be translated into EUR as if all its transactions had originally been recorded in EUR.

$$LC\ (GBP) \neq FC\ (EUR) = PC\ (EUR)$$
$$LC\ (GBP) \rightarrow Temporal\ method \rightarrow FC,\ PC\ (EUR)$$

Translation Procedures

Monetary assets/liabilities are fixed in terms of the amount of currency to be received/paid for them.

- The balance sheet is translated first, followed by the income statement and statement of retained earnings.
- Monetary assets and monetary liabilities are translated at the current rate.
    - Monetary assets include cash and receivables.
    - Monetary liabilities include accounts payable, accrued expenses, long-term debt, and deferred income taxes. Most liabilities are monetary liabilities.
- Nonmonetary assets and liabilities measured at **historical cost** are translated at historical rates.
    - Nonmonetary assets measured at historical cost include inventory measured at **cost** under the lower of cost or market rule, PP&E, and intangible assets.
    - Nonmonetary liabilities measured at historical cost include deferred revenue.
- Nonmonetary assets and liabilities measured at **current value** are translated at the exchange rate that existed when current value was determined.
    - Nonmonetary assets measured at current cost include marketable securities and inventory measured at **market** under the lower of cost or market rule.
- Shareholders' equity accounts are translated at historical rates.
- Revenues and expenses (other than expenses related to nonmonetary assets) are translated at the average rate.
- Expenses related to nonmonetary assets (e.g., COGS, depreciation, and amortization) are translated at historical rates prevailing at time of purchase of the related nonmonetary assets.

- The translation gain/loss (also known as remeasurement gain or loss) is reported on the income statement. It is the plug figure that would make net income for the year consistent with ending retained earnings (after accounting for dividends) from the translated balance sheet.

Note that the historical exchange rate used to translate inventory and COGS under the temporal method will differ according to the cost flow assumption (FIFO, LIFO, AVCO) used.

- If FIFO is used:
  - Ending inventory is composed of recent purchases so inventory will be translated at relatively recent exchange rates.
  - Units sold are from the older purchases so COGS will be translated at relatively old exchange rates.
- If LIFO is used:
  - Ending inventory is composed of older purchases so inventory will be translated at relatively old exchange rates.
  - Units sold are from the more recent purchases so COGS will be translated at relatively recent exchange rates.

Table 2-1 lists the exchange rate at which various financial reporting elements are translated under the two methods:

Table 2-1: Rules for Foreign Currency Translation

Income Statement Component	Current Rate Method FC = LC	Temporal Method FC = PC
	Exchange Rate Used	
Sales	Average rate	Average rate
Cost of goods sold	Average rate	Historical rate
Selling expenses	Average rate	Average rate
Depreciation expense	Average rate	Historical rate
Amortization expense	Average rate	Historical rate
Interest expense	Average rate	Average rate
Income tax	Average rate	Average rate
Net income before translation gain (loss)		Computed as Rev – Exp
Translation gain (loss)	N/A	Plug in Number
Net income	Computed as Rev – Exp	Computed as ΔRE + Dividends
Less: Dividends	Historical rate	Historical rate
Change in retained earnings	Computed as NI – Dividends Used as input for translated B/S	From B/S

Table 2-1: (*continued*)

Balance Sheet Component	Current Rate Method FC = LC Exchange Rate Used	Temporal Method FC = PC
Cash	Current rate	Current rate
Accounts receivable	Current rate	Current rate
Monetary assets	Current rate	Current rate
Inventory	Current rate	Historical rate
Nonmonetary assets measured at current value	Current rate	Current rate
Property, plant, and equipment	Current rate	Historical rate
Less: Accumulated depreciation	Current rate	Historical rate
Nonmonetary assets measured at historical cost	Current rate	Historical rate
Accounts payable	Current rate	Current rate
Long-term notes payable	Current rate	Current rate
Monetary liabilities	Current rate	Current rate
Nonmonetary liabilities:		
Measured at current value	Current rate	Current rate
Measured at historical cost	Current rate	Historical rate
Capital stock	Historical rate	Historical rate
Retained earnings	From I/S	Balancing figure Used as input for translated I/S
Cumulative translation adjustment	Plug in Number	N/A

Example 2-1: Foreign Currency Translation Methods

Alpha Ltd. is headquartered in the United States and prepares its consolidated financial statements in USD. The company has a subsidiary, Beta Ltd., which is based in Spain. Beta Ltd.'s financial statements for 2010 (its first year of operations) are provided below:

Income Statement and Statement of Retained Earnings For the Year Ended December 31, 2010	2010 EUR
Sales	14,500,000
Cost of sales	10,000,000
Selling expenses	950,000
Depreciation expense	200,000
Interest expense	415,000
Income taxes	850,000
Net income	**2,085,000**
Less: Dividends	800,000
Retained earnings	**1,285,000**

Balance Sheet	2010
As of December 31, 2010	EUR
Cash	1,020,000
Accounts receivable	970,000
Inventory	1,400,000
Total current assets	3,390,000
Property, plant, and equipment	4,000,000
Less: Accumulated depreciation	200,000
Total Assets	**7,190,000**
Accounts payable	405,000
Total current liabilities	405,000
Long-term notes payable	3,500,000
Total liabilities	3,905,000
Capital stock	2,000,000
Retained earnings	1,285,000
Total equity	3,285,000
Total Liabilities and Equity	**7,190,000**

For the purpose of translating Beta's financial statements into USD, the following exchange rates are given. Note that the EUR has depreciated versus USD over the year.

Date	$/€
January 1, 2010	1.35
Average, 2010	1.325
Weighted average rate when inventory was acquired	1.32
December 1, 2010 (when dividends were declared)	1.31
December 31, 2010	1.30

1. Translate Beta's financial statements into the parent's presentation currency (i.e., USD) using the current rate method.
2. Translate Beta's financial statements into the parent's presentation currency (i.e., USD) using the temporal method.

Solution:

The Current Rate Method

Under the current rate method, we first translate all income statement items to derive net income and retained earnings.

**Income Statement and
Statement of Retained Earnings 2010**

	Current Rate Method		
	€	Rate Used	$
Sales	14,500,000	1.325 (A)	19,212,500
Cost of sales	10,000,000	1.325 (A)	13,250,000
Selling expenses	950,000	1.325 (A)	1,258,750
Depreciation expense	200,000	1.325 (A)	265,000
Interest expense	415,000	1.325 (A)	549,875
Income taxes	850,000	1.325 (A)	1,126,250
Net income	2,085,000		2,762,625
Less: Dividends	800,000	1.31 (H)	1,048,000
Change in retained earnings	1,285,000		1,714,625

Change in retained earnings = Net income − Dividends
$$= 2,762,625 - 1,048,000 = \$1,714,625$$

Next, we translate the balance sheet. We use net income (from the translated income statement) to compute retained earnings and the translation adjustment for the balance sheet.

**Balance Sheet
December 31, 2010**

	Current Rate Method		
	€	Rate Used	$
Cash	1,020,000	1.30 (C)	1,326,000
Accounts receivable	970,000	1.30 (C)	1,261,000
Inventory	1,400,000	1.30 (C)	1,820,000
Total current assets	3,390,000		4,407,000
Property, plant, and equipment	4,000,000	1.30 (C)	5,200,000
Less: Accumulated depreciation	200,000	1.30 (C)	260,000
Total Assets	**7,190,000**		**9,347,000**
Accounts payable	405,000	1.30 (C)	526,500
Total current liabilities	405,000		526,500
Long-term notes payable	3,500,000	1.30 (C)	4,550,000
Total liabilities	3,905,000		5,076,500
Capital stock	2,000,000	1.35 (H)	2,700,000
Retained earnings	1,285,000	From I/S	1,714,625
Cumulative translation adjustment			−144,125
Total equity	3,285,000		4,270,500
Total Liabilities and Equity	**7,190,000**		**9,347,000**

The cumulative translation adjustment on the balance sheet is the plug figure that makes the accounting equation balance.

- We know that total assets equal $9,347,000.
- Therefore, liabilities and shareholders' equity must also add up to $9,347,000.
- Given that total liabilities amount to $5,076,500, total equity must equal $4,270,500 (calculated as 9,347,000 – 5,076,500).
- Therefore:
  Capital stock + Retained earnings + Cumulative translation adjustment = $4,270,500
  Cumulative translation adjustment = 4,270,500 – 2,700,000 – 1,714,625 = ($144,125)
  Translation gain (loss) = ($144,125)

An important point that we should highlight here is that since this is Beta's first year of operations, retained earnings on the balance sheet equals net income for the year adjusted for dividends declared (there are no retained earnings brought forward from previous years). Similarly, the entire amount of the cumulative translation adjustment on the balance sheet reflects the translation gain/loss for the current year (there are no translation gains/losses brought forward from previous years). If this were not the first year of Beta's operations, we would add the change in retained earnings over the year to beginning retained earnings to compute ending retained earnings (which is used in the computation of the cumulative translation adjustment). Further, we would look at the change in the cumulative translation adjustment over the year to identify the translation gain (loss) for the current year. An increase in the positive value (or a decrease in the negative value) of the cumulative translation adjustment would indicate a translation gain for the period.

The Temporal Method

Under the temporal method, we will first translate the balance sheet to determine the change in retained earnings over the period.

Balance Sheet	Temporal Method		
	€	Rate Used	$
Cash	1,020,000	1.30 (C)	1,326,000
Accounts receivable	970,000	1.30 (C)	1,261,000
Inventory	1,400,000	1.32 (H)	1,848,000
Total current assets	3,390,000		4,435,000
Property, plant, and equipment	4,000,000	1.35 (H)	5,400,000
Less: Accumulated depreciation	200,000	1.35 (H)	270,000
Total Assets	**7,190,000**		**9,565,000**
Accounts payable	405,000	1.30 (C)	526,500
Total current liabilities	405,000		526,500
Long-term notes payable	3,500,000	1.30 (C)	4,550,000
Total liabilities	3,905,000		5,076,500
Capital stock	2,000,000	1.35 (H)	2,700,000
Retained earnings	1,285,000		1,788,500
Total equity	3,285,000		4,488,500
Total Liabilities and Equity	**7,190,000**		**9,565,000**

Retained earnings = Total assets − Liabilities − Common stock
$$= 9,565,000 - 5,076,500 - 2,700,000 = \$1,788,500$$

We then move on to the income statement. The change in retained earnings (from the translated balance sheet) is used to determine net income for the year and the translation gain/loss.

Income Statement and Statement of Retained Earnings

	Temporal Method		
	€	Rate Used	$
Sales	14,500,000	1.325 (A)	19,212,500
Cost of sales	10,000,000	1.32 (H)	13,200,000
Selling expenses	950,000	1.325 (A)	1,258,750
Depreciation expense	200,000	1.35 (H)	270,000
Interest expense	415,000	1.325 (A)	549,875
Income tax	850,000	1.325 (A)	1,126,250
Income before translation gain (loss)	2,085,000		2,807,625
Translation gain (loss)	N/A		28,875
Net income	2,085,000		2,836,500
Less: Dividends	800,000	1.31 (H)	1,048,000
Change in retained earnings	1,285,000		1,788,500

Net income = Change in retained earnings + Dividends declared for the year
$$= 1,788,500 + 1,048,000 = \$2,836,500$$

The entire amount of retained earnings adjusted for dividends declared equals net income for the year because this is Beta's first year of operations (the change in retained earnings equals year-end retained earnings).

Translation gain (loss) = Net income − Income before translation gain/loss
$$= 2,836,500 - 2,807,625 = \$28,875$$

Balance Sheet Exposure under the Current Rate and Temporal Methods

Items translated at the *current* exchange rate are revalued (based on changes in exchange rates) from one balance sheet date to the next in terms of the parent's presentation currency. These items are said to be exposed to translation adjustment. The presentation-currency denominated value of items translated at the *historical* exchange rate does not change. These items are therefore not exposed to translation adjustment. Exposure to translation adjustment is referred to as balance sheet translation, or accounting exposure.

- A foreign operation will have a net asset balance sheet exposure when the value of assets translated at the current exchange rate is greater than the value of liabilities translated at the current exchange rate.
- A foreign operation will have a net liability balance sheet exposure when the value of liabilities translated at the current exchange rate is greater than the value of assets translated at the current exchange rate.

Whether the current period's translation adjustment results in a gain or loss depends on (1) the nature of the balance sheet exposure (net asset versus net liability) and (2) the direction of change in the value of the foreign currency (appreciating or depreciating). Table 2-2 summarizes the relationship between the trend in the exchange rate, balance sheet exposure, and the current period translation adjustment.

Table 2-2: Balance Sheet Exposure

Balance Sheet Exposure	Foreign Currency (FC)	
	Strengthens	Weakens
Net asset	Positive translation adjustment	Negative translation adjustment
Net liability	Negative translation adjustment	Positive translation adjustment

Under the current rate method:

- The parent's foreign currency exposure equals its **net asset position** in the subsidiary.
- If the parent has a net asset (liability) exposure, an appreciating foreign currency will result in a translation gain (loss), which will be reflected in an increasing (decreasing) cumulative translation adjustment on the balance sheet.
- The current rate method usually results in a net asset balance sheet exposure (unless the entity has negative shareholders' equity, which is very rare).
  - Going back to Example 2-1, the change in the cumulative translation adjustment under the current rate method is negative (goes from zero to –$144,125) because Alpha has a net asset exposure in Beta and the foreign currency (EUR) has depreciated over the year.
- Elimination of balance sheet exposure under the current rate method is rather difficult as it would require total assets to equal total liabilities (or zero shareholders' equity in the foreign subsidiary).

Items Translated at Current Exchange Rate
Total assets > Total liabilities → Net asset balance sheet exposure

Under the temporal method:

- The parent's exposure is limited to the subsidiary's **net monetary assets (liabilities)**.
- If the parent has a net monetary asset (liability) exposure, an appreciating foreign currency will result in a translation gain (loss) on the income statement.
- Most liabilities are monetary liabilities (which are translated at the current exchange rate and entail exposure to translation adjustment), while most assets are nonmonetary assets (which are translated at historical exchange rates and do not entail exposure to translation adjustment). Therefore, liabilities translated at the current exchange rate usually exceed assets translated at the current exchange rate, which results in a net monetary liability exposure under the temporal method.
  - Going back to Example 2-1, there is a translation gain ($28,875) under the temporal method because Alpha has a net monetary liability exposure and the foreign currency is depreciating.
- Elimination of balance sheet exposure under the temporal method is relatively easy as the parent simply has to ensure that the monetary assets of the foreign subsidiary equal its monetary liabilities.
  - In Example 2-1, the company could eliminate its balance sheet exposure under the temporal method by reducing the net monetary liability to zero. This could be accomplished by injecting cash (equity) into the subsidiary and using the funds to retire liabilities.

Items Translated at Current Exchange Rate
Exposed assets > Exposed liabilities → Net asset balance sheet exposure
Exposed assets < Exposed liabilities → Net liability balance sheet exposure

Translation Analytical Issues

Based on the financial statements in Example 2-1, we have calculated the following ratios:

	€	Current Rate	Temporal
Gross profit margin	31.03%	31.03%	31.29%
Operating profit margin	23.10%	23.10%	23.34%
Net profit margin	14.38%	14.38%	14.76%
Return on assets	29.00%	29.56%	29.65%
Return on equity	63.47%	64.69%	63.19%
Current ratio	8.37	8.37	8.42
Debt-to-assets ratio	0.49	0.49	0.48
Debt-to-equity ratio	1.07	1.07	1.01
Interest coverage	8.07	8.07	8.15
Receivables turnover	14.95	15.24	15.24
Inventory turnover	7.14	7.28	7.14
Fixed asset turnover	3.82	3.89	3.75

- The gross profit margin is higher under the temporal method because a lower rate is applied to translate COGS in the temporal method (1.32$/€) than in the current rate method (1.325$/€).
- The net profit margin is higher under the temporal method (14.76%) compared to the current rate method (14.38%) primarily because the translation gain ($28,875) is included in net income under the temporal method.
- The combination of a higher net income under the temporal method and a negative cumulative translation adjustment (−$144,125) on the balance sheet under the current rate method results in a lower amount of shareholders' equity under the current rate method.
- Total assets are also lower under the current rate method because all assets are translated at the current exchange rate (1.30$/€), which is lower than the historical exchange rates at which inventory (1.32$/€) and fixed assets (1.35$/€) are translated under the temporal method.

- Financial ratios calculated from Beta's financial statements differ based on which translation method is applied (current rate method versus temporal method). To analyze the impact of the choice of translation method on financial ratios, we must identify the exchange rate at which the numerator and denominator are translated, compare the relative changes in the translated values of the numerator and denominator, and then determine the impact on the ratio.
  - For example, the current ratio is different under the two methods (current rate: 8.37; temporal: 8.42) because inventory is translated at the current exchange rate (1.30$/€) in the current rate method, and at the historical exchange rate (weighted average exchange rate for inventory = 1.32$/€) under the temporal method. Since the EUR has depreciated over the year (i.e., the $/€ exchange rate has decreased), inventory (and therefore current assets) is higher under the temporal method.
  - Only the receivables turnover ratio is the same across both methods. This is because sales are translated at the average exchange rate and receivables are translated at the current exchange rate under both methods.
- Comparing the ratios based on EUR numbers to those computed for the current rate method, many of the underlying relationships that exist in Beta's EUR-based financial statements are **preserved** under the current rate method (see Example 2-2).
  - Pure balance sheet ratios (where the numerator and denominator are both balance sheet items) and pure income statement ratios (where the numerator and denominator are both income statement items) are the same in EUR and current rate method.
    - For example, the current ratio, leverage ratios, the interest coverage ratio, and profit margins are the same in EUR and current rate method.
  - Mixed ratios (where one of the inputs comes from the balance sheet and the other from the income statement) are different in EUR and current rate method.

> It is important to note that our analysis of these ratios is based on end-of-period balance sheet figures.

  - In our example, mixed ratios (turnover ratios, ROA, and ROE) are higher under the current rate method compared to the ratios based on EUR financial statements.
    - These ratios have income statement items (that are translated at the average rate) in the numerator and balance sheet items (that are translated at the current rate) in the denominator.
    - Since the average exchange rate (1.325$/€) is *greater* than the current exchange rate (1.30$/€)—i.e., EUR has *depreciated* over the year—the ratios are *higher* under the current rate method compared to the EUR financial statements.
    - If the EUR had *appreciated* over the year, these mixed ratios would be *lower* under the current rate method compared to the EUR financial statements.
- Comparing the ratios based on EUR numbers to those computed for the temporal method, all of the underlying relationships (except for inventory turnover) that exist in Beta's EUR-based financial statements are **distorted** under the temporal method. For example:
  - Receivables turnover is larger under the temporal method (15.24) compared to the ratio based on EUR amounts (14.95). Sales are translated at the average rate (1.325$/€), while accounts receivable are translated at the current rate (1.30$/€). Since the average exchange rate is greater than the current exchange rate (EUR has depreciated over the year), receivables turnover is higher under the temporal method compared to EUR financial statements.

- Inventory turnover is the same (7.14) as both inventory and COGS are translated at the historical exchange rate (1.32$/€).
- Fixed asset turnover is lower under the temporal method (3.75) compared to the ratio based on EUR amounts (3.82). Sales are translated at the average rate (1.325$/€), while PP&E and related expenses are translated at the historical rate (1.35$/€). Since the average exchange rate is lower than the historical exchange rate, fixed asset turnover is lower under the temporal method compared to EUR financial statements.
- Therefore, it is not possible to generalize the direction of distortion across ratios when using the temporal method. For each ratio we must identify the exchange rate at which the numerator and denominator are translated, compare the relative changes in the translated values of the numerator and denominator, and then determine the overall impact on the ratio.

Example 2-2: Calculating Cumulative Translation Adjustment under the Current Rate Method

An analyst gathered the following information regarding a company:

Retained earnings at January 1, 2010 = $550,000
Cumulative translation adjustment (CTA) at January 1, 2010 = $65,000
Net income for 2010 = $1,150,000
Dividends declared at December 31, 2010 = $690,000
Total assets at December 31, 2010 = $6,575,000
Total liabilities at December 31, 2010 = $3,485,000
Common stock = $2,000,000

Calculate the ending balance of the cumulative translation adjustment and translation gain for the period.

Solution:

Retained earnings at the end of the year equals beginning retained earnings plus net income for the year minus dividends declared.

$$\text{Retained earnings at December 31, 2010} = 550,000 + 1,150,000 - 690,000 = \$1,010,000$$

The ending value of the cumulative translation adjustment is the amount that must be plugged into the year-end balance sheet to make sure that the accounting equation holds (i.e., the balance sheet balances).

$$\text{Ending CTA} = \text{Total assets} - \text{Total liabilities} - \text{Common stock} - \text{Retained earnings}$$
$$= 6,575,000 - 3,485,000 - 2,000,000 - 1,010,000 = \$80,000$$

The translation gain/loss over the period is measured as the change in CTA over the year. The positive change in the CTA indicates that there was a translation gain over 2010.

$$\text{Translation gain for the period} = 80,000 - 65,000 = \$15,000$$

Differences in the Results of the Temporal and Current Rate Method

- Income before translation gain/loss is different under the two methods.
  - The current rate method uses the average rate for depreciation and COGS.
  - The temporal method uses historical rates for depreciation and COGS.
- The translation gain/loss is different under the two methods.
  - Exposure under the current rate method equals the subsidiaries' net assets.
  - Exposure under the temporal method equals the subsidiaries' net monetary assets.
- Net income is different between the two methods.
  - COGS and depreciation are translated at different rates under the two methods.
  - Under the current rate method the translation gain/loss is reported in shareholders' equity. Under the temporal method it is reported on the income statement.
- Total assets are different between the two methods.
  - Inventory and fixed assets are translated at current rates under the current rate method, but at historical rates under the temporal method.

Effects of Direction of Change in the Exchange Rate on Translated Amounts

Current Rate Method

Compared to a scenario where the exchange rate remains stable:

- If the foreign currency appreciates against the parent's presentation currency, revenues, assets, liabilities, and total equity reported on the parent's consolidated financial statements will be higher.
- If the foreign currency depreciates against the parent's presentation currency, revenues, assets, liabilities, and total equity reported on the parent's consolidated financial statements will be lower.

Temporal Method

Compared to a scenario where the exchange rate remains stable:

- If the foreign currency appreciates against the parent's presentation currency, revenues, assets, and liabilities reported on the parent's consolidated financial statements will be higher. However, net income and shareholders' equity will translate into lower amounts (assuming that the subsidiary has a net monetary liability exposure) because of the translation loss.
- If the foreign currency depreciates against the parent's presentation currency, revenues, assets, and liabilities reported on the parent's consolidated financial statements will be lower. However, net income and shareholders' equity will translate into higher amounts (assuming that the subsidiary has a net monetary liability exposure) because of the translation gain.

Table 2-3 summarizes the effects of exchange rate movements on financial statements.

Table 2-3: Effects of Exchange Rate Movements on Financial Statements[1]

	Temporal Method, Net Monetary Liability Exposure	Temporal Method, Net Monetary Asset Exposure	Current Rate Method
Foreign currency strengthens relative to parent's presentation currency	↑ Revenues ↑ Assets ↑ Liabilities ↓ Net income ↓ Shareholders' equity Translation loss	↑ Revenues ↑ Assets ↑ Liabilities ↑ Net income ↑ Shareholders' equity Translation gain	↑ Revenues ↑ Assets ↑ Liabilities ↑ Net income ↑ Shareholders' equity Positive translation adjustment
Foreign currency weakens relative to parent's presentation currency	↓ Revenues ↓ Assets ↓ Liabilities ↑ Net income ↑ Shareholders' equity Translation gain	↓ Revenues ↓ Assets ↓ Liabilities ↓ Net income ↓ Shareholders' equity Translation loss	↓ Revenues ↓ Assets ↓ Liabilities ↓ Net income ↓ Shareholders' equity Negative translation adjustment

LESSON 3: TRANSLATION OF FOREIGN CURRENCY FINANCIAL STATEMENTS: HYPERINFLATIONARY ECONOMICS

LOS 18g: Analyze how alternative translation methods for subsidiaries operating in hyperinflationary economies affect financial statements and ratios. Vol 2, pp 140–145, 158–162

Hyperinflationary Economies

In an economy that is experiencing high inflation, the local currency loses purchasing power within the local economy, and tends to depreciate relative to other currencies. As the currency loses value, translating the historical cost of fixed assets such as PP&E at successively lower and lower exchange rates causes the translated value of these assets to diminish on the parent's balance sheet (known as the disappearing plant problem).

> When a foreign entity is located in a highly inflationary economy, the entity's functional currency is not considered in determining the applicable translation method.

Practically speaking however, the value of these assets in terms of local currency would be expected to rise with inflation. While IFRS allows adjusting nonmonetary assets and liabilities for inflation, U.S. GAAP does not.

Under **U.S. GAAP**, the functional currency is assumed to be the parent's presentation currency and the temporal method is used to translate the subsidiary's financial statements. The translation gain/loss is included in net income.

1 - Exhibit 5, Volumed 2, CFA Program Curriculum 2017

Under **IFRS**, the subsidiary's foreign currency accounts are restated for inflation (using the procedures described below) and then translated into the parent's presentation currency using the current exchange rate.

- Nonmonetary assets and liabilities are restated for changes in the general purchasing power of the local currency.
  - ○ Nonmonetary items carried at historical cost are restated for inflation by multiplying their values by the change in the general price index from the date of acquisition to the balance sheet date.
  - ○ Nonmonetary items carried at revalued amounts are restated for inflation by multiplying their revised values by the change in the general price index from the date of revaluation to the balance sheet date.
- Monetary assets and liabilities (e.g., cash, receivables, and payables) are not restated for inflation.
- Shareholders' equity accounts are restated for inflation by multiplying their values by the change in the general price index from the beginning of the period, or from the date of contribution (if later), till the balance sheet date.
- Income statement items are restated for inflation by multiplying their values by the change in the general price index from the dates when the items were originally recorded till the balance sheet date.
- All items are then translated into the parent's presentation currency using the current exchange rate.
- The gain/loss in purchasing power is recorded on the income statement.

> Purchasing power gains and losses from inflation are similar to translation gains and losses from depreciation of the foreign currency when the temporal method is applied. A net monetary liability exposure combined with hyperinflation gives rise to purchasing power gains. A net monetary liability exposure combined with foreign currency depreciation gives rise to translation gains.

Under this method, a company's net monetary asset (liability) position is exposed to inflation risk as monetary assets and liabilities are not restated for inflation. In an inflationary environment, borrowers (who have payables) gain while lenders (who hold receivables) lose out. Therefore, a company will recognize a purchasing power gain (loss) if it holds more monetary liabilities (assets) than monetary assets (liabilities). See Example 3-1.

Example 3-1: A Foreign Subsidiary Operating in a High-Inflation Country

Mercury Inc. formed a subsidiary in a foreign country on January 1, 2010. Selected financial statement information regarding the subsidiary in units of foreign currency (FC) is provided below:

Income Statement	2010 (FC)
Revenue	1,500
Interest expense	550
Net income	**950**

Balance Sheet	January 1, 2010 (FC)	December 31, 2010 (FC)
Cash	1,000	1,950
Fixed assets	9,000	9,000
Total assets	**10,000**	**10,950**
Notes payable	5,000	5,000
Capital stock	5,000	5,000
Retained earnings	0	950
Total Liabilities and Equity	**10,000**	**10,950**

The foreign country experienced significant inflation during 2010. The general price index (GPI) during 2010 was:

Date	GPI
January 1, 2010	100
Average, 2010	160
December 31, 2010	200

Due to the high inflation rate, the foreign currency depreciated significantly during 2010. The following table shows the exchange rate between the USD (Mercury's presentation currency) and FC:

Date	$/FC
January 1, 2010	1.400
Average, 2010	0.875
December 31, 2010	0.700

Translate the foreign subsidiary's financial statements into the parent's presentation currency based on IFRS and U.S. GAAP assuming that the foreign country falls under the definition of a highly inflationary economy.

Solution:

IFRS
- Nonmonetary items are restated for inflation (by applying the change in GPI from the date of acquisition) and then translated into USD at the current exchange rate.
- Monetary items are not restated for inflation and are translated into USD at the current exchange rate.

Balance Sheet

	FC	Restatement Factor	Inflation-Adjusted FC	Exchange Rate	$
Cash	1,950	N/A	1,950	0.70 (C)	1,365
Fixed assets	9,000	200/100	18,000	0.70 (C)	12,600
Total	**10,950**		**19,950**		**13,965**
Notes payable	5,000	N/A	5,000	0.70 (C)	3,500
Capital stock	5,000	200/100	10,000	0.70 (C)	7,000
Retained earnings	950		4,950	0.70 (C)	3,465
Total	**10,950**		**19,950**		**13,965**

The inflation-adjusted value of total assets is FC 19,950. Given inflation-adjusted notes payable and capital stock of FC 5,000 and FC 10,000, respectively, inflation-adjusted retained earnings amount to FC 4,950.

Inflation-adjusted retained earnings are then used to compute the purchasing power gain (loss) on the income statement. Income statement items are restated for inflation (by applying the change in GPI from the average GPI over the period) and then translated into USD at the current exchange rate.

Since this is the subsidiary's first year of operations, it is assumed that the purchase of fixed assets and investment of capital were undertaken on January 1, 2010. Therefore, the change in GPI when restating these items for inflation is based on the GPI on January 1, 2010.

Income Statement

	FC	Restatement Factor	Inflation-Adjusted FC	Exchange Rate	$
Revenue	1,500	200/160	1,875.00	0.70 (C)	1,312.50
Interest expense	550	200/160	687.50	0.70 (C)	481.25
Subtotal	**950**		**1,187.50**		**831.25**
Purchasing power gain/loss			3,762.50	0.70 (C)	2,633.75
Net income			**4,950.00**		**3,465.00**

Given inflation-adjusted retained earnings of FC 4,950 and inflation-adjusted revenues and expenses of FC 1,875 and FC 687.50, respectively, the purchasing power gain (loss) equals FC 3,762.50 or USD 2,633.75.

The net purchasing power gain of FC 3,762.50 can be explained as follows:

- Gain from having notes payable:
  - FC 5,000 × (200 − 100)/100 = FC 5,000
- Loss from holding beginning cash balance:
  - −FC 1,000 × (200 − 100)/100 = −FC 1,000
- Loss from increase in cash over the year:
  - −FC 950 × (200 − 160)/160 = −FC 237.50
- Net purchasing power gain (loss) = 5,000 − 1,000 − 237.50 = FC 3,762.50

Note that under this method, all FC amounts (adjusted for inflation where required) are translated at the current exchange rate so there is no exposure to exchange rate risk. Therefore, no translation adjustment is required.

U.S. GAAP

The temporal method is used to translate the foreign subsidiary's financial statements into the parent's presentation currency:

Balance Sheet

	FC	Exchange Rate	$
Cash	1,950	0.70 (C)	1,365
Fixed assets	9,000	1.40 (H)	12,600
Total assets	**10,950**		**13,965**
Notes payable	5,000	0.70 (C)	3,500
Capital stock	5,000	1.40 (H)	7,000
Retained earnings (balancing figure)	950		3,465
Total Liabilities and Equity	**10,950**		**13,965**

The translation gain (loss) appears on the income statement.

Income Statement

	FC	Exchange Rate	$
Revenue	1,500	0.875 (A)	1,312.50
Interest expense	550	0.875 (A)	481.25
Subtotal	950		831.25
Translation gain/loss			2,633.75
Net income			**3,465.00**

Since this is the subsidiary's first year of operations, the entire amount of retained earnings is attributable to the current year's net income (dividends declared equal 0).

You should note here that the purchasing power gain calculated under IFRS ($2,633.75) is the same as the translation gain calculated under U.S. GAAP ($2,633.75). This is not always the case. However, in the given scenario, there is an exact one-to-one inverse relationship between the change in the GPI in the foreign country and the value of the FC relative to the USD, which results in equal purchasing power and translation gains.

- The GPI doubled so the FC lost half its purchasing power.
- The dollar value of the FC also halved (from $1.40/FC to $0.70/FC).

Defining a High-Inflation Economy

- U.S. GAAP defines a highly inflationary economy as one where the cumulative three-year inflation rate exceeds 100%, which equates to an average of approximately 26% per year.
- IFRS provides no specific definition of high inflation, but does indicate that a cumulative three-year inflation rate approaching or exceeding 100% indicates high inflation.

Translation Disclosures and Analysis

Under both IFRS and U.S.GAAP, companies are required to disclose:

- The total amount of exchange differences (foreign currency transaction and translation gains and losses) recognized in net income. Companies are not required to separate foreign currency transaction gains and losses from gains and losses arising from applying the temporal method (translation gains and losses) on the income statement.
- The total amount of cumulative translation adjustment classified as a separate component of shareholders' equity, as well as a reconciliation of the amount of cumulative translation adjustment at the beginning and end of the period.

Further, note that:

- Disclosures relating to foreign currency translation are typically found in the MD&A section and the notes to the financial statements in the annual report.
- Multinational companies typically have several subsidiaries in different regions so the translation gain/loss on the income statement and cumulative translation adjustment on the balance sheet include the effects of translation of foreign currency accounts of all the parent's subsidiaries. Disclosures relating to the parent's exposures to individual currencies are limited.
- Because of the judgment involved in determining the functional currency, two companies operating in the same industry may use different predominant translation methods. As a result, net income reported by these companies would not be directly comparable. In order to facilitate comparisons across companies, analysts may add the change in CTA over the year to net income for the year. This adjustment where gains/losses that are reported directly in equity are instead reported in net income is known as clean surplus accounting. However, note that this adjustment would not exactly make the two companies truly comparable.

> Under dirty surplus accounting certain gains/losses are included in shareholders' equity directly under comprehensive income. Examples of dirty surplus items include unrealized gains and losses on available-for-sale securities.

Suppose that we have two parent companies (Parent X and Parent Y) that each have one subsidiary. Further, these two subsidiaries exhibit the exact same financial performance over a given period. Assume that the financial statements presented in Example 3-1 pertain to these subsidiaries and that Parent X classifies the local currency as the functional currency, while Parent Y classifies the presentation currency as the functional currency:

- Parent X, who classifies the local currency as the functional currency and therefore uses the current rate method, would report a translation loss of $144,125 (as part of shareholders' equity).
- Parent Y, who classifies its presentation currency as the functional currency and therefore uses the temporal method, would report a translation gain of $28,875 on its income statement.

Even if an analyst were to adjust the income statement of Parent X by reflecting the translation loss (reported in shareholders' equity) in net income, the companies would still not be truly comparable. The parent's choice of functional currency influences the translation method applicable and, crucially, balance sheet exposure under the two translation methods is different. Therefore, even though the subsidiaries' performance over the period was identical (in terms of their local currency), the different balance sheet exposures under the two methods give rise to a gain for one parent and a loss for the other.

Stated differently, if Parent X were to use the presentation currency as the functional currency, not only would the impact of the translation adjustment be reflected on its income statement, but it would also incur a translation gain (not a loss). See Example 3-2.

Example 3-2: Disclosures Related to Foreign Currency Translation

Grey Matter Technologies (GMT) is a U.S. multinational. The following information is extracted from the company's financial statements:

Table 3-1: Extract from Shareholders' Equity Section of Balance Sheet

	2010	2011
Common stock	1,206	1,157
Additional paid-in capital	9,254,886	8,736,214
Treasury stock	(215,236)	(452,865)
Retained earnings	1,726,547	2,314,587
Acculumated other comprehensive income (loss)	456,821	523,584
Total Shareholders' Equity	**11,224,224**	**11,122,677**

Table 3-2: Extract from Consolidated Statement of Shareholders' Equity

	2009	2010	2011
Acculumated other comprehensive income			
Beginning balance	145,283	392,560	456,821
Change in unrealized gains/losses on AFS securities net of tax	(2,345)	3,547	(10,584)
Foreign currency translation adjustments net of tax	249,622	60,714	77,347
Ending balance	**392,560**	**456,821**	**523,584**

Table 3-3: Consolidated Net Income

	2010	2011	% Change
Net income	1,358,214	1,236,811	−8.94%

Table 3-4: Selected Information from Financial Statement Disclosures

	2009	2010	2011
Revenue ex-TAC by segment			
Americas	2,589,412	2,358,112	2,158,745
EMEA	598,745	568,521	632,514
Asia Pacific	385,124	489,652	587,425
Total revenue ex-TAC	**3,573,281**	**3,416,285**	**3,378,684**
Direct costs by segment			
Americas	584,251	542,158	536,854
EMEA	110,258	113,581	132,148
Asia Pacific	132,584	145,821	212,584

The MD&A section contains the following details regarding sources of GMT's translation exposure:

- The conversion of foreign subsidiaries' financial statements into USD results in a gain or loss that is recorded as a component of other comprehensive income under shareholders' equity.
- Financial statements of international operations are translated into USD at exchange rates indicative of market rates during each applicable period.
- If foreign exchange rates as of December 31, 2010, were used for the translation exercise, revenues from:
    - Americas would have been lower than reported by $4,000
    - EMEA would have been lower than reported by 12,000
    - Asia Pacific would have been lower than reported by 35,000
- If foreign exchange rates as of December 31, 2010, were used for the translation exercise, costs from:
    - Americas would have been lower than reported by $3,000
    - EMEA would have been lower than reported by 4,000
    - Asia Pacific would have been lower than reported by 14,000

Use the information provided to answer the following questions:

1. What was the change in accumulated other comprehensive income during 2011?
2. What adjustment related to foreign currency translation was included in other comprehensive income for 2011?
3. Instead of being included in other comprehensive income, if the foreign currency translation adjustment were included in net income, what would have the change in income from 2010 to 2011 been?
4. What percentage of 2011 total revenue ex-TAC was generated by the Asia-Pacific segment? What would this percentage have been if there had been no change in exchange rates during the year?

Solution:

1. Accumulated other comprehensive income increased by $66,763 (from $456,821 at the end of 2010 to $523,584 at the end of 2011). Note that this information can be found in (1) the shareholders' equity section of the balance sheet and (2) the consolidated statement of shareholders' equity.
2. The foreign currency translation adjustment included in GMT's other comprehensive income for 2011 amounted to $77,347. The positive adjustment arises as the foreign subsidiaries (like most companies) typically have positive net assets and foreign currencies (relating to all three of GMT's geographical segments) have appreciated versus the USD over the period. We can infer that foreign currencies have appreciated versus the USD during 2011 because the MD&A section states that revenues and costs for all three foreign segments would have been **lower** if 2010 exchange rates were used instead of those from 2011.

3. If the (positive) foreign currency translation adjustments for 2010 and 2011 had been included in net income rather than in other comprehensive income, net income would have been higher for both years. The percentage decrease in reported net income from 2010 to 2011 would have been 7.38% instead of 8.94%.

	2010	2011	% Change
Net income	1,358,214	1,236,811	−8.94%
Foreign currency translation adjustment	60,714	77,347	
	1,418,928	**1,314,158**	**−7.38%**

4. Based on the numbers reported, the Asia-Pacific segment represented 17.39% of total revenue ex-TAC. If there had been no change in exchange rates during the year, the segment would have represented a slightly lower percentage of total revenue, (i.e., 16.6%).

	2011, as reported			2011, if no change in exc. rates	
Revenue ex-TAC by segment					
Americas	2,158,745	63.89%	4,000	2,154,745	64.75%
EMEA	632,514	18.72%	12,000	620,514	18.65%
Asia Pacific	587,425	17.39%	35,000	552,425	16.60%
Total revenue by ex-TAC	**3,378,684**	**100.00%**		**3,327,684**	**100.00%**

LESSON 4: MULTINATIONAL OPERATIONS AND THE COMPANY'S EFFECTIVE TAX RATE AND FOREIGN CURRENCY–RELATED DISCLOSURES

LOS 18h: Describe how multinational operations affect a company's effective tax rate. Vol 2, pp 169–172

LOS 18i: Explain how changes in the components of sales affect the sustainability of sales growth. Vol 2, pp 172–175

LOS 18j: Analyze how currency fluctuations potentially affect financial results, given a company's countries of operation. Vol 2, pp 175–176

MULTINATIONAL OPERATIONS AND A COMPANY'S EFFECTIVE TAX RATE

Generally speaking, multinational companies are liable to pay income taxes in the country in which the profit is earned. The allocation of profit across subsidiaries (and countries) is affected by transfer prices (i.e., the prices at which divisions within the company transact with each other). Entities with operations in multiple countries with different tax rates have an incentive to set transfer prices such that a higher portion of profits is allocated to lower tax rate jurisdictions. This has prompted countries to establish various laws and practices to prevent aggressive transfer pricing practices.

Most countries are bound by tax treaties that prevent double-taxation of corporate profits. For example, in the United States, multinationals are liable only for a residual tax on foreign income, after applying a credit for foreign taxes paid on that same income. As a result, the multinational owes the IRS taxes on the foreign income only to the extent that the U.S. corporate tax rate exceeds the foreign rate of tax on that income. Further, much of the foreign income earned by U.S. multinationals is not taxed until it is repatriated.

Accounting standards require companies to explain the relationship between tax expense and accounting profit in a detailed reconciliation between the average effective tax rate (tax expense divided by pretax accounting profits) and the relevant statutory tax rate. Changes in impact of foreign taxes on the parent's effective tax rate can be caused by (1) changes in applicable tax rates and/or (2) changes in the mix of profits earned in different countries (with different tax rates). See Example 4-1.

Example 4-1: Evaluating the Impact of Foreign Taxes on a Company's Effective Tax Rate

Below are the extracts from effective tax rate reconciliation disclosures of two hypothetical companies: ABC Inc. and XYZ Inc.

ABC Inc.	2012	2011	2010
Income tax using the company's domestic tax rate	26%	26.5%	26.5%
Effect of tax rates in foreign jurisdictions	4.5	3.2	2.3
Effect of nondeductible expenses	3	4.2	5
Effect of tax incentives and exempt income	(5)	(6)	(8)
Recognition of previously unrecognized tax losses	(1.8)	(1)	(0.8)
Effect of changes in tax rate	0.3	0.4	0.6
Withholding taxes	2.5	2.2	1.7
Under/(over) provided in prior years	(3.1)	(4.2)	(5.5)
Other reconciling items	0.3	0.6	0.8
	26.7%	25.9%	22.6%

XYZ Inc.: Percentage of Income before Income Taxes	2012	2011	2010
Tax at United States statutory rate	32%	32%	32%
State income taxes, net of federal benefit	0.6	2	1.1
Earnings taxed at other than United States statutory rate	(2.3)	(5)	(3.6)
Other, net	(2.2)	(2.8)	(1.5)
Effective tax rate	**28.1%**	**26.2%**	**28%**

Based on the information provided, answer the following questions:

1. Which company's home country has a lower statutory tax rate?
2. What was the impact of multinational operations on each company's effective tax rate for 2012?
3. What do ABC's disclosures suggest about the geographic mix of its 2012 profits?

Solution:

1. ABC's home country's statutory tax rate (26% in 2012) is lower than XYZ's home country statutory tax rate (32% in 2012).
2. The impact of foreign taxes/multinational operations on ABC's effective tax rate can be gauged by looking at the line item labeled "Effect of tax rates in foreign jurisdictions." This line item indicates that multinational operations increased ABC's effective tax rate for 2012 by 4.5%. For XYZ, we look at "Earnings taxed at other than United States statutory rate," which indicates that multinational operations lowered XYZ's effective tax rate by 2.3% in 2012.
3. Changes of profit mix between countries with higher or lower marginal tax rates result in changes in the tax rate impact of multinational operations. Multinational operations increased ABC's effective tax rate by 4.5% in 2012, but by only 3.2% in 2011. This more significant impact in 2012 could indicate that ABC's profit mix in 2012 moved to countries with higher statutory tax rates.

Additional Disclosures on the Effects of Foreign Currency

Disclosures of multinational companies can help analysts better understand the impact of fluctuation in exchange rates on the company's performance.

Disclosures Related to Sales Growth

Companies often include disclosures related to the impact of exchange rate movements on sales growth in (1) the MD&A and sometimes in (2) other financial reports such as company presentations to investors and earnings announcements. For multinationals, sales growth can be attributed to changes in:

- Price;
- Volumes; and/or
- Exchange rates.

Analysts should consider organic sales growth (excluding foreign currency effects on sales growth) when:

- Forecasting future performance as sales growth that comes from changes in price and volumes is arguably more sustainable than growth from exchange rate movements.
- When evaluating management's performance as management typically has greater control over sales growth from changes in volume or price than from changes in exchange rates. See Example 4-2.

> It could also be possible that the more significant impact of multinational operations on ABC's effective tax rate in 2012 could be caused by increases in statutory tax rates in countries where ABC earns profits.

Example 4-2: Impact of Exchange Rate Movements on Sales Growth

The table below provides a reconciliation of Torsem Corp's reported sales growth to organic sales growth:

	Net Sales Growth	Foreign Exchange Impact	Acquisition/Divesture Impact	Organic Sales Growth
OND09	–2%	4%	0%	2%
JFM10	–7%	8%	0%	1%
APJ10	–10%	8%	1%	–1%
JAS10	–5%	7%	0%	2%
Average				
OND09-JAS10	**–6%**	**7%**	**0%**	**1%**

For the four quarters from October 2009 to September 2010, how did changes in foreign exchange rates affect Torsem's reported sales growth on average?

Solution:

Over the relevant period, on average organic sales grew 1%. However, the company reported a decline in net sales of 6% for the period. This is the result of a 7% negative impact of foreign exchange movements. Stated differently, if there were not changes in exchange rates over the period, growth in organic sales and net sales would have come in at 1%.

Disclosures Related to Major Sources of Foreign Exchange Risk

In order to assist users of financial statements, a multinational may (1) describe the source(s) of its currency risks and approach to measuring and managing those risks (usually in MD&A) and (2) present a sensitivity analysis on the effects of currency fluctuations (usually in the additional disclosures sections of the notes). The level of detail provided varies across companies.

Study Session 6: Financial Reporting and Analysis—Quality of Financial Reports and Financial Statement Analysis

READING 19: EVALUATING QUALITY OF FINANCIAL REPORTS

LESSON 1: QUALITY OF FINANCIAL REPORTS

LOS 19a: Demonstrate the use of a conceptual framework for assessing the quality of a company's financial reports. Vol 2, pp 195–197

Quality of Financial Reports

Conceptual Framework for Assessing the Quality of Financial Reports

There are two interrelated attributes used for assessing the quality of a company's financial statements: (1) financial reporting quality and (2) earnings quality.

- Financial reporting quality refers to the usefulness of information contained in the financial reports, including disclosures in the notes.
    - High-quality reporting provides information that is useful in investment decision making in that it is relevant and faithfully represents the company's performance and position.
- Earnings quality (or results quality) pertains to the earnings and cash generated by the company's core economic activities and its resulting financial condition.
    - High-quality earnings (1) come from activities that the company will be able to sustain in the future, and (2) provide an adequate return on the company's investment.
    - Note that the term **earnings quality** encompasses quality of earnings, cash flow, and balance sheet items.

These two attributes are interrelated because earnings quality cannot be evaluated until there is some assurance regarding the quality of financial reporting. If financial reporting quality is low, the information provided is not useful in evaluating company performance or for making investment decisions. Figure 1-1 illustrates this interrelationship and its implications.

Figure 1-1: Relationship between Financial Reporting Quality and Earnings Quality

		Financial Reporting Quality	
		Low	High
Earnings (Results) Quality	High	LOW financial reporting quality impedes assessment of earnings quality and impedes valuation.	HIGH financial reporting quality enables assessment. HIGH earnings quality increases company value.
	Low		HIGH financial reporting quality enables assessment. LOW earnings quality decreases company value.

The two measures of quality can be combined such that the overall quality of financial reports from a user perspective can be thought of as spanning a continuum from the highest to the lowest (see Figure 1-2).

Figure 1-2: Quality Spectrum of Financial Reports

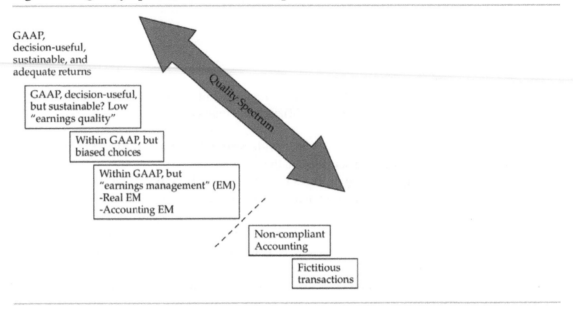

When evaluating the quality of financial statements, an analyst must consider two basic questions:

1. Are the financial reports GAAP-compliant and decision-useful?
2. Do the company's earnings provide an adequate level of return, and are they sustainable?

GAAP, Decision-Useful, Sustainable, and Adequate Returns

These are high-quality reports that provide useful information about high-quality earnings.

High-quality financial reports:

- Conform to the accounting standards acceptable in the company's jurisdiction.
- Embody the fundamental characteristics of useful information (i.e., relevance and faithful representation).

High-quality earnings:

- Indicate an adequate return on investments.
- Are primarily derived from activities that the company will likely be able to sustain in the future.

GAAP, Decision-Useful, but Sustainable?

This level refers to a situation where high-quality reporting provides useful information, but the economic reality being depicted is not of high quality (i.e., earnings do not provide an adequate rate of return or they are not expected to recur).

Within GAAP, but Biased Accounting Choices

This level refers to a situation where high-quality reporting provides useful information, but biased choices result in financial reports that do not faithfully represent the company's true economic situation.

- Management can make aggressive or conservative accounting choices, both of which go against the concept of neutrality, as *unbiased* financial reporting is the ideal.
  - Aggressive choices increase a company's reported financial performance and financial position in the current period.
    - Note that aggressive accounting choices in the current period may lead to depressed reported financial performance and financial position in later periods, thereby creating a sustainability issue.
  - Conservative choices decrease a company's reported financial performance and financial position in the current period.
    - Note that conservative accounting choices in the current period may lead to improved reported financial performance and financial position in later periods. Therefore, they do not give rise to a sustainability issue.
- Aside from biases in determining reported amounts, biases can also creep into the way information is presented. A company may choose to present information in a manner that obscures unfavorable information and/or highlights favorable information.

Note that as we go down the spectrum the concepts of reporting quality and earnings quality become less distinguishable. It is necessary to have some degree of reporting quality in order to assess earnings quality.

Within GAAP, but "Earnings Management"

This level refers to a situation where high-quality reporting provides useful information, but where earnings are "managed." Earnings management can be defined as "making intentional choices or taking deliberate action to influence reported earnings and their interpretation." There are two ways that earnings can be managed:

- By taking real actions.
  - For example, a company may defer R&D expenses until the next year to improve reported performance in the current year.
- Through accounting choices.
  - For example, a company may change certain accounting estimates such as estimated product returns, bad debts expense, or asset impairment to manipulate reported performance.

Departures from GAAP: Non-Compliant Accounting

This level reflects financial information that deviates from GAAP. Such financial information cannot be used to assess earnings quality, as comparisons with other entities or earlier periods cannot be made.

Departures from GAAP: Fictitious Transactions

The level reflects the lowest quality of financial reports, where actual transactions are omitted and/or fictitious transactions are reported.

LOS 19b: Explain potential problems that affect the quality of financial reports. Vol 2, pp 197–209

Potential Problems That Affect the Quality of Financial Reports

The basic choices that can create issues relating to the quality of financial reports include (1) reported amounts and timing of recognition and (2) classification.

Reported Amounts and Timing of Recognition

While the choice regarding the reported amount and timing of recognition may focus on a single financial statement element (assets, liabilities, owners' equity, revenues and gains, or expenses and losses), it can affect other elements as well. This is because financial statements are interrelated (think about the basic accounting equation). In the bullets that follow, we list some examples of choices and describe their impact. Note that most of these choices comply with GAAP, some of them depart from GAAP, while others are operating choices:

- Aggressive, premature, and fictitious revenue recognition results in overstated income and, consequently, overstated equity. Further, assets (typically accounts receivable) are also overstated.
- Conservative revenue recognition, such as deferred recognition of revenue, results in understated net income, understated equity, and understated assets.
- Omission and delayed recognition of expenses results in understated expenses and overstated income, overstated equity, overstated assets, and/or understated liabilities.
    - An understatement of bad debt expense results in overstated accounts receivable.
    - Understated depreciation or amortization results in overstated long-lived assets.
    - Understated interest, taxes, or other expenses result in understated related liabilities (accrued interest payable, taxes payable, or other payables).
- Understatement of contingent liabilities comes with overstated equity resulting from understated expenses and overstated income or overstated other comprehensive income.
- For financial assets and liabilities that must be reported at fair value, overstatement of financial assets and understatement of financial liabilities come with associated overstated equity resulting from overstated unrealized gains or understated unrealized losses.
- Cash flow from operations may be increased by deferring payments on payables, accelerating payments from customers, deferring purchases of inventory, and deferring other expenditures (e.g., maintenance and research).

Example 1-1: Fictitious Reports

Satyam Computer Services Limited, an Indian information technology company, was founded in 1987 and grew rapidly by providing business process outsourcing (BPO) on a global basis. In 2007, its CEO, Ramalinga Raju, was named "Entrepreneur of the Year" by Ernst & Young, and in 2008, the World Council for Corporate Governance recognized the company for "global excellence in corporate accountability." In 2009, the CEO submitted a letter of resignation that outlined a massive financial fraud at the company. The company's decline was so rapid and significant that it came to be referred to as "India's Enron."

In late 2008, the World Bank terminated its relationship with the company after finding that Satyam gave kickbacks to bank staff and billed for services that were not provided. These initial revelations of wrongdoing had the effect of putting the company under increased scrutiny. Among other misconduct, the CEO eventually admitted that he created fictitious bank statements to inflate cash balances and to show interest income. The CEO also created fake salary accounts and took the money paid to those "employees." The company's head of internal auditing created fictitious customer accounts and invoices to inflate revenues.

The external auditors did not independently verify much of the information provided by the company. Even when bank confirmations, which were sent to them directly as opposed to indirectly through Satyam, contained significantly different balances than those reported by Satyam, they did not follow up.

Explain each of the following misconducts with reference to the basic accounting equation:

A. Transactions with World Bank
B. Fictitious interest income
C. CEO's embezzlement
D. Fictitious revenue

Solution:

A. Upon billing for fictitious services, the company would (1) increase an asset account (e.g., accounts receivable) and (2) increase a revenue account (e.g., service revenues). If it reported the kickbacks offered, the company would (1) increase an expense account (e.g., commissions paid) and (2) either increase a liability (e.g., commissions payable) or decrease an asset (e.g., cash).

   Overall, the company's income, net assets, and equity would be overstated.

B. Fictitious interest income would result in (1) overstated income, (2) overstated assets (e.g., cash or interest receivable), and (3) overstated equity. These overstatements were hidden by falsifying revenue and cash balances.

C. The embezzlement of salaries of fictitious employees resulted in (1) an increase in expenses (e.g., salaries) and (2) a decrease in assets (e.g., cash). The understatement of income and equity was covered by the real but fraudulent decrease in cash, which was hidden by reporting incorrect revenue and cash balances.

D. Fictitious revenues would result in (1) overstated revenues, (2) overstated income, (3) overstated assets (e.g., cash or accounts receivable), and (4) overstated equity.

Classification

While choices relating to reported amounts and timing of recognition usually affect more than one financial statement element, classification choices typically relate to how an item is classified within a particular financial statement. Consider the following examples:

- A company that wants to understate accounts receivable in order to mask liquidity or revenue collection issues can reduce the accounts receivable balance by (1) selling them externally, (2) transferring them to a controlled entity, (3) converting them to notes receivable, or (4) reclassifying them within the balance sheet and reporting them as long-term receivables. Although these amounts would remain on the balance sheet as receivables of some sort, the accounts receivable balance itself would be lower, resulting in a favorable change in measures such as days' sales outstanding and receivables turnover.

- A company that wants to lower the ending inventory on its balance sheet for the current year can do so by reclassifying certain inventory costs as other assets. It could justify the classification on the grounds that those units of inventory are held in preparation for future product launches and are not expected to be sold within a year or one operating cycle. While the reasoning appears logical, the change in classification poses analytical problems as it results in (1) an increase in the inventory turnover ratio, (2) a reduction in the number of days of inventory on hand, and (3) a decrease in the current ratio. Further, a time series comparison of these ratios will produce an inconsistent history if the amount of inventory that would have been classified as "other assets" in prior periods is not disclosed.

- A company that wants to inflate reported cash flow from operations can do so by classifying activities such as sales of long-term assets as operating activities (instead of investing activities). The company can also capitalize rather than expense operating expenditures to achieve the same outcome, as the related outflow would be classified as an investing instead of as an operating activity.

- A company that wants changes in the value of its financial investments to flow through other comprehensive income rather than the income statement can classify them as "available-for-sale" instead of "held-for-trading."

Table 1-1 lists a selection of potential issues, possible actions/choices, and warning signs of low-quality financial reporting:

Table 1-1: Accounting Warning Signs[1]

Potential Issues	Possible Actions/Choices	Warning Signs
• Overstatement or non-sustainability of operating income and/or net income 　○ Overstated or accelerated revenue recognition 　○ Understated expenses 　○ Misclassification of revenue, gains, expenses, or losses	• Contingent sales with right of return, "channel stuffing" (the practice of inducing customers to order products they would otherwise not order or order at a later date through generous terms), "bill and hold" sales (encouraging customers to order goods and retain them on seller's premises) • Lessor use of finance (capital) leases • Fictitious (fraudulent) revenue • Capitalizing expenditures as assets • Lessee use of operating leases • Classifying non-operating income or gains as part of operations • Classifying ordinary expenses as non-recurring or non-operating • Reporting gains through net income and losses through other comprehensive income	• Growth in revenue higher than that of industry or peers • Increases in discounts to and returns from customers • Higher growth rate in receivables than revenue • Large proportion of revenue in final quarter of year for a non-seasonal business • Cash flow from operations is much lower than operating income • Inconsistency over time in the items included in operating revenues and operating expenses • Increases in operating margin • Aggressive accounting assumptions, such as long, depreciable lives • Losses in non-operating income or other comprehensive income and gains in operating income or net income • Compensation largely tied to financial results

1 - 2017 CFA Program Curriculum Volume 2, Exhibit 4.

Table 1-1: (*continued*)

Potential Issues	Possible Actions/Choices	Warning Signs

• Misstatement of balance sheet items (may affect income statement)
  ○ Over- or understatement of assets
  ○ Over- or understatement of liabilities
  ○ Misclassification of assets and/or liabilities
	• Choice of models and model inputs to measure fair value
	• Classification from current to non-current
	• Over- or understating reserves and allowances
	• Understating identifiable assets and overstating goodwill
		• Models and model inputs that bias fair value measures
		• Inconsistency in model inputs when measuring fair value of assets compared with that of liabilities
		• Typical current assets, such as accounts receivable and inventory, included in non-current assets
		• Allowances and reserves that fluctuate over time or are not comparable with peers
		• High goodwill value relative to total assets
		• Use of special purpose vehicles
		• Large changes in deferred tax assets and liabilities
		• Significant off-balance-sheet liabilities

• Overstatement of cash flow from operations	• Managing activities to affect cash flow from operations • Misclassifying cash flows to positively affect cash flow from operations	• Increase in accounts payable and decrease in accounts receivable and inventory • Capitalized expenditures in investing activities • Sales and leaseback • Increases in bank overdrafts

Quality Issues and Mergers and Acquisitions

Mergers and acquisitions provide opportunities and motivations to manage financial results.

- Companies that are finding it difficult to generate cash may acquire other companies to increase cash flow from operations. If the acquisition is paid for in cash, the outflow will be reported under investing cash flow (note that there may even be no outflow if the acquisition is paid for with equity), while reported consolidated cash flow from operations will include the cash flow of the acquired company. Note that this boost to cash from operations may or may not be sustainable.
- A potential acquisition may create an incentive for management to use aggressive choices or even misreport. For example:
  - Acquirers making an acquisition for stock may manipulate their reported earnings prior to the acquisition to inflate the value of shares being used to pay for the acquisition.
  - Target companies may be motivated to make choices to increase reported earnings to secure a more favorable price for their company.
  - Acquiring companies may try to manipulate earnings upward after an acquisition if they want to positively influence investors' opinion of the acquisition.
- Misreporting can also be an incentive to make an acquisition. Studies have suggested that companies engaged in intentional misreporting are more likely than non-misreporting companies to make an acquisition. They are also more likely to acquire a company that

would reduce the comparability and consistency of their financial statements (e.g., by targeting companies that have less public information and less-similar operations).

- Acquisitions also provide opportunities to make choices that affect (1) the initial consolidated balance sheet and (2) consolidated income statements in the future. As we learned in a previous reading, when a business combination occurs, the acquirer must measure and recognize all identifiable assets acquired and liabilities assumed at their fair values as of the acquisition date. The excess of the purchase price over the recognized value of the identifiable net assets acquired is reported as goodwill. Because goodwill is not amortized, management may understate the value of net assets acquired to understate depreciation/amortization charges going forward in order to inflate reported net income.

GAAP-Compliant Financial Reporting that Diverges from Economic Reality

Certain accounting standards can give rise to financial reporting that may not be reflective of economic reality, making it less useful for analysis. Consider the following examples:

- Recognition of asset impairments and restructuring charges in a single accounting period is consistent with most GAAP, even though they are both likely the results of past activities over an extended period. Analysts should, therefore, consider whether:
  - Similar events occur regularly enough such that they should be factored into estimates of permanent earnings.
    - If this is the case, analysts should "normalize" earnings by allocating the current restructuring/impairment charge(s) over past periods as well as the current period.
  - They should be regarded as one-off items that provide little information about the future earnings of the company.
    - If this is the case, analysts should simply exclude the item from normalized earnings.
- Other items that are commonly encountered by analysts include the following:
  - Revisions to estimates, such as the remaining economic lives of assets. An analyst may question whether the change has been deliberately timed to achieve a desired outcome.
  - Sudden increases in allowances and reserves. An analyst should consider whether prior estimates presented a biased version of economic reality.
  - Large accruals for losses (e.g., environmental or litigation-related liabilities). An analyst should consider whether a prior period's earnings have been overstated because of the failure to accrue these losses earlier.
- Some economic assets and liabilities may not be reflected on the financial statements (e.g., leases classified as operating leases, research and development (R&D) expenses, sales order backlogs). In these cases, the company holds assets that should produce future economic benefits for the company, but are not reflected on its financial statements.
- Finally, analysts must consider whether certain items presented in other comprehensive income should be included in their analysis as net income. Examples of these items include unrealized holding gains and losses on certain investments in equity securities and unrealized holding gains (and subsequent losses) on long-lived assets accounted for using the revaluation model (IFRS only).

LESSON 2: EVALUATING THE QUALITY OF FINANCIAL REPORTS

LOS 19c: Describe how to evaluate the quality of a company's financial reports. Vol 2, pp 209–213

LOS 19d: Evaluate the quality of a company's financial reports. Vol 2, pp 209–213

Evaluating the Quality of Financial Reports

As mentioned earlier, when it comes to evaluating the quality of financial statements, an analyst is essentially looking to answer two basic questions:

1. Are the financial reports of high quality (i.e., are they GAAP-compliant, and are they decision-useful)?
2. Are the earnings of high quality (i.e., do they provide an adequate level of return, and are they sustainable)?

General Steps to Evaluate the Quality of Financial Reports[2]

1. Develop an understanding of the company and its industry.
   * Understanding the economic activities of a company provides a basis for understanding why particular accounting principles may be appropriate and why particular financial metrics matter.
   * Understanding the accounting principles used by a company *and* its competitors provides a basis for understanding what constitutes the norm—and to assess whether a company's treatment is appropriate.
2. Learn about management.
   * Evaluate whether the company's management has any particular incentives to misreport.
   * Review disclosures about compensation and insider transactions, especially insiders' sales of the company's stock.
   * Review the disclosures concerning related-party transactions.
3. Identify significant accounting areas, especially those in which management judgment or an unusual accounting rule is a significant determinant of reported financial performance.
4. Make comparisons:
   * Compare the company's financial statements and significant disclosures in the current year's report with the financial statements and significant disclosures in the prior year's report.
     * Are there major differences in line items or in key disclosures, such as risk disclosures, segment disclosures, classification of specific expense, or revenue items?
     * Are the reasons for the changes apparent?
   * Compare the company's accounting policies with those of its closest competitors.
     * Are there significant differences?
     * If so, what is the directional effect of the differences?
   * Using ratio analysis, compare the company's performance with that of its closest competitors.

---

2 - 2017 CFA Program Curriculum Volume 2, pages 209–210.

5. Check for warnings signs of possible issues with the quality of the financial reports. For example:
   - Declining receivables turnover could suggest that some revenues are fictitious or recorded prematurely, or that the allowance for doubtful accounts is insufficient.
   - Declining inventory turnover could suggest obsolescence problems that should be recognized.
   - Net income greater than cash provided by operations could suggest that aggressive accrual accounting policies have shifted current expenses to later periods.
6. For firms operating in multiple segments by geography or product—particularly multinational firms—consider whether inventory, sales, and expenses have been shifted to make it appear that a company is positively exposed to a geographic region or product segment that the investment community considers to be a desirable growth area. An analyst may suspect that this shift is occurring if the segment is showing strong performance while the consolidated results remain static or worsen.
7. Use appropriate quantitative tools (discussed in the next section) to assess the likelihood of misreporting.

Quantitative Tools to Assess the Likelihood of Misreporting

Beneish Model

Based on several studies aimed at identifying quantitative indicators of earnings manipulation, Messod D. Beneish came up with an expression for computing the probability of manipulation (M-score).

$$M\text{-score} = -4.84 + 0.920\,(\text{DSR}) + 0.528\,(\text{GMI}) + 0.404\,(\text{AQI}) + 0.892\,(\text{SGI})$$
$$+ 0.115\,(\text{DEPI}) - 0.172\,(\text{SGAI}) + 4.670\,(\text{Accruals}) - 0.327\,(\text{LEVI})$$

M-score = Score indicating probability of earnings manipulation
DSR (days sales receivable index) = $(\text{Receivables}_t/\text{Sales}_t)/(\text{Receivables}_{t-1}/\text{Sales}_{t-1})$

- A change in the relationship between receivables and sales may indicate inappropriate revenue recognition.

GMI (gross margin index) = Gross margin$_{t-1}$/Gross margin$_t$

- A decline in the gross margin may motivate companies to manipulate earnings.

AQI (asset quality index) = $[1 - (\text{PPE}_t + \text{CA}_t)/\text{TA}_t]/[1 - (\text{PPE}_{t-1} + \text{CA}_{t-1})/\text{TA}_{t-1}]$

- PPE = Property, plant, and equipment
- CA = Current assets
- TA = Total assets
- A change in the percentage of assets other than in PPE and CA may suggest excessive capitalization of expenses.

SGI (sales growth index) = Sales$_t$/Sales$_{t-1}$

- Managing the perception of continuing growth and capital needs from actual growth could predispose companies to manipulate sales and earnings.

DEPI (depreciation index) = Depreciation rate$_{t-1}$/Depreciation rate$_t$

- Depreciation rate = Depreciation/(Depreciation + PPE)
- A declining depreciation rate may indicate that the company is understating depreciation to manipulating earnings.

SGAI (sales, general, and administrative expenses index) = $(\text{SGA}_t / \text{Sales}_t)/(\text{SGA}_{t-1}/\text{Sales}_{t-1})$

- An increase in fixed SGA expenses suggests decreasing administrative and marketing efficiency, which may induce management to manipulate earnings.

Accruals = (Income before extraordinary items – Cash from operations)/Total assets

- Higher accruals may suggest earnings manipulation.

LEVI (leverage index) = $\text{Leverage}_t/\text{Leverage}_{t-1}$

- Leverage = Debt/Assets
- Increasing leverage could induce management to manipulate earnings.

The *M*-score in the Beneish model is a normally distributed random variable with a mean of 0 and a standard deviation of 1.0. In order to determine the probability of earnings manipulation suggested by an *M*-score, one simply needs to look up the normal distribution statistical table. For example, an *M*-score of –1.49 indicates that the probability of earnings manipulation is 6.8%.

- The higher the *M*-score (i.e., the less negative the number), the higher the probability of earnings manipulation.
- Generally speaking, a probability of earnings manipulation greater than 3.75% (corresponding to an *M*-score greater than –1.78) is considered a higher-than-acceptable probability of manipulation.

Example 2-1: Application of the Beneish Model

The following table presents the variables and Beneish's *M*-score for ABC Company:

	Value of Variable	Coefficient from Beneish Model	Calculations
DSR	1.2	0.92	1.104
GMI	1.2	0.528	0.6336
AQI	0.7	0.404	0.2828
SGI	1.2	0.892	1.0704
DEPI	1.1	0.115	0.1265
SGAI	0.7	–0.172	–0.1204
Accruals	0.1	4.67	0.467
LEVI	0.5	–0.327	–0.1635
Intercept			–4.25
M-score			–0.8496
Probability of manipulation			19.77%

1. Using an *M*-score of –1.78 as a cutoff, would the results presented lead an analyst to conclude that ABC is a likely manipulator?
2. What do the values of DSR, GMI, SGI, and DEPI (all greater than 1) indicate regarding the company?

Solution:

1. Based on the results presented, an analyst would likely conclude that ABC is an earnings manipulator. The M-score (-0.8496) is higher than the cutoff (-1.78), indicating a higher-than-acceptable probability of manipulation (19.77% versus 3.75%).

2. Indications are as follows:
   - A DSR greater than 1 indicates that the ratio of receivables to sales has increased. This may suggest that ABC has employed inappropriate revenue recognition practices (e.g., the company may have shipped goods prematurely to recognize revenue that actually belongs to later periods). It is also possible that ABC's customers are having trouble paying the company.
   - A GMI greater than 1 indicates that gross margins have fallen this year. The deteriorating financial performance may induce management to manipulate earnings.
   - An SGI greater than 1 indicates that sales have increased this year. It is possible that the company has employed aggressive revenue recognition practices to manage perceptions of continuing growth and/or to obtain capital required to support growth.
   - A DEPI greater than 1 indicates that the depreciation rate is lower this year. It is possible that the company is playing around with depreciation methods/ estimates to manipulate reported earnings.

Other Quantitative Models

Studies found several variables that can be useful for detecting misstatement, including accruals quality, deferred taxes, auditor change, market-to-book value, whether the company is publicly listed and traded, growth rate differences between financial and non-financial variables (e.g., number of patents, employees, and products), and aspects of corporate governance and incentive compensation.

Limitations of Quantitative Models

- Accounting is only a partial representation of economic reality. Underlying cause and effect relationships can only be determined by a deeper analysis of actions.
- Managers have learned to test the detectability of earnings manipulation tactics by using models (such as the Beneish model) to anticipate analysts' perceptions. As a result, the predictive power of these models has declined.

LESSON 3: EARNINGS QUALITY

**LOS 19e: Describe the concept of sustainable (persistent) earnings.
Vol 2, pp 214–222**

LOS 19f: Describe indicators of earnings quality. Vol 2, pp 214–222

EARNINGS QUALITY

While the term "earnings quality" encompasses earnings, cash flow, and balance sheet quality, we focus specifically on earnings in this section. As mentioned earlier, high-quality earnings (1) are sustainable and (2) represent an adequate rate of return. Further, the conclusion that a particular company has high-quality earnings assumes that reporting quality is also high.

Indicators of Earnings Quality

Recurring Earnings

Generally speaking, reported earnings that contain a high proportion of non-recurring items (e.g., discontinued operations, one-off asset sales, one-off litigation settlements, one-off tax settlements) are less likely to be sustainable and are therefore considered low-quality.

Example 3-1: Non-Recurring Items (Enron Corp.)

The following table provides selected information from the consolidated income statement of Enron and its subsidiaries for the year ended December 31, 2000.

(In millions)	2000	1999	1998
Total revenues	$100,789	$40,112	$31,260
Total costs and expenses	98,836	39,310	29,882
Operating income	$1,953	$802	$1,378
Other income and deductions			
Equity in earnings of unconsolidated equity affiliates	$87	$309	$97
Gains on sales of non-merchant assets	146	541	56
Gain on the issuance of stock by TNPC, Inc.	121	0	0
Interest income	212	162	88
Other income, net	–37	181	–37
Income before interest, minority interests, and income taxes	$2,482	$1,995	$1,582

Notice the following:

- Enron's "operating income" varied drastically from year to year, falling by almost 60% in 1999 (from $1,378m to $802m) before rising by more than 100% in 2000 (to $1,953m).
- On the other hand, "income before interest, minority interests, and income taxes" shows a smooth upward trend, rising by 26% (from $1,582m to $1,995m) in 1999 and by 24% (to $2,482m) in 2000.

- "Gains on sales of non-merchant assets" and "gains on issuance of stock by TNPC" appear to be non-recurring items:
    - Even though gains on sales of non-merchant assets are realized in each of the three years, these gains have nothing to Enron's core energy distribution operations.
    - Gains on the stock sales are only realized in 2000.
- "Equity in earnings of unconsolidated equity affiliates" and "other income" are both non-operating items and are highly variable.
- The smooth upward trend in Enron's income is a direct result of the non-recurring and non-operating items. Further, these items also represent a significant portion of the company's "income before interest, minority interests, and income taxes." For example, in 1999, these two items accounted for more than 50% of the total [= ($309 + $541 + $181) / $1,995].

For the purpose of analysis, it is important to include non-recurring items when making historical comparisons and in developing input estimates for valuation. However, analysts should always keep an eye out for classification shifting when estimating recurring or core earnings. Evidence suggests that classification shifting does exist as companies (1) reclassify normal expenses as special items and/or (2) shift operating expenses to discontinued operations in order to inflate recurring earnings. Because evidence of classification shifting typically only emerges after the fact, analysts should carefully scrutinize income-decreasing special items, especially if the company reports relatively high operating earnings over the period as a result of classifying the item as non-operating.

Companies also understand that investors focus on recurring or core earnings. Therefore, in addition to reporting net income (on the face of the income statement), many companies voluntarily disclose pro forma income (also known as adjusted income or as non-GAAP measures) that excludes non-recurring items. Further, a reconciliation of pro forma income to reported income is also provided. However, analysts must recognize that some companies may be motivated to classify an item non-recurring if it improves a performance metric that is important to investors. For example, Groupon, an online discount provider, excluded online marketing costs from reported pro forma income on the grounds that these customer acquisition costs were non-recurring costs and that it planned to reduce the customer acquisition part of its marketing expenses over time. However, the SEC determined that the measure was misleading and subsequently required the company to restate its pro forma income. The point is that although voluntarily disclosed adjustments to reported income can be informative, an analyst should review the information to ensure that excluded items are truly non-recurring.

Earnings Persistence and Related Measures of Accruals

Earnings persistence requires (1) sustainability of earnings excluding items that are non-recurring and (2) persistence of growth in those earnings. The higher the persistence of a company's earnings, the higher its intrinsic value. Persistence can be measured by the coefficient β in the following model:

$$\text{Earnings}_{t+1} = \alpha + \beta_1 \, \text{Earnings}_t + \varepsilon$$

Earnings have (1) a cash component and (2) an accruals component. The accruals component arises from accounting requirements to recognize revenues/expenses in the period that they are earned/incurred, not at the time of cash movement. For example, a sale of goods in one period results in accounting income in the period the sale is made. If cash is expected to be collected in the next period, the difference between reported net income and cash collected represents an accrual.

> Accruals can roughly be estimated as net income minus operating cash flow.

$$\text{Earnings}_{t+1} = \alpha + \beta_1 \text{Cash flow}_t + \beta_2 \text{Accruals}_t + \varepsilon$$

- Studies have shown that the cash component of earnings is more persistent than the accruals component, so β_1 tends to be greater than β_2. The larger the accruals component of earnings, the lower the level of persistence and, therefore, the lower the quality of earnings.

An important distinction can be made between discretionary and non-discretionary accruals.

- Discretionary accruals arise from transactions or accounting choices outside the normal, which are possibly made with the intent to manage earnings.
- Non-discretionary accruals arise from normal transactions.

There are two ways to identify abnormal discretionary accruals:

1. Model the company's normal accruals and then identify outliers. A company's normal accruals are a function of economic factors (e.g., growth in credit sales, which would be expected to result in an increase in accounts receivable, and growth in the amount of depreciable assets, which would be expected to increase depreciation expense). Total accruals are then regressed against factors that are expected to give rise to normal accruals, and the residual of the regression is used as a measure of abnormal accruals.
2. Compare the magnitude of total accruals across companies. To make the comparison relevant, accruals are typically scaled (by average assets or average net operating income). A high amount of accruals indicates possibly manipulated, low-quality earnings.

A relatively strong signal that earnings are being manipulated is when a company reports positive net income, but with negative operating cash flows. Allou Health & Beauty Care, Inc. provides a good example of such a warning sign. The company was a manufacturer and distributor of hair and skin care products. Its financial statements for the years 2000–2002 showed positive revenue growth, fairly stable gross and operating margins, and positive net income each year, all suggesting that the company was reasonably stable. However, the company reported negative cash flow from operating activities for each of the three years, raising questions regarding its sustainability as a going concern. The explanation offered for this disconnect between positive net income and negative operating cash flow was that the company's accounts receivable and inventory had witnessed a marked increase over the period. Subsequently, it was found that the company had fraudulently inflated the amount of sales and inventory for those years.

Note that although significant accruals can suggest earnings manipulation, it is not necessary for all fraudulent companies to have sizeable accruals. WorldCom Inc., which was subsequently found to have issued fraudulent reports, showed cash flow from operating activities in excess of net income for each of the three years before the discovery was made. The company accomplished this by improperly capitalizing certain operating costs instead of expensing them, thereby classifying related cash outflows as investing outflows (instead of as operating cash outflows). An analyst who only focused on net income and cash flow from operations may have concluded that WorldCom's earnings were of high quality, but one who also considered cash flow from investing activities may have seen the bigger (correct) picture.

LOS 19g: Explain mean reversion in earnings and how the accruals component of earnings affects the speed of mean reversion. Vol 2, pp 222–223

Mean Reversion in Earnings

Research has shown that extreme levels of earnings, both high and low, are mean reverting (i.e., they tend to revert to normal levels over time).

- A company that is performing poorly will either shut down or scale back operations to minimize losses and upgrade its management and strategy to improve earnings going forward.
- A company that is earning abnormal profits will eventually face competition that will reduce its profit margins over time.

These findings hold a valuable lesson for analysts. Extremely high/low earnings should not simply be extrapolated into the future when constructing forecasts. Instead, analysts should focus on projecting normalized earnings over the relevant valuation time frame. In making these projections of future earnings, analysts must develop a realistic cash flow model and realistic estimates of accruals as well. The cash component of earnings tends to be more persistent than the accruals component. Therefore, if earnings have a significant accruals component, they will be expected to revert toward the mean more quickly, especially if the company has a higher-than-normal amount of accruals in its earnings.

Beating Benchmarks

Generally speaking, earnings that meet or exceed analysts' consensus forecasts typically result in share price increases. Studies have shown that a statistically significant proportion of earnings announcements just manage to beat forecasts compared to the proportion that fall short of those forecasts, which has been interpreted by some as evidence of earnings management. While this interpretation is open to debate, analysts should be wary of companies that consistently report earnings that exactly meet or only narrowly beat forecasts, as they may be managing reported earnings.

External Indicators of Poor-Quality Earnings

Two external indicators of poor-quality earnings are (1) enforcement actions by regulatory authorities and (2) restatements of previously issued financial statements. Analysts obviously strive to recognize companies with poor earnings quality before they become known to the public, but they should still be alert to external indicators and be prepared to reassess investment decisions.

LOS 19h: Evaluate the earnings quality of a company. Vol 2, pp 223–236

Evaluating the Earnings Quality of a Company

Case 3-1: Revenue Recognition: Sunbeam Corp. Premature/Fraudulent Revenue Recognition

Sunbeam Corporation was a consumer goods company. In the mid- to late 1990s, it appeared that its new CEO had engineered a turnaround at the company by cutting costs and increasing revenues. Unfortunately, the reality was markedly different.

- Sunbeam had included one-time disposals of product lines in revenues for 1Q97 without providing appropriate disclosures.

- In 1Q97, the company had booked revenues from sales of goods to a wholesaler, where (1) the wholesaler had not accepted ownership risks, and (2) the wholesaler could return the goods if it desired with Sunbeam picking up the cost of shipment both ways. Because the risks of ownership had not been transferred to the wholesaler, Sunbeam should not have recognized the associated revenue. All of the goods were returned to Sunbeam in 3Q97.
- Sunbeam offered aggressive discounts and other incentives to induce customers to order more goods than they would normally, and often gave customers return rights on these purchases. This inflated current period revenues by pulling future sales into the present (referred to as channel stuffing). Sunbeam did not disclose this policy.
- The company also engaged in bill-and-hold revenue practices, where revenues were recognized upon invoice issuance, while the goods remained on its own premises. The accounting requirements for these unusual transactions to be recognized as revenue are very strict: The buyer must (1) request such treatment, (2) have a genuine business purpose for the request, and (3) accept ownership risks. These requirements were not met, so Sunbeam should not have recognized the associated revenue.

Sunbeam engaged in channel stuffing and bill-and-hold transactions purely to accelerate recognition of revenues, while buyers were able to take advantage of its eagerness to sell without accepting any of the risks associated with the inventory. In the words of the SEC, "these transactions were little more than projected orders disguised as sales." Sunbeam's disclosures were inadequate, but there were warning signs in its financial statements that should have alerted analysts to the low quality of its earnings and revenue reporting.

Table 3-1 contains annual data on Sunbeam's sales and receivables from 1995 (before the misreporting occurred) through 1997 (when earnings management reached its peak level in the fourth quarter).

Table 3-1: Information on Sunbeam's Sales and Receivables, 1995–1997

($ millions)	1995	1996	1997
Total revenue	$1,016.9	$984.2	$1,168.2
Change from prior year		–3.2%	18.7%
Gross accounts receivable	$216.2	$213.4	$295.6
Change from prior year		–1.3%	38.5%
Receivables/revenue	21.3%	21.7%	25.3%
Change in receivables/revenue	0.7%	0.4%	3.6%
Days' sales outstanding	77.6	79.1	92.4
Accounts receivable turnover	4.7	4.6	4.0

Notice the following:

- Sunbeam began its misreporting activities in 1996. Although revenues fell 3.2% in that year, they increased significantly in 1997 (18.7%) as a result of Sunbeam's aggressive revenue recognition policies. The warning sign for analysts lay in the simultaneous, and much greater, increase in the accounts receivable (38.5%), which suggests that the company may be pulling future sales into current periods by offering favorable discounts and/or generous return policies.

- The ratio of receivables to revenue increased over the period (from 21.3% to 25.3%). This could indicate one of two things:
  - Customers' ability to repay deteriorated.
  - The seller shipped goods that were not wanted by customers or recorded fictitious revenues.
- The number of days sales outstanding [Accounts receivable/(Revenues/365)] increased each year, again suggesting that there were problems relating to either revenue collection or revenue recognition. The declining trend in accounts receivable turnover (365/DSO) tells the same story.

In addition to the clues found in the financial statements, the notes to the financials contained further warning signs regarding revenue recognition. In December 1997, Sunbeam had entered into an arrangement for the sale of accounts receivable worth approximately $59 million (which were consequently not included in the year-end accounts receivable balance). If an analyst were to adjust the financial statements to include this figure in accounts receivable, the year-on-year increase in accounts receivable would have been a whopping 66.1% (compared to 38.5% based on reported results) and the percentage of ratio of receivables to sales would have been 30.4% (compared to 25.3% based on reported results).

Table 3-2 compares Sunbeam's DSO and accounts receivable turnover with its industry median.

Table 3-2: Comparison of Sunbeam and Industry Median, 1995–1997

Sunbeam	1995	1996	1997
Days sales outstanding	77.7	79.2	92.3
Accounts receivable turnover	4.7	4.6	4.0
Industry median			
Days sales outstanding	44.6	46.7	50.4
Accounts receivable turnover	8.2	7.8	7.3
Sunbeam's underperformance relative to median			
Days sales outstanding	33.0	32.5	41.9
Accounts receivable turnover	(3.5)	(3.2)	(3.3)

Notice that:

- Sunbeam's underperformance relative to its peers in the industry in terms of its DSO and accounts receivable turnover clearly arouses suspicions regarding its revenue recognition policies.

Finally, in its annual report for the year 1997, Sunbeam included an expanded footnote stating that bill-and-hold sales accounted for approximately 3% of its consolidated revenues for the year. Based on this information, Sunbeam's gross margin (28.3%), and its applicable tax rate (35%), the impact of these bill-and-hold sales on earnings for the year can be calculated as 5.9% (see Table 3-3).

Table 3-3: Effect of Sunbeam's Bill-and-Hold Sales on Net Income ($ millions)

1997 revenue	$1,168.18
Bill-and-hold sales from note	3.0%
Bill-and-hold sales in 1997	$35.05
Gross profit margin	28.3%
Gross profit contribution	$9.92
After-tax earnings contribution	$6.45
Total earnings from continuing operations	$109.42
Earnings attributable to bill-and-hold sales	5.9%

Knowing that 6% of Sunbeam's net income depended on such transactions may have helped an analyst decide against investing in the company.

Case 3-2: Revenue Recognition: MicroStrategy, Inc. Multiple-Element Contracts

MicroStrategy, Inc. was a fast-growing software and information services company that went public in 1998. Its revenue consisted of multiple deliverables, including (1) outright sales of software and (2) obligations to provide services over an extended period of time.

Generally speaking, revenue from outright sales of software (i.e., product revenue) can be recognized immediately (based on delivery terms and acceptance by customers), while service revenue should be recognized as the services are provided. For multiple-deliverable arrangements, accounting standards dictate that revenue can be recognized upon software delivery only if (1) the software sale can be separated from the service portion of the contract and (2) the service revenues are accounted for separately.

MicroStrategy's revenue recognition policy (according to its accounting policies note) did in fact meet the standards' requirements:

"Revenue from product licensing arrangements is generally recognized after execution of a licensing agreement and shipment of the product, provided that no significant Company obligations remain and the resulting receivable is deemed collectible by management.... Services revenue, which includes training and consulting, is recognized at the time the service is performed. The Company defers and recognizes maintenance revenue ratably over the terms of the contract period, ranging from 12 to 36 months."

Unfortunately, however, MicroStrategy mischaracterized significant service revenues as part of the initial software sale, thereby recognizing them earlier than it should have. For example:

- In 4Q98, the company signed a contract worth $4.5 million for software licenses and a broad array of consulting services. Even though most of the software licenses sold were for applications that MicroStrategy was going to develop in the future, the company recognized the entire $4.5 million as software revenue in 1998.
- In 4Q99, the company entered an agreement worth $14.1 million for the provision for extensive services. Again, the company improperly characterized this amount as software revenue, thereby recognizing $14.1 million of product revenue in the quarter.

Without detailed information regarding these contracts, it would be difficult for an analyst to uncover this mischaracterization between product revenue and service revenue. However, there were warning signs that may have aroused the suspicion of analysts. Table 3-4 shows the quarterly mix of MicroStrategy's revenues:

Table 3-4: MicroStrategy's Revenue Mix by Quarters, 1Q98–4Q99

Quarter	Licenses (%)	Support (%)
1Q98	71.8	28.2
2Q98	68.3	31.7
3Q98	62.7	37.3
4Q98	70.7	29.3
1Q99	64.6	35.4
2Q99	68.1	31.9
3Q99	70.1	29.9
4Q99	73.2	26.8

Notice the following:

- The proportionate share of service revenue in quarterly total revenue increased in the first three quarters of 1998, and then dropped sharply in the fourth quarter to 29.3% (when the company mischaracterized $4.5 million of consulting services revenue as product revenue).
- Subsequently, the proportionate share of service revenues increased briefly (to 35.4% in 1Q99) before beginning to decline sharply toward 26.8% in 4Q99 (when the company mischaracterized $14.1 million of service revenue as product revenue that it recognized immediately).
- There is no logical reason for such a significant variation in the quarterly revenue mix. An analyst would know (from the accounting policies note) that the company has a stated policy for recognizing revenues for contracts with multiple-deliverable arrangements. This should prompt her to consider the risk of misallocation of revenues. Any deviations from observed trends should be identified and explanations sought from management. Based on how logical management's responses are, the analyst may become more comfortable or skeptical of investing in the company.

Table 3-5 provides a summary of how to assess quality of revenues.

Table 3-5: Summary: Looking for Quality in Revenues[3]

Start with the basics

- The first step should be to fully understand the revenue recognition policies as stated in the most recent annual report. Without context for the way revenue is recognized, an analyst will not understand the risks involved in the proper reporting of revenue. For instance, analysts should determine the following:
  - What are the shipping terms?
  - What rights of return does a customer have: limited or extensive?
  - Do rebates affect revenues, and if so, how are they accounted for? What estimates are involved?
  - Are there multiple deliverables to customers for one arrangement? If so, is revenue deferred until some elements are delivered late in the contract? If there are multiple deliverables, do deferred revenues appear on the balance sheet?

3 - 2017 CFA Program Curriculum Volume 2, pages 230–232.

Age matters

- A study of DSOs can reveal much about their quality. Receivables do not improve with age. Analysts should seek reasons for exceptions appearing when they:
  - Compare the trend in DSOs or receivables turnover over a relevant time frame.
  - Compare the DSO of one company with the DSOs of similar competitors over similar time frames.

Is it cash or accrual?

- A high percentage of accounts receivable to revenues might mean nothing, but it might also mean that channel stuffing has taken place, portending high future returns of inventory or decreased demand for product in the future. Analysts should:
  - Compare the percentage of accounts receivable to revenues over a relevant time frame.
  - Compare the company's percentage of accounts receivable to revenues with that of competitors or industry measures over similar time frames.

Compare with the real world when possible

- If a company reports non-financial data on a routine basis, try relating revenues to those data to determine whether trends in the revenue make sense. Examples include:
  - Airlines reporting extensive information about miles flown and capacity, enabling an analyst to relate increases in revenues to an increase in miles flown or capacity.
  - Retailers reporting square footage used and number of stores open.
  - Companies across all industries reporting employee head counts.
- As always, analysts should compare any relevant revenue-per-unit measure with that of relevant competitors or industry measures.

Revenue trends and composition

- Trend analysis, over time and in comparison with competitors, can prompt analysts to ask questions of managers, or it can simply evoke discomfort with the overall revenue quality. Some relationships to examine include:
  - The relationships between the kinds of revenue recognized. For example, how much is attributable to product sales or licenses, and how much is attributable to services? Have the relationships changed over time, and if so, why?
  - The relationship between overall revenue and accounts receivable. Do changes in overall revenues make sense when compared with changes in accounts receivable?

Relationships

- Does the company transact business with entities owned by senior officers or shareholders? This is a particularly sensitive area if the manager/shareholder-owned entities are private and there are revenues recognized from the private entity by a publicly owned company; it could be a dumping ground for obsolete or damaged inventory while inflating revenues.

Case 3-3: Cost Capitalization: WorldCom Corp. Property/Capital Expenditures Analysis

WorldCom was a major global communications company. During the 1990s, it grew rapidly via acquisitions. In order to meet consensus earnings forecasts, the company began to engage in improper capitalization of line costs (fees paid by the company to third-party telecommunications network providers for the right to use their networks), which should have been classified as operating expenses. This improper treatment began in 1999 and continued through the first quarter of 2002. The company declared bankruptcy in July 2002.

The company's auditors (Arthur Andersen) failed to detect the fraud (for various reasons). However, while an analyst would not have been able to identify exactly what was going on at the company, the balance sheet did offer a clue that something was not right. Table 3-6 presents a time series of the WorldCom's common-size balance sheet.

Table 3-6: Common Size Asset Portion of Balance Sheet for WorldCom, 1997–2001

	1997	1998	1999	2000	2001
Cash and equivalents	0%	2%	1%	1%	1%
Net receivables	5	6	6	7	5
Inventories	0	0	0	0	0
Other current assets	2	4	4	2	2
Total current assets	7%	12%	11%	10%	8%
Gross property, plant, and equipment (PPE)	**30%**	**31%**	**37%**	**45%**	**47%**
Accumulated depreciation	3%	2%	5%	7%	9%
Net property, plant, and equipment	27%	29%	32%	38%	38%
Equity investments	NA	NA	NA	NA	1
Other investments	0	0	0	2	1
Intangibles	61	54	52	47	49
Other assets	5	5	5	3	3
Total Assets	100%	100%	100%	100%	100%

It is clear that something unusual was going on in gross PP&E, especially because there had been no change in the company's strategy or anything else over the period.

- During 1997 and 1998 (the two years prior to the year the fraud began [i.e., 1999]) gross PP&E had been 30% and 31%, respectively, of total assets.
- In 1999, gross PP&E jumped up to 37% of total assets, then to 45% in 2000 and to 47% in 2001.

An analyst who might have identified this alarming trend in PP&E would not have specifically determined that line costs were being understated. However, the buildup of costs in PP&E would have aroused suspicions that expenses were under-reported somewhere on the income statement (resulting in a corresponding overstatement of reported asset values).

Table 3-7 provides a summary of how to assess the quality of expense recognition.

Table 3-7: Summary: Looking for Quality in Expense Recognition[4]

Start with the basics
- The first step should be to fully understand the cost capitalization policies as stated in the most recent annual report. Without context for the costs stored on the balance sheet, analysts will not be able to comprehend practice exceptions they may encounter. Examples of policies that should be understood include the following:
  - What costs are capitalized in inventory? How is obsolescence accounted for? Are there reserves established for obsolescence that might be artificially raised or lowered?
  - What are the depreciation policies, including depreciable lives? How do they compare with competitors' policies? Have they changed from prior years?

4 - 2017 CFA Program Curriculum Volume 2, pages 234–235.

Trend analysis

- Trend analysis, over time and in comparison with competitors, can lead to questions the analyst can ask managers, or it can simply evoke discomfort with overall earnings quality because of issues with expenses. Some relationships to examine include the following:
  - ○ Each quarter, non-current asset accounts should be examined for quarter-to-quarter and year-to-year changes to see whether there are any unusual increases in costs. If present, they might indicate that improper capitalization of costs has occurred.
  - ○ Profit margins—gross and operating—are often observed by analysts in the examination of quarterly earnings. They are not often related to changes in the balance sheet, but they should be. If unusual buildups of non-current assets have occurred and the profit margins are improving or staying constant, it could mean that improper cost capitalization is taking place. Recall WorldCom and its improper capitalization of "line costs": Profitability was maintained by capitalizing costs that should have been expensed. Also, the overall industry environment should be considered: Are margins stable while balance sheet accounts are growing and the industry is slumping?
  - ○ Turnover ratio for total assets; property, plant, and equipment; and other assets should be computed (with revenues divided by the asset classification). Does a trend in the ratios indicate a slowing in turnover? Decreasing revenues might mean that the assets are used to make a product with declining demand and portend future asset write-downs. Steady or rising revenues and decreasing turnover might indicate improper cost capitalization.
  - ○ Compute the depreciation (or amortization) expense compared to the relevant asset base. Is it decreasing or increasing over time without a good reason? How does it compare with that of competitors?
  - ○ Compare the relationship of capital expenditures with gross property, plant, and equipment over time. Is the proportion of capital expenditures relative to total property, plant, and equipment increasing significantly over time? If so, it may indicate that the company is capitalizing costs more aggressively to prevent their recognition as current expenses.

Relationships

- Does the company transact business with entities owned by senior officers or shareholders? This is a particularly sensitive area if the manager/shareholder-owned entities are private. Dealings between a public company and the manager-owned entity might take place at prices that are unfavorable for the public company in order to transfer wealth from the public company to the manager-owned entity. Such inappropriate transfers of wealth can also occur through excessive compensation, direct loans, or guarantees. These practices are often referred to as "tunneling."
- In some cases, sham dealings between the manager-owned entity and the public company might be falsely reported to improve reported profits of the public company and thus enrich the managers whose compensation is performance based. In a different type of transaction, the manager-owned entity could transfer resources to the public company to ensure its economic viability and thus preserve the option to misappropriate or to participate in profits in the future. These practices are often referred to as "propping."

Bankruptcy Protection Models

In addition to addressing the quality of just the company's earnings, bankruptcy prediction models include aspects of a company's balance sheet and cash flow as well.

Altman Model

This model is useful because it incorporates several financial ratios into a single model to predict the probability of bankruptcy. The Altman Z-score is calculated as:

$$
\begin{aligned}
\text{Z-score} = {} & 1.2(\text{Networking capital / Total assets}) + 1.4(\text{Retained earnings / Total assets}) \\
& + 3.3\,(\text{EBIT / Total assets}) + 0.6(\text{Market value of equity / Book value of liabilities}) \\
& + 1.0\,(\text{Sales / Total assets})
\end{aligned}
$$

- Net working capital/total assets is a measure of short-term liquidity risk.
- Retained earnings/total assets reflects accumulated profitability and relative age because retained earnings accumulate over time.
- EBIT (earnings before interest and taxes)/total assets measures profitability.
- Market value of equity/book value of liabilities is a leverage ratio.
- Sales/total assets is an activity ratio.

When it comes to interpreting the model, a higher Z-score is better.

Shortcomings of the Altman Bankruptcy Prediction Model
- It uses only one set of financial measures, which are taken at a single point in time.
  - Subsequent models have used hazard models that incorporate data collected over an extended period of time to calculate bankruptcy risk at each point in time.
- Financial statements measure past performance, and reported balance sheet values assume that the company is a going concern rather than one that may fail.
  - Subsequent models have made use of market-based prediction models that view equity in a company as a call option on the company's assets. They infer the probability of default from the value of the company's equity, its debt, equity returns, and equity volatility.

Newer models have used both accounting-based and market-based data as predictive variables.

LESSON 4: CASH FLOW QUALITY

LOS 19i: Describe indicators of cash flow quality. Vol 2, pp 237–238

LOS 19j: Evaluate the cash flow quality of a company. Vol 2, pp 238–246

CASH FLOW QUALITY

Indicators of Cash Flow Quality

Discussions of cash flow quality focus on operating cash flow (OCF) because it is the cash flow component that is most important for assessing a company's performance and valuing its securities. Cash flow can be of low quality if (1) the reported information correctly reflects poor economic performance (poor results quality) and/or (2) the reported information misrepresents economic reality (poor reporting quality). For cash flows to be regarded as being of high quality, there must be higher results quality and high reporting quality.

Startups and early-stage companies can be expected to have negative operating and investing cash flows, which may be financed by financing cash flows (e.g., issuing debt or equity). For more established companies (which are the focus of this Reading), high-quality cash flow has the following characteristics:

- Positive OCF.
- OCF derived from sustainable sources.
- OCF adequate to cover capital expenditures, dividends, and debt repayment.
- OCF with relatively low volatility (relative to industry participants).

Generally speaking, OCF is viewed as being less easily manipulated than operating income and net income. However, the importance of OCF to investors creates a strong incentive for managers to manipulate amounts reported. Examples of issues relating to cash flow reporting quality are:

- Boosting OCF by selling receivables to a third party.
  - ○ A decrease in a company's days' sales outstanding may suggest this is happening.
- Boosting OCF by delaying repayment of payables.
  - ○ An increase in a company's days of payables may suggest this is happening.
- Misclassifying cash flows. Management may try to shift inflows of cash from investing or financing activities into the operating section of the cash flow statement to inflate reported OCF.

Evaluating Cash Flow Quality

Earlier in the Reading, we used Satyam Computer Services as an example of a company that was engaging in earnings manipulation. The interesting thing about Satyam was an analyst simply looking for OCF persistently lower than earnings would not have identified the company as one with potential earnings management because the company's reported OCF was always relatively close to operating profits. Recall that large differences between earnings and OCF or increases in such differences can indicate earnings manipulation.

There were, however, quite a few warning signs for analysts on Satyam's financial statements. Some of them are discussed here:

- Satyam's cash flow statement was presented in an indirect format (starting with net income). The company reported a $53 million gain on foreign exchange on forward and option contracts on its cash flow statement for 1Q08, but curiously **added** this amount to net income in calculating OCF. The correct accounting treatment for a gain is to subtract it from net income in calculating OCF (as it has already been included in net income). Despite the fact that this gain represented almost 40% of the company's profit for the quarter, the company's senior executives had no clarification available for analysts during the company's quarterly conference call, a clear signal of potential problems.

- The company's days' sales outstanding grew from 79.3 in 2006 to 96.6 days on 2007, which is a very large jump. This increase raised questions about the creditworthiness of the company's customers, about the efficiency of its collection efforts, and about the quality of the revenue recognized. Further, the allowance for doubtful accounts consistently grew at a pace faster than sales.
- Finally, the company held significant amounts of cash in (non-interest-bearing) current accounts over an extended period of time. Upon being quizzed by analysts, the company could only respond by saying that it would be moving these deposits into interest-bearing accounts shortly. It turned out eventually that these cash balances were in fact non-existent.

We also discussed the Sunbeam case at length earlier in the Reading. Next, we describe some of the warning signs found on its cash flow statement for 1997:

- The company had added non-cash charges worth $284 million for restructuring, impairment, and other costs to its net income on its indirect cash flow statement for 1996. On its indirect cash flow statement for 1997, a reversal of the restructuring accrual was subtracted from net income. This shows that the company had inflated expenses in 1996, and reversed some of them in 1997 to portray significant improvements in performance since its new CEO took over (in mid-1996).
- The company's statement of cash flows for 1997 showed significant uses of cash in the form of (1) increase in accounts receivable and (2) increase in inventory.
    - A significant growth in receivables is a warning sign that sales and income have been overstated.
    - The significant growth in inventory was caused by subsequent returns of goods from customers who had initially been shipped unordered goods. (Sunbeam shipped these items to inflate reported sales.)

Classification shifting occurs when positive cash flow items are moved from the investing or financing section of the cash flow statement into the operating section. While the shift does not affect total cash flow, it affects investors' perception of a company's cash flows and future prospects.

Accounting standards offer significant flexibility regarding classification of certain cash flows. For example:

- Under IFRS:
    - Interest paid can be classified as operating or financing cash flow.
    - Interest and dividends received may be classified as operating or investing cash flow.
- Under U.S. GAAP:
    - Interest paid, interest received, and dividends received must all be classified as operating cash flow.

Further, cash flows from non-trading securities must be classified as investing cash flows, while cash flows from trading securities are typically classified as operating cash flows. Depending on how it intends to manage its security holdings, a company is free to choose whether it wants to classify certain investments as trading or non-trading.

An example of shifting cash flows from investing to operating activities can be found in the statement of cash flows of Nautica Enterprises. Excerpts from the company's fiscal 2000 and fiscal 2001 cash flow statements are reproduced in Table 4-1 and Table 4-2.

Table 4-1: Excerpt from Nautica's Consolidated Statement of Cash Flows filed in May 2000

	Year Ended March 4, 2000
Cash flows from operating activities	
Net earnings	$46,163
Adjustments to reconcile net earnings to net cash provided by operating activities, net of assets and liabilities acquired	
Minority interest in net loss of consolidated subsidiary	—
Deferred income taxes	(1,035)
Depreciation and amortization	17,072
Provision for bad debts	1,424
Changes in operating assets and liabilities	
Accounts receivable	(6,562)
Inventories	(3,667)
Prepaid expenses and other current assets	(20)
Other assets	(2,686)
Accounts payable: trade	(548)
Accrued expenses and other current liabilities	9,086
Income taxes payable	3,458
Net cash provided by operating activities	62,685
Cash flows from investing activities	
Purchase of property, plant, and equipment	(33,289)
Acquisitions, net of cash acquired	—
Sale (purchase) of short-term investments	21,116
Payments to register trademark	(277)
Net cash used in investing activities	(12,450)

Table 4-2: Excerpt from Nautica's Consolidated Statements of Cash Flows filed in May 2001

	Year Ended March 3, 2001	Year Ended March 4, 2000
Cash flows from operating activities		
Net earnings	$46,103	$46,163
Adjustments to reconcile net earnings to net cash provided by operating activities, net of assets and liabilities acquired		
Minority interest in net loss of consolidated subsidiary	—	—
Deferred income taxes	(2,478)	(1,035)
Depreciation and amortization	22,968	17,072
Provision for bad debts	1,451	1,424
Changes in operating assets and liabilities		
Short-term investments	28,445	21,116
Accounts receivable	(17,935)	(768)
Inventories	(24,142)	(3,667)
Prepaid expenses and other current assets	(2,024)	(20)
Other assets	(36)	(2,686)
Accounts payable: trade	14,833	(548)
Accrued expenses and other current liabilities	7,054	3,292
Income taxes payable	3,779	3,458
Net cash provided by operating activities	78,018	83,801
Cash flows from investing activities		
Purchase of property, plant, and equipment	(41,712)	(33,289)
Acquisitions, net of cash acquired	—	—
Purchase of short-term investments	—	—
Payments to register trademark	(199)	(277)
Net cash used in investing activities	(41,911)	(33,566)

Notice the following:

- The cash inflow from sale of short-term investments (worth $21,116) is classified as an inflow from investing activities on Nautica's statement of cash flows for 2000. However, in the 2001 annual report, the same inflow (worth $21,116) in the year 2000 is classified as an inflow from operating activities.
- The impact of this reclassification was that Nautica's operating cash flows showed a decline of only 7% (= 78,018/83,801 − 1) from 2000 to 2001. Had the reclassification not been performed, the company's operating cash flows for 2001 would have been $49,573 (= 78,018 − 28,445), exhibiting a (more significant) decline of 21% (= 49,573/62,685 − 1) from 2000 to 2001.

The lesson here is that comparisons of period-to-period reports issued by a company can be useful in assessing financial reporting quality. If a company restates prior years' financial statements (because of an error or because of a change in accounting policy), omits some information that was previously voluntarily disclosed, or adds some item that was not previously disclosed, an analyst should aim to understand the reasons for the changes.

LESSON 5: BALANCE SHEET QUALITY

LOS 19k: Describe indicators of balance sheet quality. Vol 2, pp 246–250

LOS 19l: Evaluate the balance sheet quality of a company. Vol 2, pp 246–250

BALANCE SHEET QUALITY

When it comes to the balance sheet, high financial *results* quality (i.e., a strong balance sheet) is indicated by an optimal amount of leverage, adequate liquidity, and optimal asset allocation. There are no absolute values for various financial ratios that indicate adequate financial strength, so the analysis must be undertaken in light of the environment in which the firm operates. High financial *reporting* quality is indicated by (1) completeness, (2) unbiased measurement, and (3) clear presentation. In this section, we shall focus on high financial reporting quality.

Completeness

- Significant amounts of off-balance-sheet obligations (e.g., operating leases and take-or-pay purchase contracts) should be a concern for an analyst because reported leverage would be understated. Analysts should adjust reported financial statements by constructively capitalizing operating lease obligations and purchase obligations. This requires the analyst to estimate the amount of the obligation as the present value of future lease (or purchase obligation) payments and then to add this amount to both the company's reported assets and its liabilities.
- If a company reports investments made in other companies as unconsolidated joint ventures or investments accounted for using the equity method, the proportionate share of the parent in the liabilities of the investee will not be reflected on its balance sheet. Further, the parent's profitability ratios (e.g., net profit margin) will be overstated, as its consolidated financial statements will include its proportionate share in investee profits but not its share of investee sales. Most of the time, analysts can use financial statement disclosures to adjust reported amounts to better reflect the combined amounts of sales, assets, and liabilities.
  - However, analysts should be wary of companies that operate with numerous unconsolidated subsidiaries for which ownership levels approach 50%, as this may suggest that the company is trying to play around with ownership structures to avoid consolidating investee financial statements with its own.

Unbiased Measurement

Unbiased measurement is particularly important for assets and liabilities for which valuation is subjective. Examples include:

- Asset impairment charges. Understatement of impairment charges for inventory, PP&E, or other assets results in (1) overstated profits and (2) overstated assets. If a company reports substantial amounts of goodwill, but its market value of equity is less than the book value of shareholders' equity, it may suggest that goodwill is impaired but the impairment has not been recognized. (See Example 5-1.)
- Understatement of valuation allowance for deferred tax assets. This would result in (1) understated tax expenses and overstated income and (2) overstated assets. Significant, unexplainable variations in the valuation account can signal biased measurement.

- Valuation of investments that trade in non-active markets. If the company holds a substantial portion of its assets in investments for which no observable market data exist (meaning that valuation must be based solely on management estimates), analysts should scrutinize the values attached to those investments in detail.
- Valuing pension liabilities. Valuation of pension liabilities requires several estimates including the discount rate and other actuarial assumptions (that have been discussed in an earlier Reading). Any changes in these assumptions should be examined.

Example 5-1: Goodwill

Table 5-1 presents an excerpt from Sealed Air Corporation's income statement for 2012. Table 5-2 presents an excerpt from the company's balance sheet for 2012.

Table 5-1: Sealed Air Corporation and Subsidiaries Consolidated Statements of Operations

Year Ended December 31	2012	2011	2010
Net sales	$7,648.1	$5,550.9	$4,490.1
Cost of sales	5,103.8	3,950.6	3,237.3
Gross profit	2,544.3	1,600.3	1,252.8
Marketing, administrative, and development expenses	1,785.2	1,014.4	699.0
Amortization expense of intangible assets acquired	134.0	39.5	11.2
Impairment of goodwill and other intangible assets	1,892.3	—	—
Costs related to the acquisition and integration of Diversey	7.4	64.8	—
Restructuring and other charges	142.5	52.2	7.6
Operating (loss) profit	(1,417.1)	429.4	535.0
Interest expense	(384.7)	(216.6)	(161.6)
Loss on debt redemption	(36.9)	—	(38.5)
Impairment of equity method investment	(23.5)	—	—
Foreign currency exchange (losses) gains related to Venezuelan subsidiaries	(0.4)	(0.3)	5.5
Net gains on sale (other-than-temporary impairment) of available-for-sale securities	—	—	5.9
Other expense, net	(9.4)	(14.5)	(2.9)
(Loss) earnings from continuing operations before income tax provision	(1,872.0)	198.0	343.4
Income tax (benefit) provision	(261.9)	59.5	87.5
Net (loss) earnings from continuing operations	(1,610.1)	138.5	255.9
Net earnings from discontinued operations	20.9	10.6	—
Net gain on sale of discontinued operations	178.9	—	—
Net (loss) earnings available to common stockholders	$(1,410.3)	$149.1	$255.9

Table 5-2: Excerpt from Sealed Air Corporation and Subsidiaries Consolidated Balance Sheets

Year Ended December 31	2012	2011
ASSETS		
Current assets		
Cash and cash equivalents	$679.6	$703.6
Receivables, net of allowance for doubtful accounts	1,326.0	1,314.2
Inventories	736.4	777.5
Deferred tax assets	393.0	156.2
Assets held for sale	—	279.0
Prepaid expenses and other current assets	87.4	119.7
Total current assets	$3,222.4	$3,350.2
Property and equipment, net	$1,212.8	$1,269.2
Goodwill	3,191.4	4,209.6
Intangible assets, net	1,139.7	2,035.7
Non-current deferred tax assets	255.8	112.3
Other assets, net	415.1	455.0
Total assets	$9,437.2	$11,432.0

The company has 192,062,185 shares outstanding. These shares were valued at $18 each in December 2011, and at $14 in August 2012.

Notice the following from the information presented:

- The company's market capitalization was about $3,457 million (= 192,062,185 × $18) in December 2011 and around $2,689 million (= 192,062,185 × $14) in August 2012.
- The amount of goodwill reported by the company on its balance sheet as of December 2011 was $4,209.6m. This amount comfortably exceeded the company's market cap on that date ($3,457m). Further, goodwill and other intangible assets represented about 55% of the company's total assets [= 4,209.6 + 2,035.7)/11,432.0]
- Because the company's market capitalization is lower than the reported goodwill, it implies that the value attributed to all its other assets is less than zero. This suggests that goodwill is carried at an inflated value, and that a future write-down is likely.
- As can be seen on the company's income statement for 2012, an impairment charge worth $1,892.3 was subsequently recognized against goodwill and other intangible assets.

Clear Presentation

Although accounting standards specify many aspects of what appears on the balance sheet, companies have discretion, for example, in determining which line items should be shown separately and which ones should be aggregated into a single total. For items shown as a single total, analysts should be able to find required details in the notes to the financial statements.

LESSON 6: SOURCES OF INFORMATION ABOUT RISK

LOS 19m: Describe sources of information about risk. Vol 2, pp 250–262

SOURCES OF INFORMATION ABOUT RISK

The Company's Financial Statements

A company's financial statements can provide useful indicators of financial, operating, or other risk. For example:

- High leverage ratios or low coverage ratios can signal financial risk.
- Analytical models that incorporate various financial data can signal bankruptcy risk, and others can predict reporting risks (as discussed earlier in the Reading).
- Highly variable operating cash flows or negative trends in profit margins can signal operating risk.

Auditor's Opinion

An adverse or going-concern audit opinion on financial statements, or a report indicating weakness in the company's internal controls, would clearly be a warning sign for an analyst. However, audit opinions are based on historical information and typically do not provide information on a timely enough basis to be a useful source of information about risk.

On the other hand, a change in the auditor, especially multiple changes in the auditor, can be a timely signal of possible reporting problems. Similarly, the use of an auditor who does not appear to be equipped to adequately deal with the complexity of the company can indicate risk. Analysts should be concerned if the auditor and company management are particularly close, or if the company represents a significant portion of the auditor's revenue.

Notes to the Financial Statements

Both IFRS and U.S. GAAP require specific disclosures about risks related to contingent obligations, pension and post-employment benefits, and financial instruments.

- Disclosures about contingent obligations include a description of the obligation, estimated amounts, timing of required payments, and related uncertainties.
- Disclosures about pensions and post-employment benefits include information relevant to actuarial risks that could result in actual benefit payouts differing from the reported (projected) obligations, or investment risks that could result in actual assets differing from reported amounts (based on expected returns).
- Disclosures about financial instruments include information about credit risk, liquidity risk, and market risks, and how the company manages them.

Management Commentary (Management Discussion and Analysis, or MD&A)

IFRS requires management commentary to include a discussion of principal strategic, commercial, operational, and financial risks that may significantly affect the company. Similarly, public U.S. companies are required to present quantitative and qualitative information about the company's exposure to market risks, which should enable analysts to understand the impact of fluctuations in interest rates, and in foreign exchange and commodity prices. Although both sets of standards encourage a presentation of principal risks only, companies often include a significant amount of generic commentary. This can make it difficult for analysts to identify specific and important risks faced by the company.

Other Required Disclosures

Other required disclosures and announcements that are specific to an event (e.g., capital raising, non-timely filing of financial reports, management changes, or mergers and acquisitions) can also provide important information relevant to assessing risk.

- In the United States, public companies must file an NT (notification of inability to timely file) if there is a delay in filing of financial reports. Delays in filing are often the result of accounting difficulties, which could take the form of (1) internal disagreements on an accounting principle or estimate, (2) a lack of adequate financial staff, or (3) a discovery of an accounting fraud that requires further examination. Generally speaking, an NT filing is highly likely to signal problems with financial reporting quality.
- A sudden resignation of a company's most senior financial officer or external auditor would signal potential problems with financial reporting quality.
- A legal dispute related to one of the company's important assets or products could negatively affect the company's future earnings.
- Mergers and acquisitions could also indicate changes in the company's risk profile.

Financial Press as a Source of Information about Risk

The financial press can be a useful source of information about risk. For example, a *Wall Street Journal* financial reporter, Jonathan Weil, was one of the first people to identify problems with the accounting at Enron. Note that as electronic media via the internet expand, it is important to consider the credibility of the source of any piece of information.

READING 20: INTEGRATION OF FINANCIAL STATEMENT ANALYSIS TECHNIQUES

LESSON 1: CASE STUDY: LONG-TERM EQUITY INVESTMENT

LOS 20a: Demonstrate the use of a framework for the analysis of financial statements given a particular problem, question, or purpose (e.g., valuing equity based on comparables, critiquing a credit rating, obtaining a comprehensive picture of financial leverage, evaluating the perspectives given in management's discussion of financial results). Vol 2, pp 269–270

LOS 20b: Identify financial reporting choices and biases that affect the quality and comparability of companies' financial statements, and explain how such biases may affect financial decisions. Vol 2, pp 271–297

LOS 20d: Evaluate how a given change in accounting standards, methods, or assumptions affects financial statements and ratios. Vol 2, pg 304

Financial analysis is primarily performed to facilitate an economic decision (e.g., whether to lend to a company or to invest in a company's stock). A basic framework for conducting financial analysis is presented in Table 1-1.

Table 1-1: A Financial Statement Analysis Framework:[1]

Phase	Sources of Information	Examples of Output
1. Define the purpose and context of the analysis.	• The nature of the analyst's function, such as evaluating an equity or debt investment or issuing a credit rating. • Communication with client or supervisor on needs and concerns. • Institutional guidelines related to developing specific work product.	• Statement of the purpose or objective of analysis. • A list (written or unwritten) of specific questions to be answered by the analysis. • Nature and content of report to be provided. • Timetable and budgeted resources for completion.
2. Collect input data.	• Financial statements, other financial data, questionnaires, and industry/economic data. • Discussions with management, suppliers, customers, and competitors. • Company site visits (e.g., to production facilities or retail stores).	• Organized financial statements. • Financial data tables. • Completed questionnaires, if applicable.
3. Process input data, as required, into analytically useful data.	• Data from the previous phase.	• Adjusted financial statements. • Common-size statements. • Forecasts.
4. Analyze/interpret the data.	• Input data and processed data.	• Analytical results.

1 - Exhibit 1, Volume 2, CFA Program Curriculum 2017

Table 1-1: (*continued*)

Phase	Sources of Information	Examples of Output
5. Develop and communicate conclusions and recommendations (e.g., with an analysis report).	• Analytical results and previous reports. • Institutional guidelines for published reports.	• Analytical report answering questions posed in Phase 1. • Recommendations regarding the purpose of the analysis, such as whether to make an investment or grant credit.
6. Follow-up.	• Information gathered by periodically repeating above steps as necessary to determine whether changes to holdings or recommendations are necessary.	• Update reports and recommendations.

To illustrate the LOSs for this reading, we will analyze the financial statements of Alpha Ltd. to determine whether we should invest in the company's common stock. Financial statement information for Alpha is presented in Table 1-2 below:

Table 1-2: Alpha's Financial Statements

Balance Sheet

	2010	2009	2008	2007
Cash and cash equivalents	4,520	3,750	3,350	3,500
Marketable securities	2,200	4,554	8,250	7,120
Accounts receivable	11,950	10,800	9,565	7,825
Inventories	6,384	5,675	5,980	5,125
Other current assets	1,560	1,350	1,955	1,125
Total current assets	**26,614**	**26,129**	**29,100**	**24,695**
PP&E	15,985	14,650	12,940	11,875
Intangible assets	5,500	2,855	2,000	1,855
Goodwill	24,500	20,066	17,750	16,486
Other noncurrent assets (inc. equity investment)*	11,350	9,125	7,955	6,820
Total noncurrent assets	**57,335**	**46,696**	**40,645**	**37,036**
*Investment in associate (25% stake)	6,355	6,000	4,825	3,500
Total assets	**83,949**	**72,825**	**69,745**	**61,731**
Accounts payable	9,850	8,950	7,825	6,450
Current portion of long-term debt	17,250	11,950	13,000	9,825
Other current liabilities	3,000	3,265	4,520	3,500
Total current liabilities	**30,100**	**24,165**	**25,345**	**19,775**
Long-term debt	4,044	4,655	5,800	7,211
Pension obligations and restructuring provisions	7,550	6,455	6,600	6,320
Stockholders' equity	42,255	37,550	32,000	28,425
Total liabilities and equity	**83,949**	**72,825**	**69,745**	**61,731**

Table 1-2: (*continued*)

Selected Income Statement Information

	2010	2009	2008
Revenue	77,355	70,050	66,750
Cost of goods sold	30,625	27,820	25,655
Purchases	31,334	27,515	26,510
Average daily cash expenditures	172.5	160.4	145.5
EBIT	12,665	11,525	10,555
EBT	11,655	10,570	9,645
Share of income from associate	950	790	725
Net income	**11,250**	**9,150**	**8,150**

Selected Cash Flow Statement Information

	2010	2009	2008
CFO before interest and taxes	16,035	13,210	11,860
Cash interest paid	595	480	365
Cash taxes paid	2,620	2,455	2,250
Operating cash flow	12,820	10,275	9,245
Investing cash flow	−13,900	−9,130	−4,135

Some of the aspects of Alpha's performance and operations that we are particularly interested in examining are listed below:

- What are Alpha's sources of earnings growth, how sustainable are its earnings, and do these earnings reflect economic reality?
- What is the relationship between earnings and cash flow?
- Can the company's capital structure support its future operations and strategic plans?
- Does the balance sheet reflect all rights and obligations of the company?

In order to answer these questions, we will be performing the following:

- A DuPont decomposition
- An analysis of Alpha's asset base
- An analysis of Alpha's capital structure
- An examination of the company's segments and its capital allocation across these segments
- An evaluation of earnings quality through a study of the company's accruals
- A decomposition of the company's cash flows and an evaluation of their adequacy for the company's continued operations and strategies
- Analysis of company valuation

DuPont Analysis

DuPont decomposition isolates the components that affect a company's return on equity (ROE), which helps us identify factors that drive a company's earnings, and at the same time, highlights weaker areas. The 5-way DuPont decomposition is given as:

$$ROE = \text{Tax Burden} \times \text{Interest burden} \times \text{EBIT margin} \times \text{Total asset turnover} \times \text{Financial leverage}$$

$$ROE = \frac{NI}{EBT} \times \frac{EBT}{EBIT} \times \frac{EBIT}{Revenue} \times \frac{Revenue}{\text{Average Asset}} \times \frac{\text{Average Asset}}{\text{Average Equity}}$$

This "granular approach" isolates the impact on ROE of each of its components and enables us to identify relatively weak areas of operations whose adverse impact on ROE may be masked by other stronger areas. For example, company management may point to a steadily improving ROE as testament to their business acumen. The (albeit) impressive improvement in ROE may be primarily driven by an improving net profit margin, and focusing on aggregate ROE numbers may result in management ignoring a (simultaneously) declining asset turnover ratio whose adverse impact on ROE is being masked by the improving profit margin. Breaking down ROE into its different components can therefore highlight weaker areas that management should focus on to improve the company's performance even further.

Notice that Alpha records an investment in associate (2010: $6,355) on its balance sheet and share of income in associate (2010: $950) on the income statement. This indicates that Alpha uses the equity method to account for its investment in the associate. In order to focus on Alpha's core operations, we need to remove the impact of the associate on Alpha's reported performance. Specifically we need to:

- Remove the value of this equity investment from Alpha's total assets so that the analysis can focus exclusively on Alpha's asset base.
    - This adjustment results in an improvement in asset turnover.
- Remove its share of the associate's net income from Alpha's reported net income to focus exclusively on Alpha's profitability.
    - This adjustment results in a decline in the NP margin.
- Since we have no information regarding how the investment in the associate was financed, we do not make any adjustment to the financial leverage ratio.

Based on the information provided in Table 1-2, we can decompose Alpha's ROE as follows (Table 1-3):

Table 1-3: DuPont Decomposition for Alpha Including the Investment in Associate

Income Statement Information

	2010	2009	2008
Revenue	77,355	70,050	66,750
EBIT	12,665	11,525	10,555
EBT	11,655	10,570	9,645
Income from associate	950	790	725
Net income	11,250	9,150	8,150

Table 1-3: (*continued*)

Balance Sheet Information

	2010	2009	2008	2007
Total assets	83,949	72,825	69,745	61,731
Investment in associate	6,355	6,000	4,825	3,500
Stockholders' equity	42,255	37,550	32,000	28,425

Extended DuPont Analysis

	Tax Burden	Interest Burden	EBIT Margin	NP Margin	Total Asset Turnover	Financial Leverage	ROE
2008	84.50%	91.38%	15.81%	12.21%	1.0154	2.1759	26.98%
2009	86.57%	91.71%	16.45%	13.06%	0.9827	2.0499	26.31%
2010	96.53%	92.03%	16.37%	14.54%	0.9868	1.9645	28.19%

In order to evaluate the company's performance on a stand-alone basis, we need to remove the effects of its investment in the associate. (See Table 1-4.)

Table 1-4: DuPont Decomposition for Alpha Excluding the Investment in Associate

Extended DuPont Analysis

	Tax Burden	Interest Burden	EBIT Margin	NP Margin	Total Asset Turnover	Financial Leverage	ROE
2008	76.98%	91.38%	15.81%	11.12%	1.0840	2.1759	26.24%
2009	79.09%	91.71%	16.45%	11.93%	1.0634	2.0499	26.02%
2010	88.37%	92.03%	16.37%	13.32%	1.0713	1.9645	28.02%

Note that we have not recalculated the financial leverage ratio after excluding the investment in associate. We could subtract the investment in associate from total assets and equity, but given that we do not know how this investment was financed (all debt, all internally generated cash flow, or a mix of debt and equity), such an adjustment would be arbitrary. In our analysis, we have implicitly assumed that the mix of debt and equity used to finance the investment in the associate is similar to the pre-existing capital structure of the parent.

Analysis:
- There is an upward trend in the net profit margin for Alpha with and without the associate. However, there has been a (slightly) disconcerting increase in the contribution of the associate to Alpha's aggregate profit margin. The associate contributed 1.22% (= 14.54 – 13.32) to Alpha's overall profit margin in 2010, up from 1.09% (= 12.21 – 11.12) in 2008.
- The financial leverage ratio has decreased over the period. Even though this trend in the ratio has hindered the improvement in ROE, it has lowered the financial risk inherent in Alpha.
- The tax burden and interest burden ratios have increased. Recall from Level I (Corporate finance) that *increasing* interest burden and tax burden ratios imply that the impact of taxes and interest charges on operating earnings has *decreased,* and has contributed to an improving ROE over the period.

Asset-Base Composition

In order to identify and evaluate any changes in the composition of Alpha's balance sheet we examine its common size balance sheet (see Table 1-5).

Table 1-5: Composition of Total Assets

	2010	2009	2008
Cash and cash equivalents	5.38%	5.15%	4.80%
Marketable securities	2.62%	6.25%	11.83%
Accounts receivable	14.23%	14.83%	13.71%
Inventories	7.60%	7.79%	8.57%
Other current assets	1.86%	1.85%	2.80%
Total current assets	**31.70%**	**35.88%**	**41.72%**
PP&E	19.04%	20.12%	18.55%
Intangible assets	6.55%	3.92%	2.87%
Goodwill	29.18%	27.55%	25.45%
Other noncurrent assets	13.52%	12.53%	11.41%
Total noncurrent assets	**68.30%**	**64.12%**	**58.28%**

Analysis:
- The increasing share of goodwill in total assets indicates that Alpha has grown through acquisitions.
- Acquisition activity can be confirmed by examining cash flow from investing activities in the statement of cash flows. The fact that there has been a substantial increase in cash outflow from investing activities over the period indicates that the company has been investing in acquisitions and other noncurrent assets.

Capital Structure Analysis

To examine Alpha's long-term capital structure we present the long-term liabilities and equity section of the balance sheet on a common-size basis. (See Table 1-6.)

Table 1-6: Percent of Long-Term Capital Structure

	2010	2009	2008
Long-term debt	7.51%	9.57%	13.06%
Pension obligations and restructuring provisions	14.02%	13.27%	14.86%
Stockholders' equity	78.47%	77.17%	72.07%
Total long-term capital	100%	100%	100%

Analysis:
- The proportion of (less risky) equity financing in Alpha's capital structure has increased over time.
- The proportion of (more risky) long-term debt has fallen.
- The proportion of other long-term liabilities (restructuring provisions and employee pension plan obligations) has also decreased.

Note that we had earlier already observed (in the DuPont decomposition) that Alpha's financial leverage ratio had decreased over the period. However, capital structure analysis allows us to get into more detail regarding the nature of liabilities. The financial risk inherent in long-term debt obligations is more severe than the risk associated with pension plan obligations/restructuring provisions. Therefore, an increase in long-term liabilities (leverage) brought about by an increase in pension plan obligations/restructuring provisions is less disconcerting than an increase caused by additional long-term borrowings. Capital structure analysis allows us to gauge the impact of both these types of long-term liabilities separately.

Given that the company's long-term liabilities are decreasing, we should ensure that there is no offsetting change in working capital accounts. We present various short-term liquidity and activity ratios in Table 1-7.

Table 1-7: Selected Working Capital Accounts and Ratios

	2010	2009	2008	2007
Cash and cash equivalents	4,520	3,750	3,350	3,500
Marketable securities	2,200	4,554	8,250	7,120
Accounts receivable	11,950	10,800	9,565	7,825
Inventories	6,384	5,675	5,980	5,125
Other current assets	1,560	1,350	1,955	1,125
Current assets	**26,614**	**26,129**	**29,100**	**24,695**
Accounts payable	9,850	8,950	7,825	6,450
Current portion of long-term debt	17,250	11,950	13,000	9,825
Other current liabilities	3,000	3,265	4,520	3,500
Current liabilities	**30,100**	**24,165**	**25,345**	**19,775**

Other data	2010	2009	2008
Revenue	77,355	70,050	66,750
Cost of goods sold	30,625	27,820	25,655
Purchases	31,334	27,515	26,510
Average daily expenditures	172.50	160.40	145.50

Working Capital Ratios	2010	2009	2008
Current ratio	0.88	1.08	1.15
Quick ratio	0.62	0.79	0.84
Defensive interval ratio	108.23	119.10	145.46
Days' sales outstanding (DSO)	53.67	53.06	47.55
Days' inventory on hand (DOH)	71.86	76.46	79.00
Days' payables	109.50	111.26	98.27
Cash conversion cycle	16.04	18.25	28.27

Defensive interval ratio = Cash + Marketable securities + Accounts receivable/Daily cash exp.
Defensive interval ratio = (4,520 + 2,200 + 11,950)/172.5 = 108.23

Analysis:

- The current ratio and quick ratio have deteriorated due to a significant increase in the current portion of long-term debt and a decrease in marketable securities.
- The defensive interval ratio has deteriorated due to the increase in daily cash expenditure and the decrease in marketable securities.
- The decrease in DOH indicates that Alpha is managing its inventory more efficiently.
- The decline in working capital ratios is mitigated by the improvement in the management of inventory and payables.
- However, DSO has also increased, which indicates that the company has become somewhat lenient in receivables management.

Segment Analysis/Capital Allocation

Analysis of geographical segments enables us to identify segments that are of greatest importance to a company, and to understand any geopolitical investment risks faced by the company.

Alpha has five geographical segments, whose revenue and EBIT information is presented in Table 1-8.

Table 1-8: Segment Revenue and EBIT Information

Revenue by Segment

	2010	% Total	2009	% Total	2008	% Total
North America	9,125	11.80%	6,250	8.92%	5,525	8.28%
Europe	31,565	40.81%	29,850	42.61%	27,625	41.39%
Asia	18,950	24.50%	16,860	24.07%	16,955	25.40%
Africa	7,800	10.08%	6,955	9.93%	6,350	9.51%
Australia	9,915	12.82%	10,135	14.47%	10,295	15.42%
	77,355	100.00%	70,050	100.00%	66,750	100.00%

EBIT by Segment

	2010	% Total	2009	% Total	2008	% Total
North America	2,250	17.77%	2,075	18.00%	1,975	18.71%
Europe	5,150	40.66%	4,655	40.39%	4,285	40.60%
Asia	2,515	19.86%	2,150	18.66%	1,850	17.53%
Africa	1,540	12.16%	1,375	11.93%	1,170	11.08%
Australia	1,210	9.55%	1,270	11.02%	1,275	12.08%
	12,665	100.00%	11,525	100.00%	10,555	100.00%

Analysis:

Segment revenue:

- The North American and African segments have grown (in terms of dollar sales) and form a greater proportion (in percentage terms) of total revenues than in 2008.
- Even though the European and Asian businesses have grown, they form a lower proportion of total revenues than in 2008.
- The Australian segment has shrunk over the period.

Segment EBIT:

- Operating earnings for the North American, European, Asian, and African segments have grown over the period.
- Operating profits of the Australian segment have fallen over the period.

The bulk of Alpha's revenues and operating earnings come from its European segment, which makes it a very important segment to the company. In order to evaluate the company's assets and capital allocation decisions, we use the segment EBIT information provided in Table 1-8, and the asset and capital expenditure distribution in Table 1-9 to construct Table 1-10.

Table 1-9: Asset and Capital Expenditure Segment Information

Assets	2010		2009		2008	
North America	18,470	22.00%	11,950	16.41%	10,760	15.43%
Europe	24,150	28.77%	23,450	32.20%	22,500	32.26%
Asia	16,899	20.13%	15,865	21.79%	15,560	22.31%
Africa	12,605	15.02%	11,160	15.32%	10,825	15.52%
Australia	11,825	14.09%	10,400	14.28%	10,100	14.48%
	83,949		72,825		69,745	

Capital Expenditures	2010		2009		2008	
North America	395	9.84%	350	9.97%	255	8.69%
Europe	1,275	31.76%	1,225	34.90%	1,150	39.18%
Asia	835	20.80%	660	18.80%	625	21.29%
Africa	740	18.43%	630	17.95%	425	14.48%
Australia	770	19.18%	645	18.38%	480	16.35%
	4,015		3,510		2,935	

Table 1-10: EBIT Margin Ranking versus Ratio of Capex Percent to Asset Percent

	EBIT Margin 2010	Capex %/Assets %		
		2010	2009	2008
North America	24.66%	0.45	0.61	0.56
Africa	19.74%	1.23	1.17	0.93
Europe	16.32%	1.10	1.08	1.21
Asia	13.27%	1.03	0.86	0.95
Australia	12.20%	1.36	1.29	1.13

Illustration of calculations to derive values in Tables 1-9 and 1-10:

North American Segment (2010):
Percentage of total assets: 18,470/83,949 = 22.00%
Percentage of total capex: 395/4,015 = 9.84%
EBIT margin: 2,250/9,125 = 24.66%
Capex%:Assets% ratio = 9.84/22.00 = 0.447

Evaluating the Capex%:Assets% (CA%) Ratio:
- A ratio greater than 1 indicates that the company is allocating a higher proportion of its capital expenditures to the segment than its proportion of total assets. If this trend continues, the segment will become more significant over time.
- A ratio of 1 indicates that the segment is being allocated a proportion of capital expenditures that equals its proportion of total assets.
- A ratio less than 1 indicates that the company is not prioritizing the segment and it will likely become less significant over time.

In Table 1-10 we have listed the segments according to their EBIT margins from highest to lowest. The table also includes the CA% ratio for the segments from 2008 to 2010.

Analysis:
- Despite the fact that the North American segment has the highest EBIT margin, Alpha has not been investing aggressively in the segment (indicated by a CA% ratio that is significantly lower than 1. We would expect Alpha to be more aggressive in this market by allocating a lot more if its capital expenditure on its North American segment than it does currently.
- Alpha's aggressiveness in Australia is also difficult to understand. The Australian market has the lowest EBIT margin (and declining sales) but Alpha continues to invest heavily in its Australian segment (indicated by a CA% ratio that is well above 1).
- Alpha's strategy as it relates to the other three segments makes more sense. Between the African, European and Asian segments:
  - The African segment has the highest EBIT margin so its CA% ratio is (appropriately) higher than the other two.
  - The Asian segment has the lowest EBIT margin so its CA% ratio is lower than the other two.

LOS 20c: Evaluate the quality of a company's financial data, and recommend appropriate adjustments to improve quality and comparability with similar companies, including adjustments for differences in accounting standards, methods, and assumptions. Vol 2, pp 297–300

In order to determine the sustainability of a company's earnings, we next evaluate the quality of its reported earnings. In a previous reading, we learned how to determine the quality of a company's reported earnings by examining its balance sheet-based accruals and cash flow statement-based accruals. The higher the proportion of a company's earnings that are based on accruals, the lower the quality of earnings.

Selected information from Alpha's balance sheets and cash flow statements is presented in Table 1-11.

Table 1-11: Selected Balance Sheet and Cash Flow Statement Information

Balance Sheet	2010	2009	2008	2007
Total assets	83,949	72,825	69,745	61,731
Less: Cash and marketable securities	6,720	8,304	11,600	10,620
Operating assets (A)	77,229	64,521	58,145	51,111
Total liabilities	41,694	35,275	37,745	33,306
Less: Long-term debt	4,044	4,655	5,800	7,211
Less: Short-term debt	17,250	11,950	13,000	9,825
Operating liabilities (B)	20,400	18,670	18,945	16,270
Net Operating Assets (A − B)	56,829	45,851	39,200	34,841
Balance sheet accruals (Change in NOA)	**10,978**	**6,651**	**4,359**	

Cash flow statement	2010	2009	2008
Net income	11,250	9,150	8,150
Less: Operating cash flow	12,820	10,275	9,245
Less: Investing cash flow	−13,900	−9,130	−4,135
Cash flow accruals	**12,330**	**8,005**	**3,040**

Based on this information, we can calculate the balance sheet and cash flow accruals ratios as follows (Table 1-12).

Table 1-12: Accruals Ratios

Accruals Ratios	2010	2009	2008
Balance sheet-based approach	21.38%	15.64%	11.77%
Cash flow statement-based approach	24.02%	18.82%	8.21%

The steady increase in the accruals ratios is a matter of concern. Increasing accruals ratios indicate that earnings quality is deteriorating.

To investigate further, we evaluate the relationship between Alpha's cash flow and earnings. Specifically, we compare operating cash flow before interest and taxes to operating income adjusted for accounting changes. Operating cash flow includes the effects of interest and tax payments, while operating income does not. Therefore, in order to make the two measures comparable, we add back cash payments of interest and taxes to operating cash flow (see Table 1-13).

Table 1-13: Operating Cash Flow to Operating Income

	2010	2009	2008
Operating cash flow	12,820	10,275	9,245
Cash interest paid	595	480	365
Cash taxes paid	2,620	2,455	2,250
OCF before interest and taxes	**16,035**	**13,210**	**11,860**
Operating income (EBIT)	**12,665**	**11,525**	**10,555**
OCF before interest and taxes/EBIT	**1.27**	**1.15**	**1.12**

The fact that OCF before interest and taxes comfortably exceeds operating income alleviates some of our previous concerns regarding earnings management.

Given that we know (from earlier analyses) that Alpha has made a number of acquisitions we examine the relationship between its operating cash flow and total assets (see Table 1-14).

Table 1-14: Operating Cash Flow to Total Assets

	2010	2009	2008
Operating cash flow	12,820	10,275	9,245
Average total assets	78,387	71,285	65,738
Operating cash flow/Average total assets	16.35%	14.41%	14.06%

Analysis:
- The cash return on total assets has increased over time, which justifies Alpha's recent acquisitions.

To remove any lingering doubt resulting from the earlier analysis of accruals we assess the relationship between Alpha's cash flow and reinvestment, cash flow and debt, as well as its debt-servicing capacity (see Table 1-15).

Table 1-15: Operating Cash Flow to Reinvestment, Debt, and Cash Flow Interest Coverage

	2010	2009	2008
Cash flow to reinvestment			
Operating cash flow (OCF)	12,820	10,275	9,245
Capital expenditures	4,015	3,510	2,935
OCF/Capital expenditures	**3.19**	**2.93**	**3.15**
Cash flow to total debt			
OCF before interest and taxes	16,035	13,210	11,860
Total debt*	21,294	16,605	18,800
OCF before interest and taxes/Total debt	**75.30%**	**79.55%**	**63.09%**
Cash flow interest coverage			
OCF before interest and taxes	16,035	13,210	11,860
Cash interest paid	595	480	365
OCF before interest and taxes/Cash interest	**26.95**	**27.52**	**32.49**

* Total debt equals total long-term debt (inc. current portion), but does not include pension obligations and restructuring provisions.

Analysis:

All the cash flow measures have been relatively strong, which puts our previous concerns regarding earnings manipulation to bed.

- Reinvestment needs are covered by operating cash flow by a factor of 3.19, which suggests that the company has ample resources for its reinvestment program. The OCF:capex ratio has not changed by much despite the increase in capital expenditures over the three years, which is a very good sign.
- The cash flow to total debt ratio (75.3%) indicates that Alpha is not highly leveraged. The company has room to take on more debt should investing opportunities arise.
  - A more subtle point is that the company has the capacity to pay off its debt in approximately 2.5 years [= 21,294/(12,820 − 4,015)] while maintaining its current reinvestment policy.
- Although the interest coverage ratio has declined, it is still quite high. The company's annual cash flow is enough to cover annual interest payments by a factor of 26.95 times, which also suggests that the company has the financial capacity to add more debt to its capital structure should it need to raise funds.

Decomposition and Analysis of the Company's Valuation

Next we move into analyzing the company's market valuation. We know that Alpha holds an equity investment in an associate, and while the associate's earnings contribute to Alpha's profits overall, we want to remove the effects of its holdings in the associate from Alpha's market value so that we can evaluate the value that the market is placing solely on Alpha's operations (also referred to as Alpha's implied value).

Suppose that the market capitalizations of Alpha and its associate are $175m and $40m, respectively. Since Alpha has a 25% equity interest in the associate, its pro-rata share of the associate's market value is $10m (= 25% × 40m). Removing the value of this investment from Alpha's overall market value gives us an implied value of $165m for Alpha.

Alpha's 2010 trailing P/E ratio based on its implied value ($165m) and earnings adjusted for the income from associates (11.25 − 0.95 = $10.3m) equals 16.02. Given a trailing P/E multiple of 19.5 for the benchmark index, we conclude that Alpha (excluding its investment in the associate) is trading at a 17.85% discount.

We have now performed sufficient analyses to be able to communicate our conclusions.

Support for an Investment in Alpha's Shares
- The growth in earnings has been achieved through internal operations, acquisitions, and its investment in an associate company.
- The company has sufficient cash flows to finance future operating and investment expenditures.
- The company's low leverage levels suggest that it has the capacity to obtain additional debt financing if investment opportunities arise.
- The company's ROE have shown an upward trend. The associate has contributed to the increase in ROE, but has not been the primary driver of earnings.
- The company's operating cash flows have consistently exceeded operating earnings, which gives us confidence in the quality of its earnings.
- The cash return on total assets has been consistently increasing, which implies that the company's recent acquisitions have been successful.
- An assessment of the company's implied value and trailing P/E ratio indicates that its shares are relatively undervalued.

Causes for Concern
- The increase in the balance sheet-based and cash flow-based accruals ratios raises concerns regarding earnings manipulation. However, these concerns are alleviated by the company's strong cash flow position.
- The company's allocation of capital expenditures is quite unusual. It seems to be over-allocating capital resources to the lowest margin segment (Australia) and underinvesting in the highest margin segment (North America). The company's allocation of capital expenditure across geographical segments must be monitored going forward.
- Impairment of goodwill in the future may cause losses to the company. Goodwill comprises almost 30% of Alpha's total assets.

LESSON 2: OFF-BALANCE-SHEET LEVERAGE AND EFFECTS OF CHANGES IN ACCOUNTING STANDARDS

LOS 20e: Analyze and interpret how balance sheet modifications, earnings normalization, and cash flow statement-related modifications affect a company's financial statements, financial ratios, and overall financial condition. Vol 2, pp 301–304

Given that companies are able to structure lease agreements in a manner that allows them to leave these arrangements off balance sheet (operating leases), analysts need to incorporate the effects of these arrangements on the company's financial performance and position by adjusting reported financial statements.

Recall that under an operating lease:

- The lessee only recognizes rental expense (equal to the amount of periodic lease payment) on the income statement.
- Periodic lease payments are classified as outflows from operating activities.
- No asset or liability is recognized on the lessee's balance sheet so there is no depreciation or interest expense recorded over the term of the lease.

In contrast, classification of a lease as a finance lease requires the lessee to:

- Recognize an asset as well as a liability on the balance sheet equal to the present value of lease payments.
- The asset is depreciated over the term of the lease, while interest expense is recorded against the liability.
- Periodic lease payments are classified partly as outflows from financing activities and partly as outflows from operating activities.

Since operating lease agreements give rise to obligations for the lessee to make periodic lease payments, and leased assets are used by the company to generate revenues, for analytical purposes, operating leases should be brought on to the balance sheet and treated as finance leases. See Example 2-1. Specifically, analysts should make the following adjustments:

- Increase assets and liabilities by present value of the lease payments. Since assets and liabilities are initially increased by the same amount, this adjustment does not have any impact on stockholders' equity.
- Increase net income by the amount of rental expense.
- Decrease net income by the amount of interest and depreciation expense.
- Reclassify an amount equal to the reduction in lease liability each period as an outflow from financing activities instead of an outflow from operating activities.

Example 2-1: Classification of an Operating Lease as a Finance Lease

An analyst gathers the following information regarding Mercury Inc.:

- Total assets = $41.5 million
- Total liabilities = $13.5 million
- Equity = $28 million
- EBIT = $4.8 million
- Interest expense = $1.5 million

The analyst also learns that the company also leases some equipment and treats the arrangement as an operating lease. Details regarding the lease agreement are given below:

- Present value of the remaining lease payments = $5.5 million
- Interest rate implicit in the lease agreement = 17.45%
- Lease term = 10 years
- Annual payment = $1.2 million

Calculate the company's reported financial leverage, total debt-to-equity, and interest coverage ratio and their adjusted values if the operating lease were classified as a finance lease. Comment on your answers.

Solution:

Financial leverage = Total assets / Total equity

> Based on reported financials = 41.5m / 28m = 1.48
> Based on adjusted financials = (41.5m + 5.5m) / 28m = 1.68
>> ○ Present value of remaining lease payments ($5.5m) is added to total assets.

Total debt-to-equity = Total debt / Total equity

> Based on reported financials = 13.5m / 28m = 0.48
> Based on adjusted financials = (13.5m + 5.5m) / 28m = 0.68
>> ○ Present value of remaining lease payments ($5.5m) is added to total liabilities.

Interest coverage ratio = EBIT / Interest expense

> Based on reported financials = 4.8m / 1.5m = 3.2
> Based on adjusted financials = (4.8m + 1.2m − 0.55m) / (1.5m + 0.96m) = 2.22
>> ○ Annual lease payment ($ 1.2m) is added back to EBIT.
>> ○ Annual depreciation expense (5.5m / 10 = 0.55m) under a finance lease is subtracted from EBIT.
>> ○ Interest expense (5.5m × 17.45% = 0.96m) on the liability recognized under a finance lease is added to interest expense.

The calculations above clearly show that treatment of an operating lease as a finance lease results in higher (worse) financial leverage and total debt-to-equity ratios, and a lower (worse) interest coverage ratio.